nothing uncertain, ... clear
& perspicuous from . . . . Like
an artist, in fact, which you are, as
well as a Poet. In the first two lines of
the Poem to Bayard Taylor, for instance,
the whole picture is contained.

    "And he lay among his books."

      "The peace of God was in his looks."
Nothing could be better or more forcible.
The Poem called "The Cathedral" made
me think of _____, where the trees are
magnificent _____, who used
to say that the woods there were "his
cathedral". "The sifting of Peter" is more
serious than you often write, though
it is perhaps the finest in the book.
But they are all so beautiful it is difficult
to pitch upon any one, & say it is better
than the others. I am glad you liked
the appearance of my little book. I
thought Jansen & his Clung got it up
in very good style. They took a great

Amy Fay, 1875

More Letters of Amy Fay:
The American Years, 1879-1916

---

selected

and

edited by

S. Margaret William McCarthy

INFORMATION COORDINATORS   DETROIT   1986

927.8
F282zm

Photographs.
Courtesy of the Preston H. Tuttle Collection, Institute for Studies in Pragmatism, Texas Tech University, and Sylvia Wright Mitarachi.

87-8534

Copyright © 1986 by S. Margaret William McCarthy

Printed and bound in the United States of America
Published by
Information Coordinators, Inc.
1435-37 Randolph Street
Detroit, Michigan 48226

Editing by J. Bunker Clark
Book design by Nicholas Jakubiak
Photocomposition by Elaine Gorzelski, Kristin Gorzelski

Library of Congress Cataloging in Publication Data
Fay, Amy, 1844-1928.
    More letters of Amy Fay: the American years, 1879-1916.

    Includes index.
    1. Fay, Amy, 1844-1928.   2. Pianists— United States— Correspondence.   3. Music— United States— History and criticism.   I. McCarthy, Margaret William, 1931-   .
II. Title.
ML417.F286A4   1986   786.1'092'4 [B]   86-2852
ISBN 0-89990-028-3

For all who work

to turn the mushroom cloud

into a rainbow of peace with justice

on planet earth . . .

Contents

Preface

Anyone who has ever read Amy Fay's *Music Study in Germany* probably has experienced a sense of incompletion upon reaching the end of the book, not because the book in itself is wanting, but because one wishes to know what happened next. One wonders, for example, about the direction Fay's life took when she returned home in 1875, and what, if any, impact she made on the cultural life of the United States. One speculates about her letter writing facility and suspects that such an inveterate letter writer at one stage of her life *must* have continued this practice throughout her life.

These questions plagued me when I put down *Music Study in Germany* after reading it in 1975, the year before the celebration of the nation's bicentennial. As with so many music researchers at that time, I wanted to celebrate the nation's two hundredth birthday by contributing in some way to the fleshing out of the country's musical history. Gathering information about Amy Fay's career in America following her return home in 1875 offered a unique opportunity to do this. I set about a search for possible letters in major research libraries in the three cities where Fay invested her professional years: Boston, Chicago, and New York. The yield was meager: three letters — two written in Chicago and one in Boston.

In July of 1977 my fortunes took a new turn. I learned that there was a National Endowment for the Humanities Fellow, Sylvia Wright Mitarachi, working at the Schlesinger Library at Radcliffe College on a project entitled "The Fay Sisters and the Curse of Eve." I contacted Sylvia to inquire if perhaps one of the sisters would by any chance be "Amy." Sylvia told me that indeed one of them *was* Amy Fay and that furthermore, Amy was her grand aunt. In addition, Sylvia informed me that she had in her possession a large cache of letters written by Amy to various family members and invited me to examine the material. When I looked through the correspondence, I found that indeed there were letters chronicling Fay's life in America every bit as comprehensive as those appearing in *Music Study in Germany*. I set about to transcribe and edit the letters; the present volume represents the fruit of that effort.

The letters presented here, with the exception of those to Henry Wadsworth Longfellow, are part of a whole collection written by Amy Fay to her family, especially to her sisters. The collection includes the German letters published by her sister Melusina ("Zina") Fay Peirce as *Music Study in Germany* as well as unpublished letters from the German period. All were donated to the Schlesinger Library in July 1978 by Amy's grandnieces, Sylvia Wright Mitarachi and Rosamund Jackson Ellis.

The fact that Zina meticulously preserved the letters suggests that she sensed that one day they might make an American sequel to *Music Study in Germany*. Such a possibility had been put forth as early as 1885 by Sir George Grove in the English preface to *Music Study*, in which he stated:

> Will Miss Fay never oblige us with an equally charming and faithful account of musical life in the States? Hitherto musical America has been almost an unknown land to us, described by the few who have attempted it in the most opposite terms. Their singers we know well, and in this respect America is perhaps destined to be the Italy of the future, if only the artists will consent to learn slowly enough. But on the subject of American players and American orchestras, and the taste of the American amateurs, a great deal of curiosity is felt, and we commend the subject to the serious attention of one so thoroughly able to do it justice.

The American letters do what Grove hoped for. One subject about which Amy writes at length is the New York Philharmonic, giving particular attention to the orchestra's organizational difficulties. She provides a running commentary on each of the various conductors to ascend the podium of that prestigious organization both before, during, and after the Mahler years. She reveals, for example, that a good deal of intrigue surrounded the replacement of Safonoff, whom she admired, by Mahler, about whom she had misgivings as a potential conductor.

After Mahler's demise in 1911, she continued to appraise the orchestral situation with reference to Mahler's successor, Stransky. Revelatory impressions appear throughout the letters in conjunction with all sorts of professional music making. Among the pianists Amy critiques are first and foremost her dear friend Paderewski as well as Hofmann, Busoni, Backhaus, Lhévinne, Carreño, and Fanny Bloomfield Zeisler. Among the violinists Fay scrutinizes are Reményi, with whom she shared the stage in her Chicago years, Kubelik, and Kreisler. Her lively statements about the New York critics versus Kubelik communicate well the antagonisms that she felt toward certain of these critics.

If Grove were alive today, he would be satisfied to see the American counterpart to the German letters in print. He would see that his questions about musical life in the States are answered to a great extent in the letters contained here. But the letters contain much more. In addition to lively accounts of America's musical life, they put forth much information about the life and manners of people of fashion at the turn of the nineteenth century, thereby enabling readers to fill in many more of the gaps in the history of the time. Such topics as life in boarding houses, dining customs and the stuff of conversation, the conduct of religious services and the contents of sermons, prevailing attitudes among the "four hundred set" towards such groups as Jews and Irish Catholics, customs of drinking and smoking (Amy indulged in both activities), recreational and leisure activities such as card playing, and attitudes toward the women's movement are samplings of the many subjects Amy addresses with humor, ease, and authority.

The letters also contain accounts of several of Amy's travels: to Lima, Peru, in November of 1902 to attend the wedding of her niece Pauline Stone to Arthur Jackson, owner of a rubber plantation in South America; in July of 1903 to France to visit Mrs. Clarence Eddy, an old Chicago friend who established permanent residence in Paris; and to Europe in July 1911 to attend the Liszt Centennial Celebrations. Amy describes travel customs such as life on ship, and during her 1903 trip to Europe she gives a vivid account of a burial at sea.

The letters permit the reader to trace the career of Amy Fay in the United States, where she achieved prominence as a concert pianist, educator, and club woman. They span her years in Chicago, in 1879-90, and her years in New York from 1890 until 1916. They describe the context in which her life unfolded, and form a natural companion to *Music Study in Germany*.

It is to Zina that the majority of the letters are written. Zina became a surrogate mother to Amy following the death of their mother when Amy was twelve. It was she who recognized Amy's talent for letter writing and saved the German letters. As Amy writes in a letter to Zina dated September 18, 1912:

> I would never have known I had a talent for letter writing if you had not
> the discrimination to discover the fact . . . without you the letters would have
> gone into the wastebasket and nobody would ever have heard of Amy Fay.

Zina herself was a "doer" — a writer, lecturer, and ardent feminist. She was married to the eminent mathematician, philosopher, and scientist Charles Sanders Peirce (who was involved in the pre-history of the computer), but they were divorced in 1883. She became a pioneer in cooperative housekeeping and the women's movement, publishing a book *Co-operative Housekeeping: How Not To Do It and How To Do It: A Study in Sociology* (Boston: J. R. Osgood, 1884). She founded the Women's Philharmonic Society of New York, worked to save both Fraunces

Tavern and the Poe Cottage (the latter an architectural landmark in the Bronx), and wrote another book, *New York: A Symphonic Study in Three Parts* (New York: Neale, 1918). She provided a powerful model for her younger sister Amy, and unquestionably stimulated the feminist posture that characterized Amy throughout her professional life.

Other letters in the present volume are addressed to Amy's brother Charles Norman Fay, a prominent Chicago businessman and one of the founders of the Chicago Symphony Orchestra; to her sister Rose Fay Thomas, a musical patron who became the second wife of the well-known conductor Theodore Thomas; to her sister Kate Fay Stone, who also was an accomplished pianist; and to her sister Laura Fay Smith, a skilled singer and water-color artist. In addition there are letters to her nieces Pauline Stone and Madeline Smith, to her nephew-in-law Arthur Jackson, as well as correspondence between Amy and Henry Wadsworth Longfellow. Some letters date from her Chicago period, and some from her travels to South America and Europe, but most of the letters date from the years when she was living and working in New York.

In their totality, the letters provide a valid point of entry into the cultural life of the nation at the turn the last century when the musical life of the country was well on the way to achieving new levels of sophistication and growth. They reveal Amy as an American observer "par excellence," as peerless as she was in her German years.

*   *   *

Many persons have encouraged and supported me in my work on the Fay letters. Conversations with colleagues at Regis College assisted me a great deal in clarifying my thoughts and I should like to mention in particular Sisters Rosenda Gill, Juan Mahan, Viterbo McCarthy, Dorothy McKenzie, Catherine Meade, Jeanne d'Arc O'Hare, and Therezon Sheerin. I am grateful to Sister Mary Oates for putting me on the trail of the Fay correspondence. The staff of the Regis College Library was of immense help to me, and I extend a special thanks to William Gallup whose ready assistance guided me through a plethora of challenges as I sought out dates, names of publishers, and information about relatives, friends, and associates of Amy Fay. I offer appreciation also to the President of Regis College, Sister Therese Higgins, who made possible the final typing of the manuscript and to my research assistant Cheryl Noiles for preparing the final copy and index.

I wish also to acknowledge the Radcliffe Research Support Award given me in 1983 which gave impetus to the speedy conclusion of my manuscript. I am grateful to the members of the staff of the Schlesinger Library at Radcliffe College for their ongoing cooperation in my search for material about Amy Fay. I appreciate the insights into the Fay family given me by Amy Fay's grandnieces Rosamund Jackson Chadwick and Sylvia Wright Mitarachi, and by Paul Mitarachi following the death of his wife Sylvia in 1981. The letters to and from Henry Wadsworth Longfellow, pp. 3-11, appear by kind permission of the Houghton Library, Harvard University. Lastly, I express my gratitude to Information Coordinators, especially to J. Bunker Clark, Elaine Gorzelski, Kristin Gorzelski, and Bruno Nettl, for seeing this book through to publication.

S. MARGARET WILLIAM MCCARTHY

Regis College
Weston, Massachusetts
August 1985

Biographical Sketch

Born in 1844 in Bayou Goula, Louisiana, Amy Fay was the third of six daughters and the fifth of nine children of the Reverend Charles and Emily (Hopkins) Fay of Louisiana and St. Albans, Vermont. Her real name was Amelia, after her grandmother Hopkins' sister Amelia Muller, but as she always called herself Amy when a little girl, it was the name by which she continued to be known. She was fine looking, noted for her blue eyes, perfect nose, and curly hair, as well as her keen sense of humor and story telling gifts.

Her father, Charles Fay, was a man of scholastic attainments, having graduated with an A.B. from Harvard University, second in the class of 1829. This class was unusually brilliant; it included the names of Oliver Wendell Homes and Benjamin Peirce (later Harvard professor, and father of Charles Sanders Peirce, to whom Amy's sister Melusina was married in 1862-83). Charles Fay was also awarded an honorary D.D. from Harvard in 1860. As an Episcopal clergyman, he was in charge of parishes at Highgate, Vermont; a school at Montpelier, Georgia; parishes in Bayou Goula and New Orleans, Louisiana; St. Albans, Vermont; and Marquette, Michigan. After retiring about 1870, he lived for two years in Cambridge, Massachusetts. He spent most of his remaining life at Grand Isle, Vermont, on the farm of his second wife, Sophonia Adams White, whom he married in 1864 when Amy was twenty.

Amy's mother, Charlotte Emily Hopkins, was a skilled musician and a natural artist with pencil, pen and ink, and brush. In addition she had executive ability which she applied whether running her home or presiding over parish organizations. She married at sixteen and died at the age of thirty-nine, when Amy was only twelve years old.

After the marriage in 1862 of Amy's older sister Melusina (Zina) to Charles Sanders Peirce, Amy, now a young woman, then went to live with them in Cambridge,

Massachusetts. She began her study of music in Boston, where she studied Bach with John Knowles Paine of Harvard and attended the piano classes of Otto Dressel at the New England Conservatory of Music. She made great strides forward musically when, at the age of seventeen, she studied piano with the Polish artist Jan Pychowski at a summer school in Geneseo, New York. The progress Amy made under Pychowski impressed her family so much that when she was twenty-one Amy was permitted to study with him in New York for one more series of lessons.

In 1869, with the encouragement of Zina, Amy managed to begin her music lessons in Germany, where she studied with the most prominent teachers in Europe until her return home in 1875. Initially the fame of Carl Tausig attracted her to Berlin. She had heard Paine remark one day, "there is a young man in Berlin who plays the piano like forty thousand devils! His name is Carl Tausig." Amy studied for one year with Tausig in his conservatory, and when he closed the school she continued her studies with Theodore Kullak, with whom she remained for three years. In 1873 she went to Weimar to put herself under Liszt's instruction. While preparing to make her European debut she met Ludwig Deppe, the noted teacher, and became so interested in his ideas at her initial interview that she decided to take lessons with him, which she did for a year and a half. Amy then returned to Weimar for a few more weeks of study with Liszt before coming back to America in October 1875, after six years absence. Although her name is always associated with Liszt in a special way, largely because of the vivid, enthusiastic impressions of the master that she etched in her letters and other writings, it was Deppe's technique for piano study that revolutionized Amy Fay's playing and that served as the method she was to use for her students in years to come.

During her European sojourn she regularly wrote letters home to her sister Zina, many of which were published in the *Atlantic Monthly* in 1874. The German correspondence was edited by Zina and published in 1880 as the book *Music Study in Germany*, largely through the efforts of Henry Wadsworth Longfellow in tandem with Zina. The book quickly gained a reputation as the "book of the age" and brought Fay immediate fame at home and abroad. Her literary portraits of the masters Tausig, Kullak, and Liszt appealed to an ever-widening circle of readers and won for her a large following, and her descriptions of Liszt remain to this day primary historical sources for Liszt scholars.

During Fay's lifetime the book appeared in over twenty-five editions. At the request of Liszt it was translated into German. In addition, it went through editions in England and France with prefaces by George Grove and Vincent d'Indy, respectively. Frequently it was given as a prize for proficiency in female institutions, and provided the incentive for numbers of American students to make a serious study and profession of music and to aspire to study in Europe. In recent years, reprints of *Music Study* have appeared periodically, the two most recent being an edition in 1965 by Frances Dillon and an edition 1979 by Edward Downes.

Biographical Sketch

Thanks to *Music Study,* we know much about Fay and her life in Germany, but the course of her life following her return to this country remains much more fragmented and obscure. Yet, the record indicates that Fay enjoyed a distinguished reputation in the United States as a concert pianist, educator, critic, and clubwoman of national prominence.

Her professional career in the United States began and ended in New York City, with a brief interlude in Cambridge and a decade in Chicago. In December 1875 the curtain went up on her public career at Chickering's rooms on Fourteenth Street in New York in a program that she shared with her older sister Melusina Fay Pierce. On that occasion, noted the famous American music critic John Sullivan Dwight, an address by her feminist sister on the subject of the duties of women preceded Amy's concert. Melusina's topic was a fitting keynote for a career that was to become linked increasingly to concerns about the proper place of women in life and art. From 1876 to 1878, Amy lived in Cambridge and presented several piano recitals there that were attended by the poet Henry Wadsworth Longfellow and Dwight, founder of *Dwight's Journal,* the most important American journal of its century.

Dwight gave her favorable reviews in his *Journal,* and noted in a review of a concert given on April 15, 1876

> . . . that this lady, in whom Liszt had taken so much interest, is destined to take a high place among our pianists, we can hardly doubt. . . .

During those years Amy played with the Theodore Thomas Orchestra. In 1878 she played at the Worcester Music Festival, where she was the first artist to introduce the playing of piano concertos at the festival, with the Beethoven B-flat major concerto with the Germania Orchestra under the baton of Carl Zerrahn.

In the latter part of 1878 she joined her brother Charles Norman Fay in Chicago and remained there until 1890, dividing her time among teaching, club work, and performing in that city and throughout the towns and cities of the midwest. She became a popular figure on such concert stages as Hershey Hall, Pratt's School of Music and Art, and the American Conservatory. In Chicago, she worked out a novel form of concert, called "Piano Conversation." These Piano Conversations involved a brief talk before each piece she was to play, and were happily described by W. S. B. Mathews as an exhibition of "exquisite musical pictures, illuminated by eloquent words." Possibly Amy Fay was a model and trendsetter in playing interspersed with the spoken word, for in 1885 the pianist William Sherwood was publicized in the *Chicago Sunday Tribune* for a piano recital he was to give before the Amateur Club of Chicago in which he was "to prelude each selection with some remarks in connection with the interpretation of the composition." In those Chicago years Amy shared the musical stage on various occasions with many notable musicians including Clara Louise Kellogg, Fanny Bloomfield (Zeisler) and Eduard Reményi. She toured the cities of the Northwest and

West with the Thursby Concert Company and played in such places as Louisville, Rochester, Detroit, Des Moines, as well as Washington, D.C.

As a teacher in Chicago, she worked diligently to promote the Deppe Method for the Pianoforte as described in the last chapter of *Music Study in Germany*. Among her students was John Alden Carpenter. She also invested much energy and effort in musical clubs, for she believed clubs could do a great deal to develop taste and understanding among amateurs. She was active in a woman's club known as the "Amateur Musical Club" and founded a club called the "Artists' Club." Fay also achieved popularity as a lecturer and writer during her Chicago days. She spoke frequently at national meetings of the Music Teachers' National Association and contributed articles regularly to *The Etude*.

After moving to New York in 1890, Amy continued her work as a performer, teacher, and clubwoman. The Board of Education frequently sponsored her Piano Conversations for the youth of the city. In New York, too, she maintained her good reputation as a teacher, although she occasionally lamented the lack of pupils, often attributing it to discrimination against women in the profession on the part of young students. But if, from a financial standpoint, Amy's New York teaching could not always be termed successful, from an artistic standpoint her results were, at least in her own eyes, "brilliant," moving her to comment in one of her letters that Deppe would have been delighted with the results of his method in America.

It was in New York that Amy's club activity reached new heights as a result of her involvement with the Women's Philharmonic Society of New York. This organization was founded by her sister Melusina in 1899, and Amy became its president from 1903 through 1912. According to the letters, the Society was very important to musical women in New York for at least a decade, offering them support in the performance, composition, theory, and history of music. As Amy writes in one of her letters to Zina dated March 1, 1902:

> Really, your Women's Philharmonic is a remarkable association, Mud, and you ought to be proud of having organized it.

Its success was due in large measure to the efforts of the founder, Zina as well as Amy, both of whom were able to support, through the activities of the organization, the serious involvement of women in music in a society where their gifts were not always valued. Fay's letters attest to her remarkable dedication to the Society as a faithful attender of business meetings, writer of reports, organizer of concerts, and overseer of various departments. Amy's long-term association with the Women's Philharmonic society of New York no doubt nurtured her feminist leanings, for her writings of the New York period address with greater frequency the topic of women and music. Such subjects as women in composition, the plight of the woman music teacher in the city, and general concern about discrimination against women in the field of music occupied her thoughts in her New York years, and she articulated her position in articles in *The Etude, Music,* and *Musical Courier.*

Amy never married but had numerous admirers through the years. During her European student days she became romantically involved with the Belgian musician William Gurickx, but her brother insisted that she end the relationship. When she travelled to Europe in 1903, she visited Gurickx in the house where he lived with his wife and daughter. Music was Amy's life, and while ostensibly she never regretted her single status, on occasion she used to wear around her neck a jeweled heart with "Gu-Gu's" picture in it.

In 1916, Amy's health began to decline and by 1919 her brother insisted that she move back home to Cambridge to live with him and their sister Rose. Her mental powers deteriorated and in her last days she became quite pathetic, as the following passage excerpted from a November 15, 1923 letter of Amy's sister Kate to her daughter Margaret suggests:

> . . . I went to see your Aunt Amy not long ago, but now that Zina is gone she is lonely and unhappy and it made me so unhappy to see her I could not get over it for several days. She wants to go back to New York of course and imagines that if she did she would be in her old boarding house and have her scholars and everything be just as it used to. She cannot understand there is any difference in her *condition*, and thinks it is only lack of money that prevents her returning there. If she went back she would be just as unhappy, for everything would be different. She could not get scholars and could not teach if she did, and if she went out alone she would get confused and lose her way, and no boarding house would be likely to take her. . . .

Amy died in Watertown on February 28, 1928, in the same nursing home where her sister Zina had died in 1923. She is buried in the family plot in Mount Auburn Cemetery in Watertown, Massachusetts.

*   *   *

In many ways, Amy Fay's life exemplified patterns and habits typical of women of her cultivated upbringing. Her education and the opportunities she had for self-development through travel and study were givens for a woman of her background. The problems she faced, however, are problems women still address today; namely, how to secure a position that brings personal satisfaction, how to be a useful member of society, how to tap into emotional support systems, and how to create new integration of traditional roles.

Biographical Sketch

The influences she experienced typify the influences women have known throughout history. Networking systems of family, friends, and teachers were woven into the fabric of her life. Her activities as a musical patron and club volunteer demonstrated her efforts to transfer the nurturing role traditionally identified with women to the larger society. In her role as critic she attempted to raise consciousness about women's musical gifts in traditional roles like performance and in non-traditional roles such as composition; as a performer she raised the level of taste of her audiences through her choice of quality repertory and spoken comments in connection with her recitals. As a clubwoman she advanced the place of women in music and the place of music in society. Her career thus made its mark on the cultural life of the nation and helped it achieve new levels of musical sophistication at the turn of the nineteenth century.[1]

---

[1] My article "Amy Fay: The American Years," *American Music* 3, no. 1 (Spring 1985): 52-62, contains other biographical particulars, as well as documentation.

More Letters of Amy Fay:

Amy Fay, 1910

The American Years, 1879-1916

Letters of Amy Fay

Chicago March 18, 1879

Dear Mr. Longfellow,

The anniversary of your birthday has just passed and I have not yet added my wishes to all the congratulations that have doubtless poured in for you. I wish you many happy returns, and I hope I may once again enjoy the honor of dining with you upon it as I did two years ago! I was most interested in reading in the "Advertizer" about the chair which the Cambridge children presented to you, made of the old Chestnut tree. What a charming idea, and your poem to them is perfectly exquisite! It seems so pleasant that the old tree has come to make its final abode by your fireside, as if in acknowledgement for your having made it famous! I wish I could take my seat in the chair this minute and listen to your delightful conversation, but as I can*not,* I like, at least, to think of *you* in it. In the sitting room of the Kelly's house, where we are boarding, there is a large engraving of you hanging on the wall. On the opposite side of the room is a register, and I often sit there warming my feet at the furnace, and as I do I warm my heart by gazing at your portrait. You sit, leaning on your hand, and gazing meditatively at me, till it seems almost as if you are about to speak. Sometimes I speak to you, and though you do not reply, you are a good listener! In this first house I was invited to dine here, was another copy of the same furniture, so it seems as if you were trying to cheer me at this distance and make me feel at home.

I have never had such desperate and protracted fits of homesickness as I have had here, notwithstanding my sister, Mrs. Peirce,[1] and my brother are both with me.

Amy Fay

And yet I am very glad that I came, and I am now beginning to like Chicago very much. It is a most imposing and interesting city. For a long time the bigness of it and the gigantic scale in which everything is done here oppressed and bewildered me. It seemed as if I never would do anything in art, but after all, I have made a formidable start, and I hope to be able to follow it up. I made my first appearance with Orchestra, in a Symphony Concert at which Reményi[2] also played and I received a good notice from Upton of the "Tribune" who is the grand critic of the Northwest. They tell me that a smile from him goes a long way out here. Reményi behaved very handsomely, and came and sat on the stage while I was playing. What a wonderful genius he is! Every time I heard him I was impressed. His playing is *so* fascinating! It made me long to go back to Liszt more than ever.

We are now making another attempt to get my book[3] published, though I know not whether it will be successful. My brother[4] took your letter to Osgood, to Jansen and McClurg here, as a preliminary. McClurg was much impressed at seeing an autographed letter from you! He has not yet read the book, but I hope he will take it on your recommendation. I have not yet told you how much I enjoyed the two volumes of your "Poems of Places" that you gave me. When I got here I was ill after the fatigue of the journey, and they were delightful reading as I was convalescing. My sister begs me to send you her best regards. We both hope you are in good health. Please remember me to the young ladies and also to Charlie,[5] and with a special remembrance to yourself, believe me.

Sincerely and gratefully yours,

Amy Fay

275 East Indiana Street
Chicago
care of Mrs. Kelly

---

[1] Melusina Fay Peirce (1836-1923), Amy's older sister who became Amy's surrogate mother after Mrs. Fay's death in 1856.

[2] Eduard Reményi (1828-98), Hungarian violinist who toured with Brahms in Germany from 1852 to 1853 and later took up residence in the U.S.A. in 1878, where he gave concerts.

[3] *Music Study in Germany.*

[4] Charles Norman Fay (1848-1944), Amy's younger brother who was a prominent Chicago businessman and a founder of the Chicago Symphony Orchestra.

[5] Charles Longfellow, son of Henry Wadsworth Longfellow by his second wife Frances Appleton Longfellow.

4

The American Years

Cambridge April 13, 1879

Dear Amy,

I was delighted to get your letter. You will not perhaps, think so, because I have not answered it sooner. I should have done so, but for innumerable interruptions, which make me as mute as the portrait you see on the wall, when you are warming your feet at the furnace.

I am glad to learn that you are happy and successful in Chicago. I am sure you will find many warm friends, but not more or warmer than you have left behind you here.

Had you been here last week you would have heard Bach's Passion Music given with great effect by the Handel and Haydn Society. Boston seems quite music mad. To show you what it is doing in its churches today, I send you the Evening Transcript, with a long, long list of the performances.

I hope that Jansen and McClurg have accepted your book, and that we shall soon see it in print. It grieves me to think that so good a book should have to wait so long for a publisher.

Do you know Rossini's *"Stabat-Mater"?"* Some portions of it are extremely beautiful; as for instance the *"Cujus Anima."* It would be lovely in one of your concerts, and lift the audience from their seats. Mr. Monti has been playing it to me of late, instead of Opera music. I am sure you would like it.

Reményi was here and took part in the Bach music. I was sorry not to see him. He is a powerful being, full of life, and energy. To meet him is like stopping to water one's horses. Is that intelligible? Hardly, but you will gather a vague sense of my meaning.

Alice[1] and Annie[2] join me in kindest remembrances to you, and Mrs. Paine,[3] and I am, as ever,

Yours very sincerely,

Henry Wadsworth Longfellow

---

[1] Alice Longfellow, daughter of Henry Wadsworth Longfellow by his second wife Frances Appleton Longfellow.

[2] Annie Longfellow, daughter of Henry Wadsworth Longfellow by his second wife Frances Appleton Longfellow, and friend of Rose Fay, Amy's younger sister.

[3] Wife of John Knowles Paine (1839-1906), American organist, teacher, composer, and first incumbent of a chair of music in an American university (Harvard), a post he held from 1875 to 1895.

Amy Fay

Chicago January 26, 1880

Dear Mr. Longfellow,

Some weeks ago I had a long letter to you nearly completed. Then came an interruption and it was never finished. Now I will try once more, and this time I hope with better result. First, I will begin by wishing you a "Happy New Year." Is not *8* the number of life? If so, 1880 ought to bring in a fresh stock of vitality and creative power. I shall expect greater things of you than ever! But no; perhaps I am wrong in saying that, for perfection cannot be improved upon, and it would certainly be foolish to attempt to gild the rose, or paint the lily! Only produce if possible *more* of those poems which are the delight of the world! How I wish I could take a flying visit to you today, and listen once more to your brilliant conversation! Rose[1] and I so often recall the delightful hours we have spent at the Craigie House, and now with the addition of that baby, it must be more attractive than ever. Babies are a great resource in my estimation, and I don't doubt that you will agree with me on this point. They are so sensible and always know what they want. There is perfect uniformity in their desires, and their whole horizon is a milky way. It must be hard for Edith[2] to bear this long separation from Mr. Dana, but still she must greatly enjoy being in her old haunt with you and the girls once more. I trust he will return strengthened and refreshed after his long cruise, and then how charming the meeting will be! The fatted calf can be killed just as well as if he were a "prodigal son."

I ought to have thanked you long ago for your last kind letter which gladdened my heart as I was starting off to Milwaukee to play in a concert there. I accepted it at once as a good omen, and such it proved to be as I had a remarkably pleasant trip. Milwaukee is a lovely little city, and is situated directly upon the lake, which is a deep blue color, and sparkles like a great sapphire. They call it the "American Bay of Naples," and it does look like Naples. There is a lovely drive all around it on top of the bluffs overlooking the water. The people in Milwaukee are very musical. Much more so than in Chicago. This particular concert that I played at was given by the Men's Club, and was consequently crowded. There were fully two thousand people in the Hall, yet the audience was so absolutely still that it seemed as if I could literally have heard a pin drop. It is a pleasure to play before an audience like that, because one feels as if one were listened to with some understanding.

A beautiful new Music Hall has just been built in Chicago in the very heart of the city, and the Chicagoans fondly imagine that there never *was* such a Hall. It *is* a gay and cheery place, and shows off the dress of the ladies to great advantage. The acoustic is admirable, and could not be better, but the stage is too shallow for beauty, and the decorations look cheap. On the other hand, there is a *foyer,* which is delightful when you come in. It is carpeted and hung with mirrors, which makes it very pleasant to promenade in, or to wait in during a performance till you can be shown to a seat. I was the first person to sound a note of music in the new Hall. What composer do you think I played? Wagner. I had some prickings of conscience, as I thought Beethoven ought to be the presiding genius of the new Hall, but I finally got over it by saying to myself that Wagner is the composer who represents progress, and is therefore better suited to Chicago. There is no denying that Chicago is a fascinating sort of place to live in, after one gets accustomed to its ways. Rose says she is less bored here than in any place she was ever in. The busy, wide-awake atmosphere gives life a hopeful aspect. Life is not less of a struggle here, but one has more heart to contend, and the very rapidity with which the city has rebuilt itself, is a constant reminder of how much can be done where there is a will.

Have you written any new poems of late? I have not seen the last numbers of the *Atlantic Monthly,* I am so out of the literary world here, that I feel as if I know nothing that is going on in it. I have read *one* book, however, that gave me a sensation. It is by Zola, and is called "La faute de l'Abbé Mouret." Have you read it? I thought it a very powerful and entirely original book. That is, if one can call a book original which takes for its fundamental idea anything so very old as Adam and Eve in the Garden of Eden. As Solomon is so fond of remarking in the Book of Ecclesiastes, "there is nothing new under the sun." But it often seems to me that an old idea with a new turn given to it, is almost better than a new idea. It is certainly more entertaining for the very reason that one has thought of it so often before, and never in that particular way. As I was saying about this book of Zola's—it is the most realistic and yet the most fantastic thing imaginable, and is full of delicious and poetic touches. In his description of the Garden of "Paradou," as he calls it, there is almost too great an opulence of fancy, and he makes all the flowers of all the seasons of the year bloom at once, which is questionable taste, I should say. I should not care to see the amaranth by the side of the violet. But that is a mere question of taste, and after all there is something magnificent in the way he heaps everything up. I never had the least desire to read "L'Aouin," which all the papers made such a fuss over, as it always seemed to me from the sketch given of it, as if it were a disgusting book done in a masterly way. But "La faute de l'Abbé Mouret" is very ideal, and has a great deal of religion in it, which seems strange for a Frenchman.

While I am on the subject of books, I cannot tell you about the vicissitudes that *my* book has gone through! About a year ago my sister sent it to Jansen and McClurg. They were much impressed with your letter to Osgood about it but, with the usual graspiness of publishers they were not content with that but wanted me to ask you to write a few lines, either a preface to the book, or stating your opinion of it in the way they could make use of. They said, and of course with reason, that that would sell the book right off, and secure them from risk. I refused to do this, because I thought it too much to ask, particularly after you had already done so much about the book and they had your opinion. So they kept the book for seven months and were evidently a good deal puzzled in their minds. Then they returned it, and wrote me a letter in which they stated that they found it interesting and "would like to see it published," but that there was too much of it and they thought it would be better to cut it down and take out everything except [that] related strictly to Weimar. Half-hour books are now the order of the day. They said that if I would do this and submit it to them again perhaps they would take it. By this time my sister, Mrs. Peirce, had gone east to spend a year with my father at Grand Isle. So she was not on the spot to make the required alterations, nor did she wish to do it. So the book has lain on the shelf till today, when my brother has sent it to another publisher here named Grieg. It remains to be seen what the upshot will be. If Grieg refuses it, what would you think of getting it published in one of the large newspapers here? Say, the "Sunday Chicago Times?" though I don't exactly fancy that, the Chicago Times reprinted the letters before, from the Atlantic. Grieg wishes my brother to assume half of the risk, as he says that not more than one book in nine upon art, reaches a sale of two thousand copies, and that as many as that must be sold in order to repay the publisher.

We have had a most remarkable winter thus far. Such mild weather and scarcely any snow at all. I suppose the cold is still in store, and I dread it, for Chicago is the coldest place when it *is* cold. Please give my love to Edith, and remember me to Miss Alice, Miss Annie, and to Charlie. Believe me as ever.

Sincerely and gratefully,

Yours

Amy Fay

379 Dearborn Ave.

---

[1] Rose Fay Thomas (1856-1929), younger sister of Amy Fay, who in 1890 became the second wife of the famous conductor Theodore Thomas.

[2] Edith Longfellow, daughter of Henry Wadsworth Longfellow by his second wife Frances Appleton Longfellow.

Chicago December 31, 1880

My dear Mr. Longfellow,

This is the last day of the old year, and I am going to send you a greeting as my last act in it. Your delightful letter gave me much pleasure, and I thank you heartily for it, as well as for the book of Poems you sent me by Rose. I read them repeatedly, I recalled *you* in every line. With some of the Poems I was already familiar through the columns of the newspapers — as the one about the armchair, and "The Windmill," both of which I thought particularly exquisite. One thing I always admire so much in your Poems, and that is, you always *open* them so beautifully. You *fix the keynote,* if I may borrow a musical expression, and put one in the mood *at once* for what follows. There is nothing uncertain, but the idea is clear and perspicuous from the beginning. Like an artist, in fact, which you are, as well as a Poet. In the first two lines of the Poem to Bayard Taylor, for instance, the whole picture is contained.

> "And he lay among his books!
> The peace of God was in his looks."

Nothing could be better or more forcible. The Poem called "The Cathedral" made me think of Pyrmont,[1] where the trees are magnificent, and of Deppe,[2] who used to say that the woods there were "his Cathedral!" The "Sifting of Peter" is more serious than you often write, though it is perhaps the finest in the book. But they are all so beautiful it is difficult to hitch upon any one, and say it is better than the others.

I am glad you liked the appearance of *my* little book. I thought Jansen and McClurg got it up in very good style. They took a great deal more interest in it after you had seen and talked with General McClurg about it. I was so much obliged to you for what you said to him. It made him pluck up heart of grace. They told me at the store that the book is selling rapidly, which I hope is proof of its success. The papers accorded it high praise, and everybody I have seen who has read it is quite enthusiastic over it. So your judgment of it is confirmed, and I cannot help being pleased, as the book was refused by several publishers, and none of them saw anything in it. Zina reduced it fully one quarter in size, and thereby left out several of the best things in it, as she considers. She has been quite inconsolable about it, now that people enjoy the book so much, and wishes she had not yielded to the clamourings of the publishers for condensation. However, I think perhaps it is just as well as it is. At any rate we have erred on the safe side.

I shall very likely go to Cambridge to spend next summer with my sister, Mrs. Stone,[3] who will then be living in her new house, in your neighborhood. How I shall enjoy seeing you all again! Cambridge always seems more like home to me than any other place. Kate writes me that Professor Peirce[4] has bought a lot next to hers, and that Osgood was looking at land there also. You will have all the music of the two concentrated right around you!

So you did not care for Sara Bernhardt? How *could* you resist her? I should like to take a season ticket and see her act every night! My brother was looking at the sketches in the beginning of each Libretto of her plays, evidently drawn by herself, and he said they are so spirited, and so full of talent as they could be! We found them intensely interesting, and indeed she must be one of the geniuses of the age! Norman said that each of these drawings, though scratchy in execution, showed such a thoroughly artistic grasp of the situation. No lack of *effect there*! My sheet is full so I have only room for my best wishes that you may have a Happy New Year! That it may be wholly bright and unclouded, is the warm desire of

Yours most sincerely,

Amy Fay

---

[1] Pyrmont, one of the residences of Amy Fay during her European sojourn.

[2] Ludwig Deppe (1828-90), German pianist, teacher, and conductor who developed a method of piano playing promoted by Amy Fay after her return home.

[3] Kate Fay Stone (1846-1928), Amy's younger sister who became the wife of William E. Stone in 1871. Mother of Pauline, Reginald, Margaret, and Amy. She was an accomplished pianist also.

[4] Charles Sanders Peirce (1839-1914), philosopher and logician, and onetime husband of Amy Fay's sister Melusina ("Zina").

Chicago February 25, 1882

My Dear Mr. Longfellow,

I remember that your birthday comes on Monday next, and I cannot resist sending you my heartfelt congratulations. I only regret that I am not in Cambridge to tender them in person, and to enjoy for an hour your delightful society. We had a momentary glimpse of Mr. Louis Dyer some weeks since and he brought us your kind message of greeting, and also the welcome news that you were in good health. I likewise received the two Papers you sent me some time ago, for both of which please receive my cordial thanks.

I was much interested in reading about the Liszt celebration in Boston, it must have been highly gratifying to the "Meister." I had a sort of little reunion of artists at my home also in his honor, which was quite a pleasant little affair. A long article appeared in the Chicago Tribune about the Boston celebration in honor of Liszt, and a great portion of it was devoted to you. It dealt long and lovingly upon our great Poet, and described him and his beautiful house in glowing colors! We are now hoping for a visit from Miss Annie, to whom Rose has already written. Tell her that if she will adventure herself into the wild west, we will do our utmost to reconcile her to it! I trust that Edith and her little family are well at last? Poor Richard has had a hard time of it this year with illness and the death of his father. My sisters send you their love and congratulations and that you may live to many more birthdays and gladden the world, is the warm wish of

Yours most sincerely,

Amy Fay

Chicago June 10, 1887

Dearest Lak,[1]

How you was? Your various letters, papers and photographs have all come to hand and received my undivided attention. . . . We have all been having a rather dull summer thus far, and nothing in particular seems to have occurred to vary the monotony of life. I have come to the conclusion that after thirty-five life is monotonous anyway. The only exciting thing about it is falling in love and getting married, and when that important question is settled one way or another, there is nothing left of an exciting nature. One can be *comfortable,* and that is all.

Rose and I went down to St. Louis for a few days, at the invitation of Thomas,[2] to hear the American Opera do "Nero." We were Thomas' guests at the Hotel, and he treated us in his usual royal style, and we had a charming visit. St. Louis is a totally uninteresting but cosey sort of place. One house is just like another, and the town is overgrown with dock weeds to an extent that is really deplorable. I could not help wishing that Mudkins[3] could spend a few weeks there and get up a "society for the annihilation of dock weeds!" I know she could not stand it a minute to see them flourishing so. They are a dreadful eyesore. The only thing beautiful about St. Louis is the park and the cemetery.

There is a very nice Opera House in the Exposition Building in St. Louis. We went with Thomas in his carriage, of course, and came in through the stage entrance. He had a private room facing upon the street in front of the Opera House, and it was quite a novel sensation to sit in it with the great conductor before the beginning of the performance and watch the people alight from their carriages and walk up the steps. They dress a great deal in St. Louis, and many of the ladies were in full evening toilette, *décolletées,* and with their hair dressed. They had slender and beautiful figures, and a great deal of style. I was glad not to see the fat women we have so many of *here*! Slenderness is quite universal there. The houses are utterly unimaginative and are exactly alike in the fashionable avenues. They are all light grey and have French roofs and deep doorways. They don't seem to have *any* of the new ideas in building that we have in Chicago, where *nobody* wishes to have a house like anybody else's.

I have been pegging away over my pupils of late till I am little short of being an idiot, and I want to have put on my tombstone, "She died a martyr to the Deppe exercises!" I have just had my annual pupil's luncheon, and subsequently my annual pupil's recital. Both were brilliant successes, and, heaven be praised, they are over! At the luncheon I had only my pupils, and after lunch I had them *all* play. At the recital I allowed only five of the best ones to play, and I had two pupils of Mrs. Eddy's[4] play. I invited over a hundred people and made it like an afternoon reception. All the furniture was taken out of the parlour, and chairs were placed in rows, and the grand piano stood at the head of the room. The pupils did so beautifully that my guests were completely taken down, and I hope it will be the means of putting some shiners into my pocky next season! Lots of flowers were sent to me, and the house was decorated with them very handsomely. I had one of my pupils play a Trio with Jacobson and Hess, and that made a sensation. Her name is Addie Smith, and she is one of my best pupils. Mrs. Eddy wrote me a splended notice, and put it in the *Indicator,* which is the musical hope of Chicago. I shall try to come to Woodstock this summer. Probably in August, if that will suit you, unless Gurickx[5] should come over then for a visit to Chicago.

Give my love to all the family and tell Madeline[6] that Pauline[7] is still here and is the most tremendous favorite with all the girls on the street.

Your loving,

Amy

---

[1] Laura Fay Smith (1841-1920), an older sister of Amy Fay who married Francis Wyman Smith in 1865. Mother of Charles Bertram, William Nelson, Frances Laura, Harvey Blatchford, Ernest Norman, and Madeline.

[2] Theodore Thomas (1835-1905), famous German-American conductor who married Rose Fay in 1890 following the death of his first wife.

[3] Term of endearment (nickname) Amy gave to her older sister Melusina, who was an ardent feminist and organizer.

[4] Mrs. Clarence Eddy, a personal friend of Amy Fay who inherited a fortune from her father and lived in Paris after 1895. Her grandson Clifford Vogel became a piano student of Amy Fay after Amy moved to New York.

[5] William Gurickx, a Belgian musician with whom Amy Fay was romantically involved during her European student days and whom she visited during her visit to Europe in 1903.

[6] Madeline Smith, niece of Amy Fay and daughter of Laura Fay Smith.

[7] Pauline Stone, niece of Amy Fay and daughter of Kate Fay Stone. Amy travelled with her to South America in 1902 to attend Pauline's wedding to Arthur Jackson.

The American Years

Dearest Mudkins,

Your letter with the check reached me on Friday, and the same day, by a curious coincidence I received from MacMillan $116.99 royalty, from June 1886 to June 1887. So I shall have the pleasure of remitting to you $58.50 in a few days! I had begun to think I was never going to get anything more out of them, as they had not sent me a cent since a year ago last June, and feared that another firm had got out an edition, which would cancel all *my* claims! You know they had already bought off one firm for 14 pounds, which, of course, came out of my royalty, after the convenient method which publishers have of making the author lose always! There is small inducement certainly to write books, as far as the *money* part of it is concerned. One must content oneself with fame.

. . . We have got some charming new neighbors from New York, Mr. and Mrs. Morgan who have taken the Herings' house. They belong to very rich and swell families in New York, and are a young couple of two years' standing. Mrs. Morgan is perhaps twenty-three, and was a Miss Edith Parsons. She is exquisitely pretty and *spirituelle.* Her husband is perhaps twenty-five or six, a quiet fellow, but very well bred. She seems devotedly in love with him, though it seems funny how such a quiet fellow could fascinate such a gay little humming bird as she is! We invited them over here once or twice, and then, one week when Lily[1] had allowed our cook to go home to take care of a sick sister, Mrs. Morgan at once asked the whole family over there to dinner (including Wilmerding who was with us!) with true New York hospitality and enterprise. We went over, and she appeared like a vision as she advanced to meet us, dressed in a ravishing toilet of red silk, with a deep yoke and cuffs of white Irish lace, and exquisite jewelry. When we went into the little dining room the table was beautifully set with superb silver, and looked very handsome. Everything was so attractive that I began to feel quite festive, when in an evil moment, Mr. Morgan, on whose right I sat, intending to be very polite, pushed my chair under me to sit down. He pushed it in too far, and somehow I caught in my soup plate as I sat down, and the whole contents were turned into my lap. I had on a blue velvet dress, and you can imagine the result! The whole front of it was ruined. They were *aghast,* and Mrs. Morgan rushed to my assistance with a napkin to mop it up, but the surface was so shiny it would not absorb it. At last I was ashamed to keep them all standing any longer, so I pretended it was all dry, and sat down. But all through dinner I could feel this soup soaking through me, and when I looked down furtively I saw puddles of it in the folds of my dress! You can fancy how uncomfortable I was! It was the worst *contretemps* I ever had happen to me, and poor Mr. Morgan was dreadfully unhappy over it. Mrs. Morgan rallied, however, and was most brilliant in conversation. Norman[2] seems to have an exciting effect on her and she regularly *went* for him. He really had to exert himself to keep up his end of the beam. But he came up to the scratch, and was awfully witty. I never saw him appear so fascinating, for he was put to his trumps, and all his power of *repartée* (which is considerable) was called out. One of the funny things he said was when Mrs. Morgan remarked, "I once heard a little boy ask his mother if 'Mary Had a Little Lamb' was in the Bible." "Why, yes," said Norman, "at least *Mary* was, and so was the lamb!"

After dinner we played cards of which Mr. Morgan, like most quiet men, is very fond, and she too. It reminded me of the old Peirce days, for they know all sorts of games! I enjoyed the evening, in spite of my misfortune. Lily has fortunately found a remnant of just two years, so I shall be able to repair damages. I thought, at first, that the dress was "gone up" altogether, for it was made up of remnants, trimmings, and all!

I am reading a very powerful story by Edgar Fawcett, which is coming out in the Inter-Ocean, about drinking. It is called "A Man's Will," and is a story in high life, in New York society. It seems to me he has struck out a new lead. Tell Rose I wish she could manage to meet him again at Mrs. Stebbins'! What do you think of Apthorp's[3] letter? I was to have played at the Artists'[4] Club this week, and this wretched illness of mine broke it all up. I had to lose all my lessons, too! Tell Rose the "Anabaptists" continue to abuse me in the *Indicator*. Goodbye, and believe me with love from all the family, as ever

Your devoted,

Amy

---

[1] Lily Fay Wilmerding (b. 1885), Amy Fay's younger sister who married Charles Wilmerding in 1889. Mother of Valeria Fay, Charles Henry, and Katherine Fay.

[2] Charles Norman Fay was known as "Norman."

[3] William Foster Apthorp (1848-1913), a distinguished American music critic.

[4] Artists' Club, a Chicago musical club founded by Amy Fay, at whose concert performers were Chicago artists and residents of the highest order.

New York March 28, 1895

Dearest Sister Rose,

. . . What have I been doing of interest lately? Well, nothing in particular. I went to hear *Lohengrin,* by Damrosches' company on Friday evening, with Nordica and Lehmann as Elsa and Ortrud, and with Krauss as the New Lohengrin. He is young and very handsome, and looks the part splendidly, but, alas, he has been indispositioned ever since he arrived, and was as hoarse as a crow. He did not have so much voice as a cat, and had to tell us almost in a confidential whisper, "Aus glanz, und Wonne kon ichher; bin Lohengrin gannant!" Sad, but true. "Oh, my blond beauty, I feel for you," said I to myself, "so to blaniren yourself, before such an audience, and between two such glorious women as Nordica and Schumann!" Schade, schade! I could just hear Krauss cussing his luck in his dressing room, between the acts, although I was promenading the *foyer* way up in the dress circle over the boxes, with Mr. Skinner, Mrs. Duane's friend. The middle act, with Nordica and Lehmann as Elsa and Ortrud, was perfectly stunning, and the opera was magnificently put on the stage. I thought Damrosch[1] conducted *finely,* although the nasty *Evening Post* keeps jumping on him every day and making insidious comparisons in favor of Seidl.[2] Finck[3] is really besotted on the subject of Seidl, and you wouldn't suppose to read his notices that anybody had ever held a Tact-Stock before. It makes me so mad, be Jabbers! I wish I could go to the Opera every night next week, when Lehmann is going to sing in nearly all the operas, and the whole Nibelungen Tetralogy will be given. There are so *many* things I want to hear next week. . . . There's the Opera, and a Recital by Huberman, and Scharwenka's "Mataswintha," and Plunket Greene's song recitals, and Beatrice Herford's awfully witty monologues, and Damrosches' Symphony concert, not to speak of the Theatres, which are full of stunning novelties.

. . . Mudkins finally decided to get over the *grippe,* and she has been very lively for the last two or three weeks, and quite rejuvenated. She belongs to *several* associations, and you never saw anyone go giddy as she has become. First she is driving down to the Mayor's office about saving the Poe cottage; now she confers with Miss Fischer uptown about the Horne Hotel for aged and indigent brain workers, like myself. Between times she has interviews with Sam Franko and musical managers about summer night concerts. Then she pours tea at the receptions of the Authors' Club, in their rooms at Carnegie Hall. Like Bryant's clouds, "*here* she stretches to the Froloc Chase, and *there* she *rolls* on the easy gale!" I never know where to find her, but as the bill has passed for greater New York, I know she is within the city limits, somewhere between Fordham and Brooklyn, which is quieting to my nerves. Occasionally, she dabbles a little at her book, and corrects a proof or two. It is well in vain I harangue her on this subject and tell her her book ought to be the object of her life, and that she *must* get it done. She is too well entertained with her various projects to concentrate. It reminds me of your numerous kinds of fancy work at the Island.

This being Sunday, I went down to Trinity Chapel and listened to one of those sermons from our dear Dr. Vibbert. He preached on the text "The last shall be first, and the first shall be last," and he told us we must not despair, but keep on trying to do our duty, and that even if we were one of the last, we might be one of the first, and that if we were one of the first, and didn't do our duty, we might be one of the last. What with brandy and water, and whiskey and water, and Dublin and whiskey, and Naples and water, my head got quite soft, and I don't know just where I stand, or whether I am among the first or the last, or the last or the first! I trust somewhere in the *middle*. You remember Dr. Holland said "Dr. Vibbert always took the middle path, and that he parted his hair in the middle!" . . . Laura Sanford[4] is getting to look so young ladified! She played at a concert here the other day, given for charity, in the large ballroom of the *new* John Jacob Astor Waldorf Hotel. There must have been a thousand people there. Laura looked exquisitely pretty in her white dress, and played exquisitely, too. She is to play at the Thursday Afternoon Club on the 10th of April. I have been invited to play at the Exposition in Nashville, Tennessee by the ladies there, on the 18th and 19th of May. I think I shall accept, as I would like to see it. Zina joins me in much love to you all . . . As ever.

Your devoted,

Amy

---

[1] Walter Damrosch, conductor, educator, and composer who organized the Damrosch Opera Company in 1894. Brother of Frank Damrosch, New York music educator, he was also conductor of the New York Philharmonic Society from 1902 to 1903.

[2] Anton Seidl (1850-98), Austro-Hungarian conductor who succeeded Theodore Thomas in 1891 as conductor of the New York Philharmonic Society.

[3] Henry T. Finck (1854-1926), American music critic of the *New York Evening Post* from 1881 to 1924.

[4] Laura Sanford, a piano student of Amy Fay from New York, whose name occurs frequently in the letters.

New York November 14, 1901

Dearest Zie,[1]

I got your nice long letter, and have been dying to write to you for days, but have been so driven every moment, I *could not*. This week I am playing three times for the Board of Education. I gave my first Piano Conversation Monday evening at a school in West 89th Street, and on Monday again, in East 27th Street. The first place was nearby, and was quite convenient, but the next one is at the end of the world, and I have four long flights of stairs to climb to get there! *This* audience will be mainly Polish Jews I expect! It is so foreign on the east side! My audience up here was a nice one, and many persons came up to congratulate me after the concert, among others a Dr. Pack who used to live in Burlington, and who knew all about us. He was a fine looking man. One young lady said she wanted to tell me that she "knew *every word* of my book by heart!" I forget her name. Another woman wanted to know where she could buy it, and "whether it would have a *beneficial effect* on young people?" I told her it had been made a prize book in schools quite often. Still another woman said she had a little nephew seven years old whom her friends thought a musical genius, and she wanted me to hear him play and tell what to do with him as she knows nothing about music. She was poor, and evidently hoped I would teach the boy for nothing. I told her I would hear him play next Saturday, and *she* went off grateful! On the whole, It will be quite a new and entertaining experience playing in these schools all over the city.

Friday A.M. Well, it has got to be *Friday,* and my letter to you not done *yet!* Last night I played down in East 5th Street, between Avenues C and D. You would not recognize *New York* over there! The signs on the shops are many of them in Hebrew characters, the women are hatless, and there is no evidence of the "four hundred" in *that* part of the city. I was told that the Polish women wear *wigs,* as it is a law that they must cut their hair when they marry, to prevent them from being attractive to other men. I did not see any, however. I went to this school with some trepidation, as I was told by Mr. Beers, the principal, that the crowd was a very lawless one, and the janitor had to clear them out with his club at a lecture with steryopticon. He said they chipped desks, and stole the pictures, etc., and that he "just *dreaded* when the lecturers came there." I said, "perhaps they will behave better at my Piano Conversation." . . . My audience, however, did not turn out as he said, and was composed of young men and girls, the *men* largely predominating. One working woman, in a short red skirt and bundled up in a shawl, of the lower classes, sat in one of the front row seats. . . . Four toughs, and one "athlete" came in. Mr. Curtis, the teacher in charge, remarked "those fellows have come in to make trouble. I had to force them to leave the preceding lecture." They sat in the back of the hall, and reminded me of the bad boys in your choral school in Cambridge who used to hang around so. The "athlete" had a club foot, and came hobbling in, but Mr. Curtis said he was well-known as one of the best around there! I began to talk punctually at eight o'clock. You can imagine I felt some trepidation to play the *Pathétique*[2] before this audience. I expected there would be talking and laughing so that I could not hear myself think. Do you know, they were as quiet as mice, all *through,* except when they were *laughing out* with amusement at my remarks! At the close, they applauded like everything, and then they crowded around me on the stage, and begged to know "when I was going to play to them again?" I told them I did not expect to play in that school again. Then they wished to know if I was going to play anywhere else? I said I was to play in School 225 on East 27th Street next Monday evening. "All right," said a beautiful girl, who was spokesman, "we can go up there *just as well. We'll come up Monday night.*" So I expect to contine the intimacy. Mr. Curtis escorted me to the car, and he said, "the concert was a *success.*" He was a cultivated and well-mannered young man. The four toughs gave no trouble, and seemed as much interested as all the rest. One girl asked me if I was a pupil of Virgil's.[3] She said she thought I must be, "by the way I played!" She was in Virgil's school. I did not tell her that he stole his method from me! Well, it was lots of fun down there and I enjoyed myself like everything. It quite inspired me to talk to that audience, it was so responsive!

On Tuesday afternoon we have the next meeting of the Piano Department of the Women's Philharmonic.[4] I invited Emma Zuck to be guest of honor, and she is going to sing a group of songs, which will be a great attraction. Mrs. Coe[5] . . . called a meeting of the whole Society last Tuesday, November 12th with the intention of changing the name to the "New York Music League." She wants to have men subscribers in the Club, but who will not have the right to hold office. This is her *ostensible* reason, but her real reason is, she is so jealous of *your* prestige as the *founder* of the Club, and of *me* as your sister, and also because the meetings of the Piano Department are such a brilliant success, that she wants to obliterate your *memory,* even, from the Club, and make it appear to outsiders entirely her *own.* I see through her, and know perfectly well what she is after. She is a most ambitious woman, and determined to *rule* to the limits of her power. She *padlocked* me, in true Donald MacLean fashion, when I rose to speak a second time, and said "no member is allowed to speak *twice,*" before I had time to utter a sentence. You know I am always short and to the point, when I speak to the Club. It never takes me but a moment or two to express myself. (They applaud everything I say.) The members of the Society had a sentiment about the name on *your* account (they did not *want* to change it) as some of them plainly said, in speaking of "our dear founder." This was like a red rag to a bull, to Mrs. Coe. She asked Miss Collins, who is 1st vice-president, to take the chair, and then she stood up and *delivered herself!* She blew her own trumpet for about ten minutes and detailed all the benefits tht she had conferred upon the Club and finally *forced* it at the point of the bayonet, to vote for changing the name. She succeeded in getting her way, but only by *one* vote! Wasn't it too bad Mrs. Donington and Mrs. Humaron were not present for if they *had been* on *my side who* would have won? Miss Hirsch, who was on my side, got up and *went out* during the balloting because she was too politic to vote against Mrs. Coe! . . . I am now doubting whether to resign or to stay in and plague Mrs. Coe. She would be *delighted* if I left, no doubt! The Manuscript Society has made me a Director, so I have that to fall back on! Give my best love to all the family and tell Norman and Rose I got their letters and checks.

With much love as ever from your devoted sister,

Amy

---

[1] Another nickname for Melusina.
[2] A piano sonata by Beethoven.
[3] Founder of the Virgil method of piano playing and professional rival of Amy Fay who, in her eyes, appropriated the Deppe Method from her.
[4] A musical organization by and for women founded in 1899 by Melusina and of which Amy was president in 1903-14.
[5] Amy's predecessor as President of the Women's Philharmonic Society.

New York November 23, 1901

Dearest Zie,

My hearty congratulations on the success of your lecture, which Rose wrote me was "the most brilliant one" she had ever heard from a woman! It was most fortunate that you were able to appear under editorial auspices, for we all know, to our cost, what magnates *swells* are, and it is the same the world over! I was telling Norman the other evening, the Smiths and the Beardsleys were just as potent in St. Albans, in the old days, as are the Astors and the Vanderbilts in New York, or Mrs. Potter Palmer and Mrs. Gleason in Chicago! Only we did not understand the question in our humble and inexperienced days! Now, if you can get into the *lecture field* with your paper, it will be a much pleasanter way of making money than keeping boarders, and you will realize the desire of your youth to be a lecturer, when we thought it such a terrible and disgraceful thing to do! It is wonderful how public opinion has changed since the days of Anne Dickinson and Mrs. Livermore!

Many thanks for the check, which will, of course, come in "very handy," as money under *any* circumstances, always does! I *could* carry along without it, though, and I am sorry you would not keep the royalty on the book, as I told you. I invited Laura to come over on Tuesday, and spend two days, and we really managed to crowd in a lot during that short time, and she ought to have gone home well satisfied. . . . She went to the concert of the Piano Department of the Women's Philharmonic on Tuesday afternoon. I had invited a Mrs. Wellman (Emma Zuck) to be the guest of honor, and she sang a group of most *beautiful* songs, in the most artistic manner. One of them, by Brahms, called "Die Mainacht," was one of the most magnificent songs I ever heard. It had a great climax at the end, and pretty little Emma came right up to the mark, in masterly style. The general verdict was, that she is singing better than ever, as she has much depth of style and conception. Another *gem* was a song by a French composer named Gabriel Fauré, called "Après un rêve." Fauré was an unknown name to *me,* but a little Frenchman I used to know, named Larapédie, who used to play in the Boston Symphony Orchestra, and who has just

19

come back from Paris, told me that he is being much talked about over there. I bought all four of Zuck's songs and learned them, at the concert. I sent out a good many programs; Miss Read[1] and Mrs. Roberts got them up; and the hall was *crowded.* The whole affair was a crushing success, they all said.

Norman came up and spent the evening on Tuesday, so Laura had a pleasant chat with him. He was as sweet and generous as he always is, and gave us five dollars to go to the Flower show the next afternoon, which we did. We had good seats, and looked on for a while, and then we promenaded, and Laura had a chance to see the swells in their boxes. We met *Bagby,* and to my surprise he stood still, *was* most cordial, and talked with us until *we* left *him,* instead of *his shaking us!* We met Jennie Dalton, whom Laura also knows, and I had a little glimpse of Mrs. Loring, so we were not without acquaintances in the crowd! Laura was carried away by the beauty of Mrs. Carley Havemeyer, who was in one of the boxes. On Wednesday morning I took Laura to the Watercolor Exhibition, in the 59th Street Gallery, which was interesting. We looked at the pictures pretty thoroughly, and then came home to luncheon, which happened to be *good* that day. About four o'clock Laura went back to Tenafly. She looked very well and really pretty, as she said goodbye.

. . . I have got through *three* of the five engagements to play for the Board of Education. The two remaining ones will take place on the evenings of December 3rd and 19th. I shan't get my money for a month later, which is provoking. The next one is at High Bridge.

. . . Just think, I have not had a single *Monday*[2] yet, nor have I made scarcely any calls. I have been so dreadfully busy! Tomorrow afternoon is Wesley Weyman's concert, so I shall be obliged to go to *that,* and put off receiving still another week.

. . . Are you going to have your lecture printed? I should think you *would. My* theory is that servants ought to live in communities out of the house, and that they should work by the hour and relieve each other. We should have day servants and night servants and they ought to be paid for their work by the hour. Then there would be no more trouble! There ought to be training schools to teach them their work, so they would go out all trained for it like nurses. My best love to all the family and with a great deal to you.

Amy

Mrs. Coe was much taken down by the crowd at the concert of the Piano Department and was most polite and attentive! They felt she had gone too far with me!

---

[1] A student and close friend of Amy Fay who was travelling companion during her European sojourn in 1903.

[2] Amy held "at homes" on Monday afternoons when she received visitors socially.

The American Years

New York December 30, 1901

Dearest Mudkins,

You must be wondering if I am not *dead,* it is so long since I have written any of the family. I finished my course of concerts in the public schools last night, thank Heaven! I now begin to feel so I could breathe out once more! You, see, practicing and reading up for the lecture part has kept me very closely at work, in addition to teaching, and managing the Piano Department of the Women's Philharmonic (now called "The New York Musical League," alas!). Then I have attended no end of business meetings, and written *quantities* of notes and letters, and I have had lots of other *jobs* also. I got my furniture out of storage and arranged my things, and hung my pictures, etc. All these things take time and thought. My wardrobe has also claimed some attention, though not *much,* and I have so little money to spend on clothes.

. . . Have you heard anything from Kate since her steamer letter? Laura and I have not, and we would like to know what she is doing with herself. . . . All your friends here miss you very much, and regret your departure. I often hear charming things spoken of you. I met Mrs. Lowell T. Field the other day, at a reception, and she said that she got forty of the old members of the Women's Philharmonic together, and they were forming a new Society and keeping the old name. She said you ought to come back and be the President of it, but I could see that she is dying to be President herself! Mrs. Coe, having got her say, and changed the name of our Society, in the very teeth of the opposition of a majority of the members, has simmered down for the present. She could not have done it but for the backing of Madames Courtney and Collins, and especially of Lillie d'Angelo Bergh. I have been so mad at them, that I have held myself very offish and aloof. The concerts of the Piano Department are the feature of interest in the Club, and we got by far the largest and swellest audiences. At our last reunion Marguerite Hall sang, and was the guest of honor. She has gained very much in her singing.

Kubelik[1] and Hofmann[2] continue to divide the honours in the concerts of Paur[3] and Gericke.[4] It is *amazing* what they can do. I have heard Hofmann reel off four concerts, magnificently within a short time. The last one was the E minor one by Chopin, which has been shelved for a long time. What a wonderful *composition* it is, and sustained on such a high and intellectual plane. It was divinely accompanied in the *Adagio* by the Boston Symphony Orchestra.

The opera begins next week, but I don't expect to get there! I hope you will return to New York, as you have not tied yourself down to Chicago, for this is your "native hearth" so to speak. I have missed you dreadfully, and find it lonesome without you. My rooms are delightfully comfortable this year, as I have furnace heat, and the sun. I like them immensely. I have moved my bed into the alcove so it leaves the room quite free. On Monday I received and four of my pupils met here, which was pleasant.

21

Amy Fay

They were Miss Read, Miss Potpin, Edith Blanc and Hattie Hill, all of them talented. I expect to have Laura over on Christmas Eve. I shall write to Norman and Rose in a day or two. . . . I hope that you will have a Merry Christmas, and send you my best love. This is not much without money to back it up with however.

Your loving sister,

Amy

---

[1] Jan Kubelik (1880-1940), Czech violinist and composer, father of the conductor Rafael Kubelik.

[2] Josef Hofmann (1876-1957), celebrated Polish pianist and head of the Curtis Institute of Music in Philadelphia in 1926-38.

[3] Emil Paur (1855-1932), Austrian conductor who was conductor of New York Philharmonic in 1898-1902.

[4] Wilhelm Gericke (1845-1925), Austrian conductor and composer who conducted the Boston Symphony Orchestra in 1884-89 and again in 1898-1906.

New York January 1, 1902

Dearest Zie,

Happy New Year! I got your letter of Christmas containing the five dollars. I alas want as my first act of the New Year to be to acknowledge and thank you for them. I was tremendously touched at your sending me money out of your *minute* income and it really seems *wrong* of me to accept. I should be so glad if by some way you could get more money. As for myself I am cudgelling my brains all the time about getting a position as musical correspondent on some paper, but it always seems impossible to make them pay for anything. Mathews[1] owes me sixty dollars but I'll really never see a cent of it although he apologized at the time he made the price for the lowness of it. He admitted, himself, that ten dollars was very little for my work. Goerlitz and Frohman were *delighted* with my Kubelik article, and they sent me one of the finest boxes in Carnegie Hall for Kubelik's matinee on Saturday afternoon, right in the center of the house. As the seats in the parquet were two dollars, I had given up going as I did not care to sit up in the top of the house and be suffocated by the crowd. I was *much* delighted to be able to sit in a grand box, like the swells and took Miss Bates and Miss Read with me. As it happened, Frohman sat in the very next box and my old friend, Mrs. Steele McKaye and her two sons and daughter, Hazel. Mrs. McKaye at once introduced me to Frohman and I had quite a long conversation with him, which was luck! He said Goerlitz wanted him to use my *article* here, and perhaps he should do so. The critics, of course, have been acting in their most divisive way, and there is a regular fight between them and the violinists here. The violinists all agree with my estimate of him, and acknowledge his enormous talent, while the critics treat him worse than they did Hofmann last winter. Frohman has come out in the Musical Courier with an article over his own signature protesting against the way Kubelik has been criticized by them. I think it is just a bid for money on their part. I am more and more convinced that everything is *business,* in music as in other things.

By the way, Jungnickel has come back to live in New York again, and he came to see me a few days ago, and inquired very affectionately after you. He is completely tired of Baltimore and says he has "wasted too many years of his life there." He regretted that you and he did not start in with orchestral concerts that time when you had the three thousand dollars, as that money was the making of Kaltemborn, and gave him *his* start. I heard yesterday that the Philharmonic will need a conductor next season, and that Paur is going back to Germany. Perhaps Jungnickel might get in there. If Theodore wants to come back to New York *now* would be the time to lay his plans. . . . So Theodore's financial burdens seem to be dropping off him. I hope *he* won't *drop off* now that it is getting to be easy sailing, at last.

Isn't it *fine* that Normie has won his suit against Slaughter? I hope this means the restoration of his *bonds,* which have been withheld from him so long. This *ought* to *increase* his income. Miss Read says she saw a large placard at Wanamaker's near the elevator advertising the "Fay Typewriter" in big letters, and telling all the wonderful things it would do! I think Normie is on the homestretch now, with his financial difficulties and right glad am I!

Laura came over on Christmas Eve, as I wrote you, and we had a very successful time on Christmas Day. I got up and went to early service. . . . I had taken Sister Laura to see Mansfield in *Beaucaire* on Christmas Eve. I think she enjoyed it, although she kept asking me "how many more acts are there?" etc. . . . Laura had not been to the Theatre for forty years, she said. The play was a very pretty one, and he impersonated a Frenchman, and turns out to be King Louis the 15th at the close of the last act, when he was supposed all through the play to be lowborn. He spoke English like a Frenchman, with an accent. . . . Fanny and Nelson[2] gave us a delightful little dinner, and were very affectionate and eager to make us feel welcome. . . .

Your loving sister,

Amy

---

[1] William S. B. Mathews, Chicago music critic.

[2] Fanny and Nelson Smith, Laura's son and daughter-in-law.

Amy Fay

New York January 9, 1902

Dearest Zie,

. . . We had a business meeting of the *"Musical League"*[1] last week, and I am happy to say, that I got my *revenge* on Mrs. Coe and Miss Collins. You ought to have seen the resignations *pour in*! The Club was evidently entirely disaffected by the changed of name, and change of principles, admission of *men,* etc. Mrs. Coe's and Miss Collins' faces grew longer and longer! Katherine Smith gave in the resignation of one woman, whose name I have forgotten, and she said quite openly, that she "had no further interest in the Society since the change of name and of *principles,* as it was no longer the *the same thing as before."* I was so *delighted,* I could have thrown my cap! Mrs. Coe has entirely come down from her top political attitude and is very chummy *now* in her manner. She is probably discovering that her demeanor did not please. The Council meeting was so small, that they could not get a quorum till I came in, and business was at a standstill. Miss Collins is now trying to crawlfish out of her mistakes, and to make out that she was opposed to the admission of men. As to the name, she said that many in the Society had not liked the name of Philharmonic in the first place. Then she said there was *another,* which was chosen by Mrs. Peirce, which was not taken by the Club. I think she made that up out of whole cloth, and she always proves to me as being so anxious to carry out *your* intentions in regard to everything. . . . Yesterday I poured tea at the private meeting of the Manuscript Society, and played Paine's "Country Scenes" which were much applauded. We had pleasant rooms at 126 East 23rd Street. I am in a hurry, must close with much love. Tell Madeline I got her charming letter and will answer it soon.

As ever,

Your loving Amy

---

[1] Formerly called the Women's Philharmonic Society of New York.

New York January 18, 1902

Dearest Zie,

. . . This has been the most interesting winter I have spent in New York, as we have such superb concerts here all the while, and the Women's Philharmonic and

Manuscripts Societies give me enough society, in a very easy and inexpensive way.
 . . . I am delighted to be able to state that I have succeeded in changing the name
of the Women's Philharmonic from the New York Musical League, back to its original
title, which you gave it. I told the members about Mrs. Field's plan of rallying the
disaffected charter members of which she had forty, and forming a new society under
the old name and constitution, and inviting you to be Honorary President of it. I
told the club that when you found you had made a big blunder, the best thing to
do was to *acknowledge* it, and *retrace* your steps as quickly as possible. Mrs. Coe,
pretty well frightened by the many resignations, and also by the inextricable confusion
to our Club which Mrs. Field's enterprise would cause, was sensible enough to see
that I was right and consented that we should return to the old name. Even Miss
Collins was eager to retract, and the Club at large is attached to the old name on
your account. So we are again the Women's Philharmonic Society, much to our *joy*.
The astute Mrs. Courtney made the discovery that the change of name was not legal,
to that of the New York Musical League, as thirty days notice ought to have been
sent out, which was not done. Also it was not voted upon in the business meeting
of the whole society, but only in the Council. It was all hurried through. Must go
to bed. It is late.

My best love,

Amy

New York February 16, 1902

Dearest Zie,

I have been wanting to write to you for many days, but have been so *wretchedly,*
on account of my cold, which has lasted for *five weeks*, and is only *just* getting better
now, I could not bring myself to take pen in hand. Alas I have been *very* busy and
have worked in spite of my cold. I played a recital for the Board of Education two
weeks ago last Thursday night, and have another one at Kingsbridge tomorrow
evening. (This is the ninth.) Tuesday evening is the concert of the Piano Department
of the Women's Philharmonic, and I had to arrange the programme last week. . . .
Yesterday (Saturday) I taught in the morning, went to Paderewski's first recital
in the afternoon. Lily came up to dinner and spent the night. At nine in the evening
was the reception to Mrs. Coe, our President, and I had to dress, and receive on
the stage, so I suppose Miss Collins and she must have asked me as *your* representative.
I wore my white lace dress. It was a *beautiful* affair held in the Chapter Room, which

The Society will be At Home to Members and
their Friends

Saturday Afternoon, February Twenty-second, 1902
From Four until Six O'Clock

Room 1
Fifty-sixth Street Entrance

Tea will be Served following the Programme

American Composers

∗

MISS JULIA E. HARD
Chairman Entertainment Committee

MADAME OLIVE BARRY
Chairman House Committee

The Women's Philharmonic
Society of New York

Founded in 1899 by
Mrs. Melusina Fay Peirce

∗

ANNUAL RECEPTION TO THE PRESIDENT

OF THE SOCIETY

Mrs. Henry Clarke Coe

Chapter Room, Carnegie Hall

Saturday Evening, February Fifteenth, 1902

From Nine until Eleven O'Clock

∗

Headquarters of the Society
Room 1, Carnegie Hall, 56th Street Entrance

THE LOTUS PRESS, N. Y.

President
MRS. HENRY CLARKE COE

∗

Officers receiving with the President

Vice-Presidents

Miss LAURA SEDGWICK COLLINS, First
MADAME LOUISE GAGE COURTNEY, Third
Miss MAIDA CRAIGEN, Fifth

Miss AMY FAY, Second
Miss LILLIE d'ANGELO BERGH, Fourth
Miss LILY STAFFORD PLACE, Sixth

Secretaries

Miss NELLIE F. HOGAN, Recording
Mrs. G. WASHBOURNE SMITH, Corresponding
Miss MARY F. SINCLAIR, Enrollment

Treasurer

Mrs. EDWIN ARDEN

∗

Miss COLLINS
Chairman of Committee of Arrangements

Programme...

†

Bass Soli—(a) On the Banks of Allen Water . . . Old English
(b) Traum Durch die Dämmerung . . . R. Strauss
(c) Die Oblösung . . . A. Hollaender
MR. RICHARD BYRON OVERSTREET
Miss CORINNE WOLERSTEIN, Accompanist

Piano Soli—(a) Pastorale. Presto . . . . . Scarlatti
(b) Etude de Concert . . . . . Martucci
(Dedicated to Mme. Delhaze-Wickes)
MADAME DELHAZE-WICKES

Soprano Solo—Aria from "Il Seraglio" . . . . Mozart
Miss LOUISE B. VOIGHT
Miss CORINNE WOLERSTEIN, Accompanist

Violin Soli—(a) Sentiment Poetique . . . . . F. Volker
(b) Mazurka . . . . . Zarzycki
MR. FRIEDRICH VOLKER
Mrs. VOLKER at the Piano

Duet—Gondeliera . . . . Henschel
Miss VOIGHT AND MR. OVERSTREET
Miss CORINNE WOLERSTEIN, Accompanist

∗

THE PIANO IS A BALDWIN

∗

MADAME KATHERINE EVANS VON KLENNER
Chairman of Programme

26

is bright and festive, and the women were very prettily dressed, and the program of music was short but *very* good, gotten up by Madame von Klenner. . . . Your name is on the programme as "founder," and it was really quite a feather in your cap. Miss Collins said she had one all ready in an envelope, to send to "Mrs. Peirce." I invited Betts and Mrs. Weyman, among others, and they both came and enjoyed it very much. Mr. Betts begged me to give you his regards. The pianist, Madame Dallage Wickes, was *brilliant,* and was from Belgium and knew Gurickx! I had not known of her before. If you could see the *intense* pleasure they all take in the club! Why, it is Miss Read's very *life,* as she has charge of the Saturday musicales. She is getting to be quite elegant and a woman of the world, receiving so much. . . .

The Dallibas (Mrs. and Gerda) came over last week for Paderewski's opera. I had to stand in line an hour to buy their tickets for them, but she invited me and Mr. Searle to go with them, so that was a compensation. I suppose Rose told you she got me a chance to write it up for the Daily News in Chicago, but I sent out a very poor article, much to my regret. They allowed me only a thousand words, and that was so little, I could not say anything to speak of. I began one *splendid* one but by the time I had got through the first act, I had already transcended my limit, so I began all over again, to try and condense it. The time was up and I *had* to take it to the office to be telegraphed, and still I had not given any idea of the opera. After Tuesday, I am going to write a complete account, to my own satisfaction, for Mathews or Florence French will take it, if nobody else will. The fact was, I was half ill, I could not get my wits together. I have learned how to do a *short* article now, I think, and I could do it another time!

We were at the opera house *all day* on Wednesday, Miss Read and I. I only had a few minutes' conversation with Paderewski, as he seems afraid to talk to me when his wife is present! He has *"gone off"* in looks, but is as fascinating as ever. Both the opera and the concert were sold out a week in advance! The opera is *beautiful,* and has some unique points. I'll describe it later. I have no more time now, so must wait till Tuesday or Wednesday before writing again. I am enjoying Lily very much and the rest has done her good. Many thanks for your last letter and with much love to all.

As ever,

Amy

New York March 1, 1902

Dearest Mudkins,

. . . We have had a *very* trying winter, and very little good weather, it seems to me. We plunge from one storm into another. You know how these drenching twelve hour rains *pour down* in New York! I really pitied Prince Henry, for it did nothing but rain while he was here, and he could have got no idea of the real gay character of New York when it is pleasant. Also, when Lily was here, it was cold and forbidding, and we had *piles* of snow. Regular New England weather. You need not be alarmed about my visiting Rose, for I had no such intention. I told Lily I could not come out until I give up my room there, which I took for the season. Anyhow, I am so hard to visit, for I do not know what to do with myself away from my piano, and if I went out to Chicago, it would be to take a room in some boarding house just as I do here. Without all my pictures and things, I should be very forlorn. There does not seem to be any solution of my fate, at present.

I wish Normie could give me the money to go to Germany in June. Liszt's monument will be unveiled in Weimar during that month, Mr. Burmeister tells me, and I should love to be there, among the "Lisztraner." My name is always associated with Liszt's, and I should like to write an account of this occasion, which will probably be the last act in the drama of Liszt's career. Paderewski gives a concert here on March 8th . . . and his opera will be going on at the Opera House at the same time in the concert. . . . The two delightful moments in the opera are the *ballet,* which closes the first act, and the opening of the last act, when you see a lake gleaming and sparkling in the hollow of the mountains, and clouds are soaring tempestuously over the moon. Manru sleeps on a rock, and nothing is going on on the stage except when he stirs uneasily in the light of the moon. The orchestra keeps playing the overture, and it is perfectly fascinating just to sit there and watch the water sparkle, and the clouds rushing gloomily over the moon. Every now and then she comes out in her virgin purity, and then Manru stirs (being a gypsy) until, when she emerges in full splendor, he rises and walks with extended arms and closed eyes towards the lake, as if hyptonized. The music, meanwhile, is *exquisite,* and in the scenery, Paderewski conveys the *gloom* and *loveliness* of the Galician Mountains. You feel remote from anything and everybody. Nothing but *mountain, water,* and *sky.* You see the long track of the moon across the lake, every time she comes forth from the clouds, and the water ebbs and flows exactly like real water. It is most deceptive! The orchestra keeps your thoughts company. This scene seems to last a *long* while, and you sit perfectly passive and let the beauty of it take possession of you and roll over you. I never saw any such effect of being alone with nature, in an opera, before. As for the ballet in the first act, the music is simply bewitching, very fast and very magnetic, and it keeps increasing in excitement. The costumes of the dancers were so pretty, too, funny little hats and breeches for those who personated the male dancers. They seemed like brownies, dancing away up there! The girls had on short skirts, and carried crooks, if I remember aright.

Anyhow, it was gayety personified, and the music was elaborated and intensified as the night went on, and became quite important in character. That ballet put you

Programme Arranged by Miss HATTIE STERNFELD.

Concerts will be given

At the Pro Cathedral, Stanton and Norfolk Streets,
early in March.
At the Educational Alliance, East Broadway and
Jefferson Street, Sunday evening, March 23rd.
At the West Side Settlement, 460 W. 44th St.,
sometime in April.
Other Concerts to follow. Dates to be announced.

"Music, in the opinion of many,
ranks second only to faith and religion".
Fraternus.

* * * * * * * *

WOMEN'S PHILHARMONIC SOCIETY OF NEW YORK,
DEPARTMENT OF MUSIC FOR THE PEOPLE.

YOUNG PEOPLE'S
CONCERT
BY THE

Piano & Violin Classes
OF

THE EDUCATIONAL ALLIANCE.
EAST BROADWAY & JEFFERSON ST.

MR. MARK FONAROFF,   MISS HATTIE STERNFELD,
INSTRUCTOR OF VIOLIN.   INSTRUCTOR OF PIANO.

MISS HATTIE GLOGAU,
ACCOMPANIST.

Saturday afternoon, March 1st 1902,
at 3:30 p. m.

IN THE ROOMS OF THE SOCIETY
No. 1 Carnegie Hall,
56TH ST ENTRANCE.

MEMBERS AND GUESTS ARE CORDIALLY INVITED.

PROGRAMME.

PART ONE.

1. CHILDRENS' ORCHESTRA, ages 6—16 years.
   a) Menuet from the septet - - Beethoven
   b) Death of Asa - - - - Grieg
   MR. MARK FONAROFF
   Conductor.

2. PIANO SOLO
   a) Knight Ruppert - - - Schumann
   b) Over the Meadow - - - Lichner
   SARAH SCHOENKOPF.

3. SONG
   Winter's Lullaby - - - DeKoven
   MASTER HARRY GOLDSTEIN

4. PIANO SOLO
   Andante et Rondo - - - Rosenheim
   MASTER MAX BASSEL.

5. VIOLIN
   a) Romance - - - Tschaikowsky
   b) Mazurka - - - Wienawsky
   MISS ROSE FRANK.

6. PIANO SOLO
   Fantasie D Minor - - - Mozart
   MISS NELLIE NELSON.

PART TWO.

(ENSEMBLE)

7. Norwegian Wedding March - Soderman
   Anitras Danse - - - - Grieg
   For two Pianos eight hands.
   1st Piano { MISS NELLIE NELSON
             { MASTER MAX BASSEL.
   2nd Piano { MISS ROSE LIPMAN
             { MISS CELIA BOORSTEIN

8. SONG
   Serenade - - - - - Schubert
   MASTER HARRY GOLDSTEIN

9. PIANO SOLO
   Cachoucha - - - - Raff
   MISS HATTIE GLOGAU.

10. VIOLIN
    Zigeunerweisen - - - Sarasata
    MASTER MICHEL SHAPIRO.

11. CHILDRENS' ORCHESTRA
    a) Sarbande - - - - Bach
    b) Chorus from Messiah - - Handel

in the best spirits, and made you feel happy as could be, in spite of the tragedy of the whole act preceding it. It wound up the first act delightfully and was an entire contrast. The third act is the most important, and Fritzie Scheff, who is a young girl, and the "enfant terrible" of the company, came out uncommonly — in it. She is the gypsy girl, Ava, who finally lures Manru away from his wife and child, and brings him back to the tribe. No doubt Fritzie Scheff has studied Calvé's Carmen, and made her her model, for her Ava, is just as vivid and forcible as Calvé's Carmen. It is full of dash and "go," and she carries off poor, weak Manru, with the aid of the familiar gypsy airs, played on the fiddle by Jagre. Paderewski makes a point of the fact that it is the *music* he loves which causes Manru to forsake his wife, and not the seductions of Ava. I meant to have put all this in the paper, but somehow Mr. Satan prevented me. Anyhow, I got *belated* on the thing and had not time, as I started *twice over* on the article. If I had sent the first one, it would have been all right, but it never does for me to fix things over in writing. I never can improve upon my *original* conception, and I get bewildered if I try to change it.

Paderewski seems much more serious and older than he did. I suppose his son's death must have been a great shock to him. His wife looks young and pretty, this time, and he seems to have eyes only for her. She is very exacting, I imagine, and keeps a close grip on him! He has given her his beautiful house in Morges, which he had wanted to sell, in token of his gratitude for her care of his son. Madame Paderewski has been ill at the Manhattan Hotel, and Paderewski is quite anxious about her. He has been off on a concert tour, and she remained here, but he runs back whenever he can, to see her. I only said "How-d'ye-do" to him at his concert, as he had the usual crowd waiting. He played his concerto with the Boston Symphony Orchestra last week, and it is *beautiful* and the orchestration is splendid. I had not heard it formerly.

This afternoon Hattie Sternfeld had her gala day at the Women's Philharmonic, Saturday afternoon. Mrs. Humaron presided at the table, beautifully costumed, and they had their "Music of the People." Really. I was astonished to see what Hattie Sternfeld had accomplished with those children in Canal Street, at the Educational Alliance. She teaches down there two days in the week, and I believe only talented children are admitted to the classes, which are formed for their benefit. Her little pupils all did extremely well and played with a good deal of brilliancy and concert effect. Then there is a good violin teacher down there, named Samaroff, and he has trained a little orchestra of boys and girls, and they played very well together. Alas he had one boy violinist, a Russian, named Shapiro, who is a born concert artist. He was *very* gifted, indeed, and advanced for his twelve years! You don't know how interesting it was to hear this concert entirely by children! Really, your Women's Philharmonic is a remarkable association, Mud, and you ought to be proud of having organized it! The room was *crowded.* I was awfully glad to hear that Normie is asked to be at the dinner for the Prince, and I hope now to see him able to resume his proper place in society. He has been *poor* for *so* long! I hoped he would send me a check on Monday, as I have only a few dollars in the bank. The two months when I don't get the house rent are awful! My paper is full, so I must close for the present, with a great deal of love as ever from your devoted sister

Amy

New York March 15, 1902

Dearest Zie,

Sembrich[1] is quite a surprise to everybody, in "Manru," as it was thought the part of Ulana would not give much scope to her vocal pyrotechnics. The role is a tragic one and calls for sincerity and depth of feeling. She threw herself into it with such intensity, that she made a very fine thing out of it, and distinguished herself in a new way. It was said before the opera was performed that Sembrich, in accepting the part of Ulana, had "sacrificed herself to her friendship for Paderewski," but she did it *so well,* that the reverse turned out to be the case, and she scored a decided success. She had not been credited with the possession of so much *heart* (or rather soul) as she manifests in the character of Ulana. On the scene before at Hedwig's cottage, where Ulana begs forgiveness of her mother, and receives, instead, her curse, the climax is reached when Sembrich utters a cry, and falls prone upon the doorstep. The is so realistic, it tightens your heart strings to hear it, and she does it with consummate art. Ulana monopolizes the first act, while Manru is the star of the *second* one. In the third, the whole gypsy tribe is on the stage, and Ava, the gypsy maiden (who wins him back to his people) is the new element. Each act increases in interest as it goes on, but the third and final one is intensely absorbing and exciting, and the music gets better and better. Bispham divided the honours with Sembrich in the first act, and was *splendid* as Urok, the uncanny, sorcerer dwarf. He did his part so perfectly, it was impossible to believe it *was* Bispham, even when you were told! It seemed as if he must actually be the dwarf he represented. He sang gloriously, too. Von Bandrowski, the Polish tenor, when seen at the rehearsal in his ordinary clothes, a grey cloth suit and grey kid gloves, looked like a man of the world, of assumed manner, who "knew it all," and took things easily. Sembrich is a brunette, while Bandrowski is blond, in their *natural* colors, and so they looked at *rehearsal,* so it was very funny to see them both at the public performance, exactly the contrary. Sembrich wore a blonde wig while Bandrowski was the darkest of gypsies, with long black, elfin locks hanging down under his hat. Bandrowski has a beautiful voice, and he comes up to his climax as finely. Still, he has not the fascination or perfection

Amy Fay

of Jean de Reszke. Nobody will ever come up to *Jean,* I suppose! Fritzi Scheff, a young German girl, made a great hit as Ava and was remarkable as the coquettish gypsy girl, who wooed Manru in the last act. Paderewski insists, however, that it is Manru's love of music, and the old violinist Jagre, who makes him forget his wife and child and become the chief of the gypsies, by fiddling to him the melodies with which he has been familiar from his childhood (and *not* the charms of Ava which mislead him). It was interesting to see Kubelik who looks like a gypsy, sitting in the front seat at the rehearsal, and hear Jagre fiddle a wild run on the violin in Manru's ear. The final scene, where Urok throws Manru over the precipice, is not well managed, as it looks as if he were carefully letting himself *drop.* It is deliberate and dramatic. The defect of the opera is that there are no show pieces for the singers. For such great artists, it is too simple. It is not so profound as Wagner, nor so ornate as Mozart. The orchestra is the best part of it. Yet, it is fascinating music.

Amy

---

[1] Marcella Sembrich (1858-1935), Polish-American singer and longtime member of the Metropolitan Opera Company.

New York April 19, 1902

Dearest Mudkins,

I suppose you are wondering why you have not received back your deed signed by Laura and myself, but I did not want to sign this without first talking over the matter with Norman. He seems to have scooted without saying good-bye and is most likely back in Chicago. I am perfectly willing to sign the deed as far as I am concerned, but I was wondering if it would not perhaps lessen Laura's income, and she is even poorer than you and I are, as she does not get fifty dollars per month from Norman as we do! I must say, I admire Laura's power of patient endurance of her lot, for how she can *bear* to live amid such gloomy surroundings, and sit down three times a day to such a *table* passes *me*! Lately I have not been able to have her come over for little visits, as I have had as very little money myself, and it is *too bad.* A trip to New York is the only oasis in her desert, but it always costs me several dollars when Laura comes over, as I always help her out in shopping, carfare, etc., when she is here, and I have not been able to spend this the last two months. She was over to spend the day a month ago, but that was the last time. The front room is occupied

32

now, as we have three more boarders, so I have no place for Laura in the house. She could take a room across the street, but that would make it more expensive. I feel the greatest sympathy for you, and it seems as if the only thing you could do is to live on your money for the present, and I think you ought to have it. But if I were you, I should try for a thousand dollars, and not take the *whole.* You could supply present needs with *that,* and still have five thousand left, whereas, if you take it *all,* there is no knowing what might happen, and you might be left without a *cent!* Will and Norman ought to see the justice of your complaints and let you have a thousand dollars from the estate and very likely you could get them to do so without much difficulty.

I went down to the Women's Philharmonic this afternoon, and there was a large audience at the customary Saturday Afternoon Musicale. Miss Hard is chairwoman of these now, and she is simply *busting* with ambition, and I don't believe she attends to anything else. She and Mrs. Roberts get up the programmes, and while they have a great deal of new talent all the while, they are a miscellaneous lot, and good, bad, and indifferent are all mixed in together. . . . The members of the Council complained vigorously at the last meeting (several of them), that Miss Hard had altogether too much music on Saturdays and that no time was left for conversation and sociability. They said it was "nothing but *concert, concert,* all the time, in the club, and *no* club life, whatever." Then I spoke up and said it was great pity that the arrangement of the chairs had been changed. Early in the season the chairs were placed around the room as in a private drawing room, and the centre of the floor was cleared. This made a charming impression as you entered the room. Miss Hard, in her ambition to have large audiences, has the chairs in rows now, like any concert hall, and you are wedged into your seat all the afternoon. The members of the Council all agreed with me on this point, particularly Mrs. Boas, who was emphatic: I told Miss Hard afterwards what had been said, as she was absent from the meeting that day, and the members took advantage of it to express their opinions. I begged her to return to the former way of placing the chairs, and to have shorter programmes. It was of no avail! Today she had all the chairs in rows again, and two *more* numbers on the programme than usual! . . . I was quite provoked with Miss Hard, for even when I played on Saturday afternoon not long ago, and wrote her a special request to put the chairs around the room, she paid no attention to my request. I will send you today's programme so you can see how ambitious it is in its general appearance.

I met today a writer by the name of Mrs. Cromwell Childs, the wife of an editor, I believe. She pitched into me for not writing more, and asked why I did not? I told her I could not get a position on a paper. She said that newspapers "pay so little, they are not worth while," and the thing to do is to try for Women's Magazines, as they pay the best. This is the time of year when the magazines and papers make changes, and engage their staff for the coming year, and she advised my going to the *Women's Home Companion,* of which Mr. Arthur T. Vance is the editor, at 5 West 21st Street. He paid *her* three hundred dollars for twelve articles on household matters. That was pretty good, wasn't it? I am going to take Mrs. Child's advice, and I was wondering if *you* could not do some writing on Women's magazines and papers as you are so peculiarly well up on the Woman question. Mrs. Childs says I must not be discouraged if I am refused a lot of times but must keep right on applying to people and *blowing my own trumpet,* that is the way to succeed. She advised trying for *Everybody's Magazine,* and for the *Ladies' Home Journal,* and said she would write me out a list of periodicals and addresses and send them to me. I thought this very kind in her, as it was all without solicitation on my part.

Do you intend to remain in Chicago all summer? I should think you would be crazy to return to your pals in New York. I have not seen Miss Vanderpoel this winter. I called once, but she was not at home. Then I invited her to a tea I gave for Mrs. Clarence Eddy three weeks ago, but Miss Vanderpoel could not come on account of other engagements. My tea for Mrs. Eddy went off delightfully, and all the guests enjoyed it. . . . Mrs. Eddy has been buying a home on the Riverside drive for her daughter by her first husband, Mrs. Vogel, who was with her, and who has a husband and three sons, the eldest of whom is eighteen. She is about forty, and a bright and pleasant woman. They have all lived abroad for *years,* but think they must come back to their own country now, to make good American citizens of their boys. I visited Mrs. Mellen, Mrs. Carter, and Mrs. Olzendam, as they will be future neighbors of Mrs. Vogel, whose house is No. 3 West 89th Street. She has returned to Europe, but will take possession in the fall.

. . . Poor Mrs. Carlson misses you a great deal, and she mourns the loss of our Flat, which was a "second house" to her she says. Mrs. Grenville Winthrop lost her brother, Mr. Oddie, and Mrs. Walsh's husband died about the same time. . . . Mrs. Walsh is frightfully lonesome without him, and what is *very hard* is, that all the large stores, nearly, Altman, Arnold's etc. where she traded suddenly made a rule not to pay anymore shopping commissions except for customers out of town, nor will they permit Mrs. Walsh to accompany the persons she shops for anymore. The result of this is such a heavy loss to her, that she is worried to death lest she cannot make a living. She wept and told me she sometimes felt as if she *"should go out of her mind."* I felt doubly sorry for her, as I know from your experience and mine how hard it is to lose your income! I was hoping Mrs. Walsh would be able to make *more* money after Mr. Walsh's death, but she has lost not only her husband but her business, and she has worked so hard! She looks very pale and changed. Mrs. Winthrop was so broken up over the death of her brother that she sees no one. Chickering Hall has just been pulled down and something else must be built there. I felt so sad to see the gap where it has stood! I called on Mrs. Chickering this afternoon and found her looking much younger and like her old self in her comfortable and handsome house. She receives on Sunday afternoons. She must have plenty of money! Good-bye with love.

Amy

The American Years

New York November 12, 1902

Dearest Pollie,[1]

I *was* so glad to hear that dear Will is better, and I hope to mercy that he will continue to improve. Your Aunt Zina sent me a cheerful note also, and she expects to leave Chicago on Thursday for New York, she says. Many thanks for the check, and I had just received a letter in regard to money matters from Norman which I enclose. Please hand it to Will, if he is able to read it. You will laugh when I tell you that the New York Morning Journal and also Evening Journal sent up for your photograph yesterday, which they wish to put in the paper (also *mine*) when they announce our departure. Zina has the only picture we had of you, the pretty one in the round frame, so I told the Journal man I would write and ask you for one. I think they must have got hold of your marriage through a friend of mine, Miss Catherine Leaky, who writes on the editorial page. I met her in the car one evening and told her we were going to Lima, and she was *much* interested. I asked the Journal men what they wanted to put your journey and marriage in the paper for? They said it was a "pretty story," and "*romantic*." All the world loves a lover, you know! Everybody seems to consider you quite a heroine, and wonderfully brave, because you are going so far to meet Arthur![2] Everybody's picture is in the paper nowadays, and it is remarkable how they get them as they do! All the heavy swells are in, just the same as everybody else. So here is your chance to become famous! I *had to be civil* to the reporters, anyhow, for if you aren't, they put in something disagreeable about you. Your Aunt Lily snubbed them once in Chicago, and they described her as a "vinegar-faced female", which she did not much relish, when she read it! This was at the time of Rose's wedding. Probably they will put me in as a "fat and buxom, but *good-natured* aunt," who will act as Miss Stone's chaperone, "elderly" or something of that sort! The people in the boarding house all want to see you. My best love to Will, and kind regards to Mrs. Kendall. Like yourself, I am writing fifteen million letters per day!

Your affectionate,

Aunt Amy

---

[1] Pauline Stone, niece of Amy Fay, who travelled to Lima, Peru, for her wedding to Arthur Jackson, owner of a rubber plantation in South America.

[2] Pauline's fiancé, Arthur Jackson.

35

Amy Fay

S. S. Segncoudas November 17, 1902

Dearest Mousie,[1]

I wonder how you are, and *hope* you are on the road to recovery and that you will have no set-backs in that most treacherous of diseases, *pneumonia!* Pauline and I are both well and are in fine spirits. We are nearing the Isthmus of Panama, and expect to land early tomorrow morning and take the train at eight o'clock. It will take us three hours by train to get from Colon to Panama. The voyage has been entirely uneventful, but very delightful. We have had balmy weather the whole way, with the exception of the very first day and night. It was rough just as soon as we got out of the harbour at New York, and the ship rolled all night. I was *very seasick,* and got rid of all I had on board, and all my *bile* without delay, and was all well for breakfast the next morning, to the surprise of all! Mr. & Mrs. Todd and their little boy have proved to be very agreeable companions and Mr. Todd has paid me every attention, including glasses of champagne, cocktails before meals, and beer at luncheon! Mrs. Todd is a pretty and dainty little woman, who is something on Kate's style, with her trim little figure, and is always "*tirée* à quatre épingles"! Her dress is perfection for the sea. Mr. Todd is quite a *dude* also, and the boy is a dear little fellow, and very convincing. We have not made any acquaintances on board, though there are twenty-six passengers with the exception of Madame Castro of Panama, who admired my playing on the piano (we have a good Steinway, fortunately) and whom I have pressed into service to help me with my Spanish everyday, and who gave me quite a little start in the language. She was born in Denmark, but is a resident of Panama, where she has a husband and eight children. One little boy is her sole companion. I find Spanish quite hard, as it is not at all like French or German, and I am only *beginning* to get used to the sound of it. Pauline has not yet tackled it, as she has been writing notes ever since we started.

The late afternoon is the most delightful part of the day, as the sunsets and cloud effects are beautiful. Also the moonlight, late at night, has been enchanting. The air is so soft, it is a caress to the cheek! I have been wishing you were with us to breathe it, for no trip could be better for a sore lung than this one! I hope you may yet make it someday. We passed Cuba about sunset day before yesterday, and had a beautiful view of its bold and mountainous coast against the brilliant yellow sky, The outline of the mountain top was exquisite. There were also some steep ramparts of rock and precipices to be seen in the foreground. I was sorry I could not run over and pay a call to my friends the Bruwaerts. M. Bruwaert has been made minister of France to Cuba, and I had a very nice letter from Madame Bruwaert just before I left New York, saying she wished I would come to Cuba, but without the least idea I was about to sail close by in a couple of days! The *real* sight seeing of our trip will begin on the other side of Panama, I opine. We passed the island of San Salvador, now called Watkins Island, where Columbus landed, in the evening, and saw the light house. Till now we have had only *water, water, water!* The ocean is a *very big place!*

Our captain is a jolly old tar! Pauline sits on his left at table and he finds her very attractive, evidently. She is looking well and pretty, and is happy over the near approach of Arthur. The ship is extremely comfortable and cosy, not being one of those *monster* ones! (The table is very nice.) I have been diligently *perusing* the *Conquest of Peru* by Prescott which Lily was thoughtful enough to send me, and am quite primed about Lima. Madame Castro says it is not hot there and is delightful. I suppose Pauline told you of the five baskets fruit and the lovely roses which greeted her on board from Arthur's New York relatives. Mollie Lyles and a few others came to see us off, including Zina, who said she should write you. Probably Norman has got home by this, and he must have been discouraged to hear of your illness, as were we *all*. Give my regards to Mrs. Kendall, and believe me, with *much love*.

As ever,

Amy

---

[1] Nickname for Will Stone, Amy's brother-in-law.

Areguipa January 4, 1903

My Dear Pauline,

I have got back to Areguipa, as you see, and have been with the pretty Spanish lady I told you of, I don't feel sure of her name yet. As near as I could make out she said it was Senora Louise, but it can't be that! She gave me a card with the name of Alfredo Biscardi on it, but I could not be sure it was the name of her husband, or the person she is going to visit in Mollendo. We had magnificent weather on Lake Ticicaca on Friday, and the view was much clearer of Mount Sorata than I have seen it before. Those same priests were on board, but also a French Jesuit, a man of great brilliancy and education, with whom I had rather an amusing time. He was driven out of France with the rest of the Jesuits, and has been in South America twelve years, he told me. I made him help me with my Spanish, and it was *lots of fun!*

I should have liked to talk to him *all day,* but it would have attracted attention, so I could not, and he was much too wary an old fox for that! He had a fine opera glass, which he lent me to look at the scenery with. He lives at Areguipa, but I do not know his name. I am sure he is a fine preacher! I am going to buy a mantilla, so I can go into the cathedral here, for they tell me there is a very remarkable pulpit in it, the devil holding the world on his back! It is carved in wood, and came from Europe. If you are still in La Paz, I am going to ask you to get a photograph of that old fountain in the Plaza, as it is the only thing Conway has not got in his book. To think I did not get *one snap shot,* or even learn to use my Kodak in La Paz! Was there ever such a fizzle as my stay there! I shall hardly dare face the family when I return!

I have picked up a lot in my Spanish, and it was a source of great amusement on the boat, at the table. Everybody went into shrieks of laughter over it when I began to try to talk, but they enjoyed my efforts so much, *I kept on.* I came to the Hotel Ingles in Areguipa, thinking I might be able to speak English here, and possibly meet some Americans. It turned out to be a third class hotel, and I can't eat the food atall, but the *location* is splendid. It is near the railroad station, and in full view of those three glorious mountains with the fields of barley across the road. Last night it was *too beautiful for words!* Senora Louisa left for Mollendo this morning, so I am alone here. I am going up to the Gran Central Hotel for breakfast! I found some Americans here, of the rough and ready kind who will help me with my shopping. One is Mr. Hawley, who is in McCord's office, and who knows Arthur. He said he would bring Mr. McCord to see me today. I met McCord, in fact, at the station when I went to see the Senora off. He looks like a dried up American business man, but was very polite, and said he would "see me later"! You don't know what a pleasure it is to have some money in my purse once more! I have been so strapped since we landed at Callas! It seems nice to be going *home* again, too! The ride over the mountain was not so hard yesterday *though long,* as the weather was beautiful, and we had a better class of passengers. I was not sick at all. I shall go to Mollendo on Tuesday, and from there to *Lima.* Give my love to Arthur and with a great deal yourself, I am

Aunt Amy

The weather is hot here today. I am glad to see the *sun.* I was so cold in La Paz! My regards to all friends there.

Mollendo January 14th, 1903

My Dear Pauline,

This afternoon I take the steamer from here to Lima, having arrived here last Sunday afternoon. I remained in Areguipa one week, in order to familiarize myself a little with the city, and also to get my *washing* done. Such a lot of it had accumulated, I could not let it go any longer. I had a very pleasant time in Areguipa, as Mr. McCord seemed to take a fancy to my "age and infirmities" and he invited me to luncheon and dinner every day except the last one, and *that* day Mrs. Hawley invited me. I was thus released from eating the horrid food at the Hotel Ingles and lived on the fat of the land, with plenty of cocktails, wine and beer! That charming young lawyer, whom you met at the Gran Central, is a great pet of Mr. McCord's, and he takes all his meals at McCord's house, so *we three* had many a cosey time together! He was lovely to me! Most obliging and attentive! He is only twenty-three. Mr. Hawley's family lives in the second story of the McCord mansion, and a lovely home they have up there! A broad piazza arms all around, and Mrs. Hawley has fitted up a nice corner on the shady side of it, with table, working-chairs and rug, with pretty *plants* in pots, and there she just *lives* in the open air. She is unusually sweet and refined, and I had a delightful day with her on Saturday, when she invited me for the afternoon and to stay to dinner. Mrs. Hawley is one of our nice American housekeepers, and she gave me a *delicious dinner.* Mr. Hawley has a fine collection of Indian curiosities, butterflies, etc. Many things I had never seen before. Mrs. Hawley has a number of *superb* Chinese shawls, sold by the old aristocratic families in Areguipa, compelled to part with them to pawnbrokers, by poverty. They are the handsomest I ever laid my eyes on, and I was *wild* to have some! She uses them as draperies in her rooms, and they are *beautiful.* If you ever return to Areguipa do try and get one of those shawls. A woman comes around and sells them regularly. They are *unique.* There was a black one all embroidered in the most gorgeous colours, on the piano, and another one, *café au lait,* also worked in colours, then she had a pure white one, and a red one, with magnificent *fringe* which hung down so gracefully! The silk is a splendid quality, so thick and lustrous, and I should think it was imperishable.

I had a very pleasant journey down here on Sunday, as Mr. McCord had arranged for me to travel with the Gibsons, in his private car, which we had all to ourselves. Mrs. Gibson was a Providence girl, a Miss Butts, I think she said. She was in Cambridge very often, and knows the people there well. . . . Mr. Gibson is an Englishman, and a manager of a gold mine in Bolivia. His wife says he is at home only three months in the year. They are young people, and Mrs. Gibson does not look more than twenty-eight years old! (very attractive.) She has three little children, two of them are babies. Mr. McCord has allowed them the use of the Station House while they are here. You remember it, that pretty house with the flowering trees in front, where I wanted so much to go? They invited me to lunch and to spend the day yesterday. I went, and had a *delightful* time. The trees are a perfect blaze of red flowers, and humming birds were fluttering around them. We sat on the piazza and had a fine view of the breakers. Mrs. Gibson is artistic, and she is a good housekeeper, so the luncheon was as *good* as it could be. After lunch I got my Kodak, and Mr. Gibson, who is an expert, showed me all about how to use it, and we took pictures of the house. Last evening our friends the Lees carried me off to their house, and the Gibsons also, and we had a pleasant time *there*. Mr. Gibson is going on with me to *Lima* so I shall be all right *there*. Mrs. Gibson says she hopes you will come and look her up if you ever return to Areguipa. She has the prettiest house *there*; she says. I wish I had seen it. It is built like a pagoda, and stands in the middle of a garden! Well, I must close this letter. I hope you and Arthur and Mr. Todd are well and that you are safe *at home!*

With love as ever,

Aunt Amy

P.S. Your photographs of New York city got in my bag by some mistake. I return them to you. Tell Mr. Todd I bought *four* antique rings in Areguipa this time! I had a good time shopping with Mrs. Morgan, the wife of the proprietor of the Hotel Ingles, as she speaks English. Last night the moonlight was *gorgeous* on the breakers here. It seems very pleasant to be going *on board* again. I shall get to New York about the 5th of February. I do *hope* I shall get my room back again! I shall be so sorry if I do not! Write to me soon and tell me how you are getting on with your housekeeping and how you like Sorata. Give my regards to Mr. Todd, and tell him I hope he is well again. . . .

Amy

New York February 4, 1903

My darling Pauline,

I arrived home yesterday morning (Monday), our ship getting in at nine o'clock, but it was nearly eleven before I reached 94th Street on account of the usual delay at the wharf with the custom house officials. I did not have any duties to pay, however, which was a consolation! . . . Miss Read was overjoyed at my return, as she was very lonely while I was away, and *all* the boarders were most warm in their welcome which was pleasant. Miss Schmidt, the pretty blonde, has got engaged during my absence, to a man with whom she has been in love for five years (a journalist on the "Press"), so she is *radiantly* happy. I had thought Miss Schmidt and Mr. Bishop would make a match, but this is not the case, and he is now devoting himself to Miss Sherwood! I think you met her once at our Flat in 56th Street, did you not?

40

She is the daughter of the pianists,[1] you may remember, and comes from Boston, and has been on the stage. My friend, Miss Bates, gives Miss Sherwood singing lessons *gratis,* for the pleasure of teaching her, she has such a lovely voice and is so talented!

Your Aunt Zina is boarding in Staten Island at 95 Tompkins Avenue, the same street as Laura Sanford Hoffman lives in, and near her. I had not been in my boarding house half an hour when your Aunt Zina came in, and we had a long talk. She staid all day, and brought me some lovely flowers. She told me of the deaths of our Aunt Matilda Camp, Mama's sister (an old lady over eighty. I don't think you ever saw Aunt Matilda, as she lived in Washington. She was Ethel Camp's grandmother) and also that of Will Ellis who succumbed to asthma on February 1st, and was buried yesterday. . . . James Peirce wrote your Aunt Zina a most affectionate and *lovely* letter announcing Will Ellises death to her. I thought it was awfully nice of Jim to do this. . . . You ought to see *my mail!* Such *heaps* of letters and invitations, it makes my eyes *ache* to read them, with my glasses so long! I filled the wastebasket with envelopes. There was a check of fourteen dollars, from England, royalty on the *English* edition of my book, over a month old! . . . I have been unpacking and getting my room in order all day and will see about a piano tomorrow. Give my love to Arthur, and write me how you like your new home? I suppose Mr. Todd has left you. If not, remember me to him and believe me, with such love to yourself

As ever

Your affectionate,

Aunt Amy

---

[1] Mr. & Mrs. William Sherwood.

New York June 14th, 1903

My Dear Arthur,

Your very sweet letter of April 22nd reached me on June 3rd and it was a long time on the road! I was mighty pleased to get it particularly as the long promised one from Pauline with our *account* in it has not materialized! . . . Will wrote me that you were about to give your first dinner party (I wish I could be one of the guests!), which must have been an exciting event. It seems that Margaret has had the measles but she is probably over them by this time. I expect to see her ere long, for I shall sail for Europe on the 1st of July, in the Holland-American ship, the *Statendam*. It will seem quite natural to be on the ocean again. I am going to visit Mrs. Clarence Eddy, and old friend of mine who formerly lived in Chicago, but who has been in Paris for seven years, where she has a handsome apartment. She has invited me to stay *"just as long as I want to,"* so I shall stay there two or three months, I expect, returning to New York in October. As Mrs. Eddy is a rich woman, I hope to have a comfortable time as her guest, and I like her very much *personally,* so I think we shall be congenial. She will perhaps take a summer villa at Malmaison, a suburb of Paris. Mr. Eddy has taken to himself the "skizmatic tints of the rainbow," as Charlie Peirce used to say. That is, he has fallen in love with a cousin of Mrs. Eddy's, after being married for twenty-five years. (See what dangers lie before you!) As a result, he and his wife have parted company, and I shall slip into his snug berth. . . . My pupil, Miss Read, who lives in the house here, will go with me to Paris, although she will take board somewhere. We shall go sightseeing together. Mrs. Eddy wrote that I should be perfectly free to come and go as I pleased. I shall have to get acquainted with Kate and the children all over again! I have not had a *line* from Kate since last fall, but she owes two letters. I feel quite proud that Margaret led the school and got the highest marks. My sister Zina (Mrs. Peirce) has been with me for a month or more, tell Pauline. I have never been able to send the baby pin to *"Dorothy"* because I have forgotten the address. Will thought it must be to Mrs. Lawton's baby, but he did not know the address either. Professor Paine bobbed in and made me a call a few weeks since. He was in New York to see about his opera, which he hopes will be produced here at the Metropolitan Opera House winter next . . . and Norman was here a fortnight ago, besides Will Stone's being on twice. . . . Give lots of love to Pauline for me, and I hope she will come out of the forest unscathed and that *you* will not have the horrible fever again. With much love and many thanks for your letter, my dear nephew, I am affectionate

Aunt Amy

Will was looking *finely,* and he enjoyed hearing about you from me.

July 8, 1903

Dearest Zie,

Wednesday has come around *again* and still we are on the broad ocean, but we expect to reach Bologne on Friday. I shall get off there, as Miss Read and the

The American Years

Fairlambs and I continue on to Rotterdam, in order to see *Holland.* Amsterdam and Rotterdam are within two hours ride of each other, so we can do these cities in a very short time. Then we shall proceed through Leyden and Delft to Antwerp and Brussels, and so on to Paris, where I shall arrive about the 17th. We have had perfect weather till now, with the exception of Sunday, when it *rained,* but nobody has been sick in our party, and this is the steadiest ship I ever was on. You hardly feel the motions, and we have had *no rolling at all,* which is *so* uncomfortable when you are in your berth, and prevents sleep. We shall get to Rotterdam early Saturday morning. I found a nice letter from Mr. Munger when we came on board, written from Xenia, Ohio, his home, and he was a *second* time the *only one* of my friends who remembered me on the steamer! Curious that *he* should have, was it not? It was *sweet* of him anyway, and you remember he went down to see me off at South America and brought me a book, and also was at the wharf to greet me on my return and to help me carry my things. I think I shall have to remember him in *my will!* Tell Mrs. Downing her flowers were *beautiful,* so fresh and sweet; I enjoyed looking at them *all day* and smelling them. Miss Read and I put our flowers over the looking glass in our stateroom in the evening, where they were very decorative, and our companions were *impressed!* We had our usual lunch, and two very nice women were in the lower berth, neat and well dressed, and just as presentable as *we are!* They were Mrs. York from San Juan, and Miss Anna Wolfe, from Chicago, and were strangers to *each other* as well as to *us.* Mrs. York lives in Mexico, and she is a very pretty woman, young, and strikingly like Madame Bruwaert, I was struck with the resemblance to "Lucie King" the other evening, when Mrs. York was dancing, she had that same brilliance in the ballroom that Madame Bruwaert used to have before she was married, at Bournique's dances. Besides the Fairlambs and Miss Read, we have Miss Read's French teacher, Madame Carpentier, in our party, and she is a remarkably interesting conversationalist, cultivated and thoughtful, and with a good deal of French *espirit.* I like her very much, and she is a cunning little woman, like Jenny Wren, *"always dressed in brown!"*

The ship is very crowded, and there are many Jews, Germans and Dutch, and lots of *children* on board, mostly little boys. Still, there are some aristocratic persons too, as for example, the Comte Louis de Pressigny, of Poitiers, France, who was presented to me last evening, and who has travelled all over, even to Arabia. He is a great talker, spare of frame, and wears the curiously made clothes which French men always have. Why is it there is such difference in the cut of French *tailors* and French *dressmakers,* I wonder; The *men* always look so *strapped* across the chest, just the contrary principle of the cut for women! Monsieur le Comte went to New York for three weeks only and has returned not at all pleased with our city, which he found *"ugly and dirty,"* he says. However, we will go over again later, and he may change his mind another time. He is a bachelor . . . a thorough gentleman, agreeable and *very elegant* in *manner.* The dining room is neat and the table is very good, we find, in the second cabin, and our *state room* is nice too, although *pretty crowded* for *four* sizable women! Only two of us can dress and undress at a time, but there are no cockroaches or *B's* of any kind, and we have clean linen and plenty of towels. On the whole, we have had a delightful time excepting on the rainy Sunday, when we could not get out on deck. There is only a small parlor upstairs, which is the chief drawback in bad weather, as there is nowhere to go, and we have to take to the dining room.

. . . A poor young man in the steerage died of consumption on Saturday night, and was buried on Sunday at midnight. He was a Russian Jew, only twenty-two years old, and rejected all religious administrations from the priest. A few of us sat and got leave from the captain to see him drop overboard. It was a wild and gusty night and it was raining at intervals. The ocean was all tossed up, and the waves showed their teeth, in the darkness, as far as we could see. The body was carried from the depths of the hold, wrapped in a blanket, and sewed up in canvas and looked like a mummy. They laid it on the deck and then took it to the rear end of the ship and laid it down. In the meanwhile one of the sailors had taken down the flag of Holland, and this was rolled around the body. Then a portion of the railing at the corner of the ship was opened and the body was placed on a board and carried to the opening, where it was rented on the edge, shoved half way out over the sea. The officer in charge muttered a short sentence which ended with *"Peace to his ashes."* He then counted *one, two, three;* the sailors tipped up the board, and the corpse, which was weighted, slipped silently into the water. The waves came to *meet it.* They covered it with a wreath of foam, and then swept it from sight *forever!* We heard *no splash,* the young man was *gone!* Although so simple, the funeral was impressive, and was done in about five minutes. When the body was brought from the hold, we formed a little procession and marched behind it to the opening in the railing. Comte de Pressigny and Mrs. York were the nearest, and the Comte took off his hat. One of the other men whispered to his mate, *"Otez donc votre casquette,"* and they all uncovered. This was the only word spoken, as the *"corpse to the ramparts we hurried."* When it was shoved overboard, we all stood for some seconds, *"deep into that darkness peering,"* until the board was withdrawn, and the railing replaced. *One* woman wept bitterly, so the poor young man had *some* tears shed over him, as he lay on the floor on the deck while the flag was wound around him. He had not a friend or relative on board! As I gazed back over the broad ocean, it was *very grand,* indeed, and there was something *fine* about being consigned to so vast a space, at that hour of the night, with all the wind of heaven blowing a dirge over you! We were all more excited than we were aware of, and none of us slept very well after this gruesome event.

I have been *much* amused at Mr. Fairlamb's tactics during this voyage, and the success with which he has contrived to get admission to the first cabin. In the first place, although a member of the *second* cabin, he had armed himself with a letter of introduction to the captain, which he lost no time in presenting.

As soon as he got on a friendly footing, his *next* measure was to get himself made chairman of a committee to celebrate the *Fourth of July*. This was to be in a saloon of the *first class* passengers, and so it was a first rate *coup* on Fairlamb's part, as he had no end of consultations and hurryings to and fro. A concert was arranged for the afternoon, and in the morning there were speeches and singing of the "National Airs," with a special "national air" of *Fairlamb's own* tucked in, of which he brought a hundred copies with him. These he subsequently presented to the singers, thus advertising his hymn. He also had a song of his sung by a *solo* gentleman at the concert in the afternoon. He has held rehearsals and played accompaniments. You can readily see how thick Fairlamb soon got with the first class cabin! Miss Read and I were asked to play at the concert. Miss Read played a group of three pieces, while I was *twice* on the program, and I played the Kreisleriana by Schumann; and Paderewski's second Minuet and Bizet's "L'Aurore" for the other number. The saloon is a very large one and it was crowded. I was very much pleased when Fairlamb announced that "Miss Amy Fay was going to play," to be greeted with long and hearty applause. I had to bow several times from side to side and finally bumped *hard* against a pillar which I did not see, I was so confused, in turning to go to the piano. I played all right, though, and the audience was really *affectionate* in its applause. I felt as if the people were *fond of me,* as I used to in the Women's Philharmonic. Some of the ladies came up and spoke to me about my book. They wanted to know if I was *The Amy Fay,* to which I replied, *"Yes."*

I discovered three acquaintants from Chicago in the first cabin; they were Mr. and Mrs. Mittellochulte and Mr. Eddy, *not Clarence,* but a man who said he had sung in a concert in Austin, Illinois, where I once had played. I had completely forgotten *him* and the *concert* but recalled it dimly after a while. We have a band of music on board, which gives us three evening concerts a week, and plays twice a day on deck. It is enough to make you *die laughing* to see the German Fraus start up and dance, but they dance *well,* no matter how fat they are! The other day the band played a waltz, and one fat Frau jumped up and began to whirl, and was presently joined by two others, still bigger, and the way they bounced around, like big rubber balls, in the passageway between decks, was fun to see! I don't know *when* I have been so entertained!

We have had *two* balls on deck, the second was last night, and it was pretty. Gorgeous *moonlight.* The people of both cabins intermingled, and the deck was closed in with awnings and sprinkled with sand, and lit with colored lamps. Many dressed in light silks, and looked very fine. . . . We now have reached Friday afternoon, and I shall get to Bologne this evening about eleven o'clock. *Lots of flirtations* are in full blast, and the kisses are flying about! As there are a number of young ladies, students, and people of all sorts *spooning.* The Count is carrying on three or four at a time, but does not omit to come to *me* between times. I find him quite amusing.

Amy Fay

Well I must conclude this long letter, as supper is served. I hope you have not been *too* lonesome since I left, and that it was not too much trouble to put away my clothes and bric-a-brac. . . . Miss Read wants me to tell you that she arranged my hair twice a day and also that I am "catching on" to the new way *myself,* which she thinks very "encouraging." We had an impromptu performance in the second cabin the night before last, at which we both played, and anybody that *could,* got up and did something. The affair was arranged by a young German from Cleveland, who is a *wit,* and he made a very funny speech himself. He is Mr. Fellinger, and he is going to be a priest. He brought everybody of note on board into his speech with a witticism on each person. No names were spoken but all were recognized. We passed the Isle of Wight this afternoon, and the weather is *divine.* I have been studying Spanish and tackling French, German and English. The last two days have been extremely jolly in the second cabin. Lots of students are on board, and they make things lively. On the evening of the *Fourth,* we had some fireworks, and the students of Harvard, Yale, and Cornell, were on different decks, and three different bands, cheering themselves and each other. *Cornell* did not get much notice, but Yale and Harvard paid *each other* their compliments and "rah, rah, rahed!" Give my best love to all, and remember me to the Marshalls and to Mrs. Downing.

Your loving,

Amy

Chatou July 24, 1903

We drove from Paris to Chatou in about an hour. The road lay through the Bois and was ideally beautiful. When we emerged from the woods we descended along a gradual hillside from which we could look about and see "les immesures horizons de Paris" as Zola says. This city is stupendous and wholly different from any other. The repose, the dignity, the beauty and at the same time the dashing gaiety of it forms a wonderful combination. Then the endless historical association and the poetic charm which stimulate the intellect and the mind that it is no wonder Paris is the magnet which attracts the world. The French themselves can never get over this astonishment at it and when they say "Paree!" with a wave of the hand, you feel unutterable things.

Chatou is an exquisite suburb and all the places are kept up like those at Newport. Flowers, turf, and trees are everywhere and the gravel walks are combed with a fine tooth comb every day by the gardeners. We are quite near Bougival on the Seine and the other day we stood over there by way of the river from which face the lovely seats of the rich, each one more beautiful than the other. Crossing a bridge we came to the house of Tourgenyev, the great Russian novelist, where he is said to have died in the arms of Madame Viardot Garcia, the famous singer and the sister of Malibran. This is the most electric dwelling you can imagine set on high ground which with charming houses are full in flower and trees and automobiles whizzing about and the Seine winding in and out . . . according to which way he went - out of the *front* or the *back* door he had his lovely river view of the deep retirement or of the wood.

The most utter silence and seclusion prevails out here and I long to see some people about. In driving you hardly see a soul and the French are so awfully exclusive with their high walls and tall gateways that you can only get tantalizing glimpses of their Paradise. The swells abroad do not permit that free-hearted open view of their estates that ours do! I should think Europeans would enjoy Newport for that very reason, though perhaps they think we make ourselves too common! But how much better for a house to have its beauty visible than to be peered in when one walks or drives by those endless blank walls! The American plan is far better (as our plans always are) and happier. Coming back here the other day from after a day in Paris I had to stand and ring the bell and wait for the servant to come and open the gate so that I could get into the house. That's the way they live here.

Chatou August 3, 1903

Dearest Norman,

When you get this letter it will be near your birthday, and I want to wish you "many happy returns" of the same. I wish you could be over here and spend it with me and we would have a fine time together driving to St. Germain, which is not far from here. I am having a quiet but delicious summer at Mrs. Eddy's in Chatou. It seems to be a fashionable dwelling place hereabouts: Chatou, Croisy, Bougival, St. Germain, etc., everywhere beautiful villas with exquisitely kept grounds, quantities of flowers, roses peeping coquettishly over the highwalls, and the river Seine winding peacefully through the country at large. To reach St. Germain we climb a long but gradual hill, and when you come out on the top you are high over Paris, and have an extended view of the city in any direction, for many miles, all embowered as it is in the trees, like a village. It is wonderful how they have preserved the *trees* here, and you have this verdure everywhere, besides the great forests. The French think *so much* of a forest! There is one in St. Germain of over eleven hundred acres, with lovely roads cut through it and you can lose yourself there in the woods, as *we* did the other day, and it was three hours before we got home! The Bois de Boulogne is a wood covering 2250 acres of ground, and that is the scale they have things on in Paris. Our Central Park in New York is but a small affair in comparison. In the St. Germain forest there are often little cleared out spaces in the shape of a star and the roads diverge from it so that you see these leafy arcades in every direction as you drive across it. You hardly know which road to choose they are *all* so beautiful. There is a good deal of small game in this forest, and we saw the quail and rabbits dart across the path as we went along. There are so many outdoor resorts where the poor can go on Sundays and holidays in Paris, that I should think their lives would be very happy here. They avail themselves to the full of it, too. Mrs. Eddy is furnishing a new apartment she has taken in Paris near the Champs Elysées, and in the same block where Jean de Reszke lives. We drive into town every other day, and while she is shopping I go sightseeing with Miss Read or the Dallibas. Jim Dallibas *looks* perfectly well, and he will probably live a long time in spite of his sufferings. He has his ups and downs, of course, and is much better some days than he is others. They are at a nice little hotel, the Colombia, 16 Avenue Kleber, not expensive, and very comfortable. They will go to London for September, and have taken their passage for America on October 2nd. Miss Read has about decided to go to London with them, and sail from Liverpool in time to get back to her school, September 13th. . . . They all want me to go with them, too, but I don't know whether I will or not, yet.

Kate and the children are in Switzerland with Grace Koenig and her family, but they will return to Paris to see me. The weather has been too cold to be enjoyable there, so far. . . . Tell Lily Miss Read is boarding in just such a place as *she* had when she was in Paris at Mme. Bordes! It is a *pension* kept by two sisters, the Soeurs Lasalles, and is an excellent place to hear French spoken. Miss Read pays seven francs per day, the table is excellent, and she has a nice room and the use of a good piano in the salon. Readie is fixed quite to her mind. The address is 35 Rue Vineuse, and the house is near the Trocadero. A young English officer is the only *man* boarding there, and Miss Read says the whole family is devoted to him! I wrote to Mrs. Hallowell, but she is spending the summer in Normandy. She will very likely have to run over to Paris this month on some art business, in which case I shall see her. She has been automobiling with Mrs. Potter Palmer, who is in Paris at present. Mrs. Eddy and I are going to call on Mrs. Palmer.

Was not poor Donoghue's[1] suicide a *dreadful thing!* I was horror stricken by it, and shall never cease to regret this loss. He looked so bright and handsome when I saw him in June. He was wild with happiness over a commission to paint the portrait of a rich woman in New York and after all, the portrait was *rejected.* Poor fellow, his luck was *too bad,* and he could stand it no longer. I hope *your* courage will not give out under all the strain you have to endure. I feel so anxious about you all the time, as this strike must be the most devastating thing to contend with, but I hope you will be up to the situation and *never say die!* You have carried things through so splendidly before! Good bye dearest Brudder with much love to all from

Amy

---

[1] A New York painter and a friend of the Fay family.

Chatou August 5, 1903

Dearest Zie,

I got your two letters of July 15th and 16th. I did not intend to be so long in answering them, but as Mrs. Eddy and I drive into Paris about every other day, I have not had much time to attend to my correspondence. . . . I was . . . rejoiced to hear that the long threatened recognition of your services in some *substantial* way from the Fraunces Tavern Chapter[1] friends, finally materialized. I hope you *will* be able to complete the plates of your book with the money! I always believe in finishing a job one has already spent a great deal of time over, and if that book is as much a part of your life as you have asserted it was, it is your *duty* to *finish and publish it,* be the consequences *what they may.*

Yes, I had heard of Donoghue's death before I got your letter, from a Boston sculptor here named Mr. Brooks . . . I was *horror stricken* at it, of course, and terribly *shaken* by it. Poor fellow! If he only could have held out a few days, the black fit might have passed and *some* success *might* have reached him! I feared for him that evening, when he was in such high spirits over the portrait, and dreaded lest his hopes should be dashed to the ground. I can't remember whether I wrote a note of farewell before I left, but am afraid I did not. Probably the portrait was not a *likeness* and that was why it did not suit. I don't believe *that* was Donoghue's strong point. Did you go and see the picture? He was *so* interested in it, and said he was going to make it something *"quite different"* from other people's portraits. I declare, I think it was *too bad* they did not at least send Donoghue a check for his *time,* even if the portrait *was* rejected! I hope Mrs. Fiske felt remorse at being the cause of such a tragedy! I think there never was a man who had such hard luck as Donoghue had! *Nothing* seemed to succeed with him, even those exquisite little statuettes of his, which one would think the dealers might have appreciated. We *never* can replace him as a friend, for he was a *unique* person, and I always felt it a privilege to have such a first rank artist in our circle. It seems strange that *you and I could not help him,* but it was like the music of Charles Hopkins.[2] People did not see the beauty of it as they *ought to have done!* I hope you took care to mend the pedestal of my precious little *Isolde.* I wonder what Donoghue did with the one he offered to give Nordica, which she refused? I had it in my mind to buy it as soon as I could scrape up the money after I came home. I felt *dreadfully* that I could not send him twenty-five dollars a year ago when I was in Staten Island, and he wrote me he would let me have it "for anything I would give for it!" Only think of it, I could not afford *that small sum* at the time! . . . One wonders why it was, such genius as Donaghue had should go unrewarded from the world, for he certainly worked hard! I hope he left some record as to *where* his statues are stored away in cellars, but probably nothing will ever be done with them, even if he *did.* I should like to know if the Sophocles is in the Field Museum? I know Donoghue *tried* to sell it in Chicago, but I think he did not succeed in doing so. *That* was conceded to be a masterpiece by everybody, and it ought to be taken by the Museum *now,* if it was not before, as Donoghue won the first prize on it at the World's Fair. I think it was the mistake of his life that he settled in New York instead of going back to Chicago. *Out there* his friends might have rallied round him and could have had a better chance. I am sure that *everybody* who knew Donoghue must have had a severe shock at the manner of his death. It made *me* wakeful for a week, as I kept going over it in my mind *a great deal,* and I was going to beg you to invite him to dinner, and send you his address again. I was telling Gurickx about him in Brussels, and was wishing I could give *him* a statuette of Isolde to put in his music room in Gurickx's new house. *He* would have appreciated it.

You can't imagine how charming Gurickx was! He is very little changed except that he wears a beard now. His hair and beard are much darker, almost black, with a few grey hairs scattered through them. He looks older, of course, but is more attractive than ever. I wrote him a note when I arrived in Brussels and then went out with Miss Read. When I returned to the hotel, I found a *magnificent* bouquet of roses from him and a note in my room, in which he bid me welcome and said he should call at five on Tuesday afternoon, which he did. The next morning he took me to see his fine large house in the suburbs, which is just being finished. It has a beautiful situation with extended views from all the windows, and a garden around it in which were many roses already planted in bloom. His grand piano was in the drawing room, and was the only furniture in the house except two chairs. The painters were putting the finishing touches on the interior. Gurickx had built his house in the style of some of the old houses in Bruges, with steps on the roof, and on top just a little *bear* in metal or wood, of which he was very proud. "Voilà mon petit ouvre qui regarde, pour voir qui vient," said Gurickx. He must be very well off to have such an establishment, or else his wife must have money. His position as

Professor with the Royal Conservatory is a good one, and he wears in his buttonhole a ribbon which is a decoration from the King. In the afternoon Gurickx invited me to his town house to hear his best pupil play, and he asked me to bring Miss Read also. His wife was not visible, as she is near her confinement, but I observed her sitting in the window upstairs as we drove up in the cab. She is *petite,* with dark hair and eyes, and is young and pretty. They have only one child, a little girl ten years old, named "Germaine." Isn't that a pretty name? She was at boarding school, so I did not see her, but she is the *idol* of her *father.* Gurickx is very happy in his marriage, and he has probably made a wise selection, with his usual judgment and discrimination. I hope the *next* child will be a *boy,* and then he will have everything! His pupil was taking a lesson as we entered, and was a young girl about eighteen with a lot of sentiment in her face, a typical "jeune fille." She had a sheet of paper with a large repertoire of pieces on it from which Gurickx asked us to select what we wished to hear. Her name was Cécile Callebert and she had just taken first prize at the *concours* this summer. She played with a *finished technique* and was thoroughly well schooled. Her expression was *musical* and agreeable, but neither dashing nor dramatic, and she did not have as much character and style as my pupils have. I should have expected more *brilliance* from a pupil of Gurickx's. Her *Bach* playing was *exquisite,* and was the best thing she did. I made Miss Read play two pieces afterwards, and she did very well. I was much pleased at the effort she made, and I think that Gurickx was a little surprised. After the music was over he rang for some wine and refreshments, and we had a pleasant chat till about six o'clock, when we took our leave. I did not see Gurickx again as he had to go to Ghent the next day, when he was to be one of the jury at the concours of the conservatory there, and *we* were going to Paris.

His house was pretty and homelike, and he did the honours with much grace. Miss Read thought he was a good deal agitated inwardly, by his *manner,* and I daresay he was! He had reason to be, with his wife upstairs and me downstairs! I was "en grande tenure," and wore my new blue silk costume and flower hat (Readie did my hair!). It was a stunning get-up, and did not *look poor!* Miss Read wore her light grey dress with the white lace trimming and her white lace hat. Gurickx and I had each played one piece to each other at the country house, in the *morning,* as we left the field to our pupils in the afternoon. He asked after *you,* by the way. I did not make things unpleasant for him, but just talked on general subjects gaily and impersonally. Altogether it was a nice little episode to meet him again, and we mutually avoided any reference to the past! He *looked at me affectionately,* though, and as if he still had a *lot* of sentiment! I was glad for him that he had to go to Ghent the next day, when he could have a chance to think things over, away from his wife. I showed him a copy of my book[3] and he was delighted with the picture in it and exclaimed, "You must give me a copy like that!" So I gave him the book, and he gave me his photograph, a very good one.

Amy Fay

Brussels has grown and improved immensely and is not a very imposing city. It is chuck full of art and I was greatly impressed with it. I think Gurickx did wisely to return to his own country, where he has a *fixed position* and for him New York would have been a poor exchange. His wife, too, suits him a great deal better than *I* would have done so it is all right. He was *stirred up* at seeing me again, though, and possibly had some regrets. You ought to have seen the servant maid at Gurickx's house. Such a *pink* of French neatness and prettiness! The house, too, was as neat as wax, quite equal to Kate in daintiness and order. The walls were old tapestry on silk and the carpet was red in the parlour, and the colours were perfectly chosen.

I am having a quiet but very enjoyable sojourn at Chatou, and Mrs. Eddy, Miss Bullet, and I get on most harmoniously together. If Donoghue's death had not cast such a pall, I should be perfectly happy, as there is no effort about life here, and everything is lovely about me. Mrs. Eddy usually invites somebody on Sunday to pass the day. Mme. Nevada and her husband (Dr. Palmer) and her daughter, who is sixteen years old, came out the first Sunday I was here, also two American ladies, and the sculptor, Mr. Brooks, who told me about Donoghue's death. I talked a great deal with Nevada, who is a lovely little woman and much more interesting than I should have supposed. She is very fond of Loie Fuller, the *danseuse,* and praised her beautiful and generous nature, giving her immense credit as an artist. She says that Loie is always creating and growing and that she gave an entirely new impulse to art in Paris, which is also warmly acknowledged by artists here. The *other* dancer, Isidora Duncan, who has made such a *furor* here, owes a great deal to Loie Fuller, who helped her financially and every other way, but she has proved utterly ungrateful, and has even disparaged Loie's dancing and tried to injure her benefactor! Miss Duncan dances with only a thin gauze over her, so you see her figure as if she had nothing on! She is trying to convert the world to *naturalism* in art. She *was* in New York about the time I gave my concert and Eleanor Norris danced, so it is very probable that your article was the source of Isidora Duncan's inspiration. The *Tribune* quoted it, you remember.

Next Sunday Mrs. Eddy has invited Alexander Guilmant, the famous organist, and his wife and son, Alex Schwab and his sister. Schwab is living in Paris now, and I met him on the street, as I wrote you. Mrs. Eddy enjoys hearing me practice Charlie Hopkins' "Surfeit of Toil" and "L'Addio" very much. She came into the parlour to ask the names of the pieces, and she said they were "so beautiful!" She wants me to play them for Guilmant. I have not studied the pieces yet.

The drives and walks here are a never failing delight, as this is a place full of old chateaux and large estates with stately iron gates, tall and gilded, and with lions carved in stone in front of them. Louis the 14th had a favorite residence out here. It is the quintessence of aristocratic France, this neighbourhood. Miss Read spent the day here last Sunday and she is in good spirits now and enjoyed herself hugely; we drove to the forest of St. Germain all the afternoon. My clothes do very well,

52

only I wish I had another for morning wear! The weather is cool and showery, like our April but lovely in between times. Give my best love to Laura and Madeline, and with a great deal to yourself I am

Your devoted sister,

Amy

---

[1] Melusina Fay Peirce was responsible for the restoration of Fraunces Tavern in New York City.
[2] Charles Jerome Hopkins, uncle of Amy Fay who was about the same age as Zina.
[3] *Music Study in Germany.*

Paris August 14th, 1903

Dearest Rose,

I wonder how you are getting along, and whether you have had *hot* weather to visit you! Paris is a cool place in summer, almost too cool for us Americans, as we are used to being *baked,* and we have a shower two or three times a day. Fortunately the rain is of short duration and seems to be a kind of family watering pot of darling nature's, to freshen the flowers. They get a drenching here just as they do in the greenhouses at home, and this continual moistening keeps them in splendid condition. Chatou is gay with them everywhere you go, and they do make the country very attractive here. I have never seen such a profusion of geraniums before. Every house has great waves and beds of them in the yards and along the fences, and on each side of the doorstep.

Yesterday was *Sunday,* which is Mrs. Eddy's day for company, and she has a party come out from town to luncheon always. Yesterday she had Alexander Guilmant, the organist, and his wife and son, the latter a very nice and sensible young man. Schwab and his sister, Miss Schwab, were here also, and Arthur Mees and his wife were invited but did not accept, as they were leaving Paris. Theodore's ears ought to have burned, for we all talked about *him,* and I brought down your photograph group to show the company, which was looked at with much interest. Schwab is writing a book of reminiscences about the artists he has known, and he said he would like to have the photograph of Theodore made by Platz to put into it, as he is writing

53

about *Theodore* among others! He said he should give him "full credit for what he had done for music in America," *malgré* some little private differences he had with him! It was at the epoch of the New York Festival when he said that Theodore gave the program to the *Herald* in advance, contrary with his agreement with Schwab to give them to *all* the papers *the same day*. Schwab was business manager, I believe. He is a *great gossip,* is Schwab, but he is entertaining as he knows all about the musical profession. Guilmant was as sweet and simple as possible. Mrs. Eddy wanted me to play for him, so I *did* play a lot of pieces, and he was very complimentary, as was his son.

Mrs. Eddy has got a fine Steinway piano for me to practice on, I am happy to say. The one which was in the house was a deplorable instrument, and could not be used for company. One morning she came down and she said, *"If you are going to practice, I am going to get a good piano!"* This was joyful news to *me,* you may be sure, and she kept her word! I had been trying to study on the old piano, but could not use the pedals at all, as the loud one would stay down all the while if you touched it, and the soft one would not work! Well, I think Mrs. Eddy enjoys having some music, especially when she has guests out here on Sunday for the day, and it *is* a great relief from conversation. I played the "Addio" by Charlie Hopkins, and Guilmant liked the theme so much that he sat and improvised upon it a long time. Tomorrow I am invited to luncheon with the Jim Dallibas' at the hotel Columbia, and afterwards to tea at Mrs. Charles Thayer's, who is a cousin of theirs, and who lives in Paris. Mrs. Eddy drives me into Paris about three times a week, and while she is engaged with her dentist and with her shopping for her new apartment, I go sightseeing with Miss Read and the Dallibas.

I am overcome with the *beauty* of Paris, and it is certainly *grandiose,* the scale upon which it is laid out! The drive through the *Bois* is *delicious,* to begin with, and the view of the whole city from the top of a hill is impressive. The churches and the Louvre interest me more than anything, and the more I go to the picture galleries, the more I *want* to go! The gardens of the Tuileries are so spacious and so gay with flowers, and there are such *magnificent* groups of statuary everywhere, they are wonderfully striking and ornamental. Then the Seine winding along, spawned with low and graceful bridges, and flanked on each side with grand old buildings, is another feature of the landscape. I don't wonder the French are in love with Paris, and it must be a never ceasing source of inspiration to live here. But I should hate, nevertheless, to be patriated, as so many Americans are here. After all, it is more satisfactory to live in *your own* country, and *be a part of it, I think!*

Mr. Eddy[1] is hovering round Paris, much to Mrs. Eddy's amusement, but there are no signs of readjustment between them, as yet! He is going to visit Louis Lombard in Lugano, Italy, the paper said, so that will put a quietus on Mrs. Eddy's and *my* going there, as Mrs. Eddy proposed doing when I arrived here! Louis Lombard, you may remember, was a musician in Buffalo, who became a millionaire by his marriage and who has one of the finest places in Italy. I should like to go to Italy, but don't want to have to spend the money to do so. I can't do it, Mrs. Eddy would like to have me spend a year with her, she says! I am going home, though, in October. . . .

With much love as ever,

Amy

---

[1] Clarence Eddy became estranged from his wife.

Chatou August 15th, 1903

Dearest Zie,

Your letter of July 28th is at hand, and I also received the *Leader* and the extracts you sent with it, for all of which *many thanks!* Mrs. Eddy has many magazines and papers. She takes the *Musical Courier* and the *Leader* and she buys *Town Topics,* so you need not trouble to send any more cuttages. I had not read the papers *thoroughly,* however, so those you sent were new to me, just the same, and interested me very much, particularly the speech of the German Emperor about Folk-Song which I thought contained some sound sense in it. Mrs. Eddy had my name put in the Paris *Herald* the other day, as her visitor in Chatou, and this morning I received the following note:

> "Mademoiselle! Veuillez me dire si vous êtes *l'auteur* du charmant volume '*Music Study in Germany?*' J'en ai immensement jouis [*sic*]! C'est bien écrit, et je vous fais mes complements. Seriez vus disposée à aller à Munich entendre *Wagner?* Veuillez me l'écrire,
> Wien, Hotel Krantz
> Mme de Belostotsky
> 12 Août"

From this name, I conclude the writer of this letter must be a Russian lady or Pole living in Vienna. I shall answer it today, and will let you know the result later. There are some splendid performances of Wagner's operas going on in Munich now, for a month. Kate wrote me about them, and asked if I would go with her and hear a cycle of them, but I could not spend the money to do so, much as I would enjoy it.

I *should* like to go to Berlin the 29th of September for the unveiling of Wagner's statue and the five days' Festival which will follow it, but am afraid my finances will not admit of *that,* either. It is so provoking to be tied *financially* when I have not been here for such a long time, and there are so many things I want to do! I feel as if I *must* go to Hamburg to see Fal Timm, as she is now seventy-one years old, and one does not know how much longer she may be alive. Mrs. Eddy wants me to return next summer and arrange to be with her a whole *year,* and perhaps I may do this. . . . Yesterday Mrs. *Will* Dallibas made a luncheon party for me, and I met there Mrs. Dunlap of Chicago, who has lived in Paris with her husband ever since they lost their money seven years ago. She is looking about the same as when I saw her last, except somewhat stouter. . . . As I wrote you in my last letter, Mrs. Eddy had a little party last Tuesday, consisting of Guilmant, the organist, Madame Guilmant, their son, who is a very agreeable young man, Schwab, and his sister. . . . We talked music and artists all day long, and Guilmant was very charming. At Mrs. Eddy's request, I played a lot of pieces for him (she has a fine Steinway piano for me now!) ending with Charlie Hopkins' *"Addio,"* which he thought was beautiful, and he sat down and made a long and clever improvisation in it, weaving in a theme from Beethoven's Sonata Pathétique very ingeniously, which I had *also* played, and mingling the two pieces together. Guilmant has a set scheme for improvising, and he does it on scientific principles. So much in one key, so much in a contrasting key, then in the minor, and with an episode or two of a different kind, then a finale in which all the thoughts are presented and interwoven. He is not a *natural* improvisor, like Charlie Hopkins, but he is a *fine musician,* without originality. Both Guilmant and his son praised my playing warmly, and the old man said I had a *"remarkable memory".* I did not play the *"Surfeit of Toil"* for Guilmant, as I did not know it well enough to do it full justice, alas he improvised so long that "dinner was served," and we had to go into the dining room. Schwab was entertaining, as newspaper men always are, and we talked about his book he is writing on artists he has known. He will put Theodore into it, he says, and will do him full justice as a leader of orchestra. We talked about the American Opera Company, and I tried to make Schwab see that it was one of Theodore's most *brilliant achievements,* but don't know whether I succeeded in making any impression, though he backed down a little finally, as he was under the conviction that *Seidl* was *the* great conductor of opera, because he was with *Wagner.* Schwab has probably already written up Seidl as *the* great Wagner conductor, and he can't alter his work, probably.

The most interesting thing I have seen in Paris is the School of *"Beaux Arts,"* . . . It was something wonderful to go through *salle after salle,* and see all the arrangements for study they contain and the splendid collections of statuary (one room contained the Michelangelo casts) and pictures which the pupils draw from. We were shown the picture which got the *Prix de Rome* this year. The subject was the *"Prodigal Son,"* and it was done by a young man named Monochablou who comes of a whole family of artists, but is only twenty-four years old, himself. It was a wonderful picture, so *dramatic,* and the *light* on the group of the father and son was remarkably managed. The son was kneeling down, and the father had *rushed forward* to bend over and embrace him, with the true paternal passion, while in the distance the mother is seen coming down the path and shading her eyes with her hand from the sun, to see if it is really her son! Back of all the personages in the picture is a fine landscape. There is a burst of sunshine on the father as he bends over and clasps his son, his arm around his neck, as he kneels there. There were two other pictures from other competitors on this same subject, which was given out by the committee, but they did not compare in talent with that of Monochablou. To the left of the picture is seen the house in the distance, from which the father had run to meet his son *"while he was yet afar off!"* It was a fine conception, finely executed and really *affecting,* it was so impetuous and full of feeling! We had to go into the basement to see the prize pictures which were heaped together their frames against the wall. The fact is, they have so *many* pictures by the pupils in the Beaux Arts, they don't know what to do with them! We went through room after room of the competitions of *other* years which are hung as closely as they can be placed to each other, to save the space. It would seem to be a hopeless task to achieve distinction as an artist in *Paris,* and I should think there would be *many suicides* here! I don't see how they can possibly sell their things. . . .

The monument to Victor Hugo, by Barrias, is simply *stunning* and must have cost an *awful* lot of money! It is in the center of the Place Victor Hugo, so there is plenty of space to see it to advantage and it was put up only last year (1902), in February. Things are done on such a *grand scale* here! St. Gaudens' *Sherman* monument looks as if it were copied from a monument to Charlemagne, *here,* which stands near Notre Dame. It reminds you of it the minute you see it only the horse is held by a man instead of a woman. The composition is very much the same, and St. Gaudens *must* have had it in his mind, one would think, though perhaps unconsciously. . . . Give my best love . . . to all the family, and with a great deal to yourself, believe me, as ever

Your devoted sister,

Amy

Chatou August 23rd, 1903

Dearest Zie,

. . . Yesterday we devoted to the statuary in the Louvre, and it was *awfully* interesting. We first took the collection of modern sculptures, which fill several large *salles,* and there were many sculptors of the seventeenth and eighteenth centuries whose names were unknown to me, but who had done *significant* things! Only the great dead artists are in the Louvre, you know, the great *living ones* being in the Museum of the *Luxembourg,* which we had gone through the day before, Houdon, Canova, and Barye were the only familiar names to *me* in the modern sculptures of the Louvre. I was very glad to see the original bust of Washington by Houdon and also that one of Voltaire. The latter is the most *brilliant* face you can *possibly imagine,* and is considered Houdon's best work. Washington has a thoughtful and rather *sad* expression, but is interesting, and the *mouth* is very characteristic. On the statue of *"Cupid with his dart,"* by Antoine Tassaert, there was an awfully clever inscription by Voltaire—as follows:

"Qui que tu sois, voici ton maître
Il l'est, le fut, on le doit être."

Wasn't that *just like* his wit? There was one *standing* statue of *Spartacus,* by Foyatier, which was so like Andrew Brooke (Mr. Stuart's pupil) that he might very well have stood as a model for it (*Very Handsome*). It is a pity Mr. Stuart can't own it, as he is *madly devoted* to Brooke! Miss Read and I were both struck by its *amazing* resemblance, and it had Brooke's pose, when he *sings,* to the *life!* One of the most beautiful things was a statue of *"Napoleon just awakening to immortality,"* by a great sculptor named Rude. He is half sitting up on his bed, and the eyelids seem *just about* to open. A laurel wreath is on his head, and his perfect features are severely and delicately cut. It is *ideal. Canova* had some exquisite groups, and the well known one of Cupid and Psyche kissing each other, was in one of the *salles,* in the *middle* of it. While were were looking at the "Modern Sculptures" Miss Read happened to turn back the leaves of the guidebook and she caught the name of the *Venus de Milo.* Neither of us had remembered about *her,* and we *flew* to the salle where *she* stands *above* in her glory. You see her a *long way off* through two of three other salles, and she looks so glorious and stately as you approach that you see *right off* how *immensely superior* she is to *all* other statues of women! It is as great a difference as Raphael's *Sistine Madonna* over all *other* Madonnas! Strange, how one artist can have so much more genius than *all* the artists, isn't it? In spite of the innumerable casts one sees of the Venus de Milo, you *must* see the original, to grasp the *wonderful* youth and beauty of it. I had forgotten what an exquisite *mouth* she has, just like a Cupid's bow, and the lovely girlish oval of the face, and the freshness and plasticity of the figure, which looks alive, and the majestic intellectuality and purity of the statue. She is *indeed* a *goddess,* and you feel that man may have *aspired* to her, but that he has never *touched her!* It was too fortunate that Readie did not leave Paris without seeing the *Venus de Milo,* one of the most precious things in it! Very likely

I should have, too, if she had not glanced through the inestimable Baedeker and read the name by chance. I don't know how we came to overlook it. I saw the statue when I was here before but don't think I *took it in.* It looked entirely different to me.

Tomorrow evening Readie and I are going to the opera for the first time, and I shall spend the night at her *pension* so we can have one *more* day together on Tuesday for sightseeing. It is very fatiguing, and you have to get used to walking immense distances in Paris, there is no convenience here like our cable cars and omnibuses, which stop at every corner, and go every minute. Here you must go the *"arrêt"* before the thing will stop, and if it is *full* you are not allowed to get in, but must remain standing five or ten minutes until the *next one* comes along! It is impossible to get anywhere *quickly* in Paris. You can take the underground railway (called the Metropolitan) but you always have to walk several *long* blocks to get to it, and generally wait for a train. Then you have a long walk at the other end, when you get out! Cabs are the only comfortable way of going about but they cost twenty cents, besides a *pour-boire* for the driver. It counts up very fast, so we don't take them except when it is unavoidable. The weather is cold and rainy most of the time, though you get about between showers. It is impossible to dress up here without getting wet. The rare occasions when the sun shines for a few minutes the weather is delicious, but it goes right in again! With all its heat, I prefer our climate. . . .

You will be pleased to hear that Mrs. Eddy has invited me to go to the Wagner Festival at Berlin as her *guest.* Of course, I could not refuse such an offer as *that,* so I *am going.* She got tickets for everything and it will be a most elaborate occasion. The prospectus is bound in pink, a little book, with a gold medallion of Wagner on the cover. There will be a reception at the House of Parliament on the evening of September 29th, a *banquet* at the Winter Garden of the Central Hotel on Thursday evening, October 1st, and a gala opera on Saturday evening, October 3rd, besides *lots* of concerts, the unveiling of the statue, and the Farewell Gathering at the Zoological Gardens October 5th in the afternoon. I am wondering if my grey satin, black lace, and blue embroidered silk will carry me successfuly through these occasions? Mrs. Eddy is bound to go to them *all,* and it will cost her a pretty penny for us both! However, I'm in for it now, and no mistake! . . .

I shall sail for home from Hamburg October 10th probably, and will not go second class this time, so I must pay full fare. I have now about sixty-five dollars in my purse. I shall have to pay a deposit when I engage my passage, of at least twenty-five dollars, so *hurry up Factolus!* Mrs. Eddy and I took a drive to Bougival the other day. She has had her eye on a *"grande* propriete" on the other side of the Seine which is for sale. It has a forest on it and there is a superb view for miles, as the house is on the crest of the hill. She is passionately fond of old trees, as the French think so much of a forest, as every now and then we get out of the carriage and peer through the gate of this place. . . .

I *was* so relieved to hear that the strike seems to be nearing its end, and that

Norman is in better spirits, and I do hope he will have some good luck *now*. It would be nice if Mrs. Case came to New York to live, wouldn't it? Did the Marshalls stay in town all this time, and is Miss Marshall having that operation in prospect? Ms. Bullett, Mrs. Krehbiel's sister, is still with Mrs. Eddy and she is nice and friendly to me. It keeps us from being lonely to have her in the house, and I like her very well. . . . Give my best love to all the family. Grace Koenig returns on the 28th and will come out next Sunday she says in her letter. . . . What do you hear from Rose and Theodore? I have had no word from Rose since I left New York. I hope your *book* is progressing. With the best love, as ever.

Your devoted Amy

August 30, 1903

Dear Rose,

   . . . Miss Read told Mme. Loudrillon about the "Book of the Age,"[1] and she was *wild* to get hold of it and translate it. I sent her a copy and she went right to work on it. To my delight I found that she has made a *capital* translation of the Liszt part, which she will submit *first* to the editor of one of the Reviews here, and I hope it will be accepted. If these letters make a *hit*, Madame Loudrillon will then translate the whole book. This is a good scheme, I think. It gave me *great pleasure* to read her translation, and her mother said she was "*so interested* she wanted her to *keep on* reading the book aloud," from which I hope the editor will be similarly disposed. I think this was *great luck*, my finding a translator right off, and such a good one! This alone would make my trip worth while. . . .

   The weather has *at last* taken a turn, and the *last two days* are like our early June, and the *sun shines* once more! We have had rain nearly every day, and a chill *coldness* until now. Mrs. Eddy and I drive over to the forests of St. Germain on Marly-le roi, in the afternoons, and then we get out and walk in the woods and the carriage follows us till we are tired and get in again. Marly was a favourite residence of Louis the Fourteenth, and he had a beautiful chateau out there, which was razed to the ground, but the pond in front of it is still there. . . .

   I suppose you know that Mrs. Eddy has invited me to go to the Wagner Festival in Berlin, which will open September 30th and will last til October 5th. The tickets for the Festival alone cost seventy-five dollars! *Most generous* of her to take me! There will be grand doings, a banquet, reception, gala opera, concerts, unveiling of his statue, and a final afternoon reunion in the Zoological Garden. I hope to meet some of the *big musicians* there.   Vincent d'Indy is going for one! Also, Glasounov [Glazunov] Rimsky-Korsakoff, and many others. *You* and *Theodore* ought to be there also. I sail for New York on October 8th from Hamburg steamer Augusta Victoria, and now goodbye for today.

Your loving,

Amy

---

[1] The name given *Music Study in Germany* by Ethelbert Nevin.

Chatou September 4th, 1903

Dearest Zie,

I have written *you* four letters, *two* to Rose, and *one* to *Norman,* which is not a bad record for an absence of two months, particularly when you deduct eleven days at sea. I am leading as quiet a life here as if I were at Woodstock, and there really is not very much to write about.

Miss Read sails from Glasgow tomorrow, and you must get her to tell you all about our trip in Holland, which was so surprising and full of novelty. Oh, those Dutch *painters* were wonderful, and so were the *churches.* I don't wonder the artists all want to go to Holland and that it is so much a great artistic center. Through Miss Read my book is getting translated into French, as she told Mme. Loudrillon about it, with whom she boarded in Paris. This was the place recommended to her by Mrs. Vogel, Mrs. Eddy's daughter. Mme. Loudrillon was wild to see the Book of the Age and to translate it and I lent her the copy I had with me. She began with the Liszt letters, which she will submit to the editor of one of the Reviews here. If he accepts them, she will translate the rest of the book. I went in last week to read her translation, and to my great surprise it is splendidly done, and I shall be much disappointed if it is *not* accepted. There is not much enthusiasm about music in Paris, however, so they may not care for the letters. . . .

Best love to all,

Amy

Amy Fay

Chatou September 9th, 1903

Dearest Zie,

... I have taken my passage, as I wrote you, for October 8th, from Hamburg, on the Auguste Victoria and shall hope to be in New York by the 18th. When I arrive, I shall *pitch into my profession harder than ever!* I am glad I got in with the *Jews* last Spring, and shall continue to do so, for they take their lessons *regularly,* even if they can't pay as much as other people do! They also bring *other* pupils. I want to keep up my concerts for the Board of Education this winter and I wrote to Dr. Leipziger in June, so I hope there will be no difficulty about my getting engagements. ... It does seem a shame that man in Brooklyn can't give you the money to furnish that boarding house instead of expecting *you* to do it, and then you could go ahead with it. Could you not propose to him to furnish it one room at a time, as you gradually fill it up, and not try to furnish the whole house at once? Perhaps he could *begin* that way, or could not Miss Vanderfroel get you the money through her friends? She has such confidence in you. Have you written to Morowitz? He was so interested in your 81st Street venture that time! I am so afraid Normie will end like Donoghue and kill himself sometime, it scares me to pieces to think of it! September 11 ... Your second letter with the check and the family letter reached me last evening, for all of which my best thanks. It was a pleasure to hear directly from Laura and from Madeline again. *Too bad* Norman had to suspend Madeline's allowance. He must, indeed, be in a bad way, or he never would have done it. I felt so sorry to have you send on this royalty from the book, for you have such a *pittance* to live on, you really ought to have it. ... This week there was a dinner party given by Schwab and his sister, and I had to take a cab from the station in town and back, as Mrs. Eddy was ill and did not go. I went in the train instead of the carriage. Miss Bullet went with me. As Schwab is a Jew, the guests were all Jews but ourselves. He took me in on his arm, and opposite me was a man about thirty years old, whom he did not introduce to me. My conversation was largely with this individual, as Schwab devoted himself to eating his dinner. He had a long nose, eyes very closely set, and a high, screamy voice, which set my ears on edge! It was really hard for me to speak to him on that account. He turned out so clever, however, and everything he said suited me *so exactly,* that I began to get very much interested in him in spite of his personality. After dinner he *continued* to talk to me, and finally he said that he was a "Wagner melomaniac" and that he was going to paint the *whole* of the *Meistersinger,* and that he is *now* doing *"Parsifal"* in a series of twelve pictures, which were ordered by Knodler and *must* be in New York by December! Well, I pricked up my ears at *that* as you may well suppose, and suddenly I had an intuition, and I said to him, "There were two very extraordinary exhibitions given at Avery's some years ago. I have forgotten the artist's name, but one of the pictures was called the "Dawn," a forest, with a figure shooting out arrows of light. There was *another one* with the *Devil* seated up on the tower of Notre Dame." *"I am the man,"* said he, "who painted those pictures." He gave me his card, and the name on it was *P. Marcius Simons, 156 Boulevard Pereire.* I at once recalled the name, for I was carried away with those pictures, and always have wished to meet this painter, but never expected to! You will doubtless remember his exhibitions. It was way back in *1896* when we were at Mrs. Merrill's and I took Laura Sanford to see them. Well, you may imagine how surprised and *delighted* I was to see Simons! I told him we thought the second exhibition not so good as the first one, but more exaggerated, and we thought perhaps he was going mad! He said that many of the *pictures were unfinished* and that a card of explanation ought to have been addressed to the public. It seems that the dealer took everything Simons had in his studio but he made him such a good offer he could not refuse it, and he let all his things go—good, bad, and indifferent, just as they were! I told him I thought it was a mistake to do that, as it gave a false impression. That picture of the *"Dawn"* I had longed to have for my own, it was so full of genius. He said it was bought by Robert Cutting in New York (how the swells do get everything, don't they?). The upshot of our interview is that I am to visit Simons' studio and see the four Parsifal pictures he has *ready.* He is painting *tooth and nail* on the others and I asked him if he was doing them separately or together? He said "together." He cares a great deal more for music than for painting, he says, and were it not for this order, he would be at Munich listening to Wagner cycles! "Outside *of my own work* I don't busy myself with *art at all,"* he added!

At this point Schwab asked me to play, which I was very pleased to do, as I was in good practice and had such a genius as Simons for a listener, and I did play several pieces, my *very best.* They all clapped their hands, and Schwab called over to me, *"You are accepted,"* as if he were a manager and I were playing *on approval!* There was a pretty young singer, an American, named Miss Parkinson, Marchesi's crack pupil, and she sang after I finished playing, very charmingly but nothing *great.* Then Miss Bullet and I took our leave. The ride through the streets of Paris, singularly quiet, and lit up by brilliant moonlight, was wonderfully beautiful. Oh—this city! You ought to see it! It is simply *limitless* in its possibilities. My steamer, the Auguste Victoria, sails from Hamburg October 8th. I suppose Miss Read will be back when you get this. Do tell me whether her trunks turned up before she sailed! I was all upset about them. With much love to all and especially to your dear self.

As ever your loving,

Amy

63

Amy Fay

Dearest Zie,

Kate and the children have *at last* returned to Paris, now that I shall be leaving in ten days! They arrived on Monday and were out here to luncheon today and spent the afternoon. Mrs. Eddy is *lovely* about entertaining and she is always glad to invite my friends and seems really to *enjoy* having them. . . . We are going to move into town next Tuesday, and I will have a week in Paris before leaving for Berlin September 28th. . . . Miss Mary Münchoff, the charming singer from Omaha, who lives in Berlin with the sculptor, Professor Uphues (pronounced "Oopoose") and his wife, has been visiting Mrs. Eddy for the last two weeks, having come on to catch up with Madame Marchesi and to have her dresses made. I believe I told you about her before, and how she went to Baden-Baden to sing a concert at which Gaye played, the other day. It was an orchestral concert given in honor of the Grand Duke there. She had a great success, and was invited to a supper after the concert, given at the house of a *swell,* who turned out to be the *very* Madame Lineu at whose house in Antwerp I was invited to meet Liszt at dinner, when I was in Brussels in 1885. Miss Münchoff told Madame Lineu that I was at Mrs. Eddy's house and she remembered me, and sent her compliments to me. It is strange that I should have been thinking about Madame Lineu only a short time ago, and wondering about her. She lives in Brussels now, Miss Münchoff said. Yesterday I went to the cemetery of Père la Chaise with Miss Münchoff and the Herr and Frau Professor, and we had a very interesting, though fatiguing afternoon there. . . . I find the Professor very interesting and original and envy Miss Münchoff the artistic training she gets from being with him so much. It is like our going to the Thomas concerts. (Kate was *delighted* to get the book of programmes and the photographs, tell Rose, which I have just given her. I do think Kate appreciates Theodore better than *anybody!* She is always talking bout him! Mrs. Eddy took quite a fancy to Kate at luncheon and got much interested in her conversation about Theodore's concerts.)

The French conception of a cemetery is the strangest thing for such a spacious city as Paris, and all they seem to think of is to *save space.* So many houses have gardens in the rear! The tombs are put just as closely together as houses in a block, and there is no grass plot whatsoever. The allées are paved, but are *shaded with trees,* fortunately. There are very few flowers growing, and the graves have *bead* wreaths laid upon them. It is *cold* and *artificial!* On the other hand, there is much fine sculpture by distinguished artists. Balzac's tomb had his head in bronze upon it; and there was a bronze book and pen lying there to represent his work. In a sequestered nook *Daudet's* handsome head looked down at you from behind the tomb . . . a family mausoleum, with palm leaves droping down the sides of the tomb and wreathing the top of it, in bronze. This was the most beautiful one I saw. Molière and la Fontaine were lying next to each other and above them were two sarcophagi not long shaped, but square like Longfellow's. On top of Fontaine's was a fox sitting, with tail curled up, so cunning and roguish, and there were bas-reliefs of little wild animals around the base. This was a *charming* monument, with nothing of *death* about it, but on the contrary, it represented LaFontaine's *life* work! I have been reading Béranger's poems over again, which are all about grisettes on *La gloire de France,* and they touch the hearts of his countrymen! He is such a simple, jolly bohemian, with a sentiment of a *poet* and the *finesse* of a *man of the world!* He would be impressed with his own monument, if he could see it! It is a great big tablet with bronze medallions on which is inscribed *"Béranger, le poète national de France!"* Nearby is the tomb of his *"Lisette,"* to whom he wrote so many amorous lines, who died at the age of 79! Her real name was Frère, and on her stone is inscribed an exquisite poem by Béranger to her, wherein he tells her that *"près de sa beauté"* he felt himself *a king!* We would not have known about Lisette's grave had it not been for the kindly instruction of a policeman who took a shine to Miss Münchoff and conducted her slyly to it! Think of that *grisette* who was common property being buried near Béranger, Molière and LaFontaine! Chopin's monument has been mutilated by some brute of a relic hunter and the forefinger and thumb of the statue of the muse bending mournfully over her harp have been broken off! It is a particularly painful thing to a *musician* to see the *hand* broken! Only the stumps of these two fingers remain. This monument was erected to Chopin by his friends, of whom Liszt was one. It is a statue of a woman sitting on the tomb with a lyre in her lap over which she is grieving and a very pretty monument. The most curious of all the monuments is that of *"Abélard and Héloise"* which, of course, everybody wants to see. It has been lately restored, and there is a good space around *this* monument, which is planted with flowers and protected by an iron fence, so the relic hunters can't get to *it.* The wire and bead wreaths are done away with which used to cover the tombs, and the two bronze figures lie side by side under a Gothic panoply. Abélard died in 1141 and Héloise in 1163; what a *long time ago!* Sarah Bernhardt has designed a handsome tomb for herself, and put her name on it, although as the guide says, she is still *"alive and kicking!"* We were amused to see that somebody had laid a bouquet of flowers upon it as a tribute! I am sorry now that I did not cast a glance at the tomb of Lefébure-Wély, the composer of the immortal *"Monastery Bells,"* although I was in the neighborhood of it. But, as I was going by I said to myself, *"Oh, that old trashy piece,* I don't care anything about the author of it!" That was a great mistake on my part, for anything which has become known the *world over* is worthy of attention! Alfred de Musset's tomb has a portrait bust of him on it, with regular features, not especially individual or fascinating, as Daudet's is. Chaplain, the painter, had a monument which "departed from religious tradition *very freely,"* as the Professor said with a grin! A female figure *bare of draperies* held up his palette and brush, and his bust looked down upon her with *no* disapprobation in his eye! There was not much of the religious element about *that,* as it was a *rear* view of the female, which is not ideal! There was *one* monument which would be *lovely* for Charlie Hopkins and Cicely. Two tombstones stood side by side, of light grey marble, and from each proceeded a bronze arm and hand, one of a man and the other of a woman. They *clasped hands* as if they were joined *after death,* and they formed an arch over the two stones. It looked *so loving!* Thought it a beautiful idea for a married pair, and the Professor said it was *"gar nicht sebel"* — not at all bad! Well, I expect you are tired of hearing about tombs and monuments, so I will conclude my remarks on this subject.

We were about dead when we got back to Chatou it was so far, and Miss Münchoff went to bed soon after dinner, and lay there till nearly noon the next morning, to "rest up." It did not take *me* that long to recover! You get a fine view of Paris from Père la Chaise. I went to the Opéra Comique the other night to hear an operetta by Gustave Charpentier called *"Louise,"* which is the sensation of the hour, and was splendidly given. Mlle. Clara Friché was the Prima Donna, and she was very fine from the French point of view, a handsome woman. The piece of work of *"réalisme et de rêve à la fois"* — *"de réalisme franc et violent: de rêve imprécis et charmant,* etc." The theatre is a *very* beautiful one, all white and gold, with exquisite statues holding up the golden drapery above the drop curtain, and garlands of gold leaves on each side of the stage. There was one scene in the opera of *Paris,* lit up by night, which was extraordinary. . . . Give my love to Readie and I do *hope* she got her trunks before she sailed. Much love to you all from

Your affectionate sister,

Amy

September 29, 1903

The Wagner Festival

We left Paris at one on the afternoon and arrived in Berlin punctually at nine the next morning, September 29th. We had a luxurious journey in a first-class compartment which was practically a little room to ourselves with dressing closet adjoining. I slept very well and realized how the world "se mova" since my girlhood days in the seventies when there were no sleeping cars on the railroad. We drove to this standard and excellent pension and while Mrs. Eddy went to procure our tickets to the festival I made my way to my fellow teacher and promoter of "the Deppe" piano method — Miss Elizabeth Caland.

The American Years

Fräulein Caland[1] lives in a large artistic apartment in Goethe Strasse in Charlottenburg and she was overjoyed to see me. Her studio is charmingly artistic with grand piano and pictures of great artists, etc. . . . She does not grow weary in the good cause. She was born in Holland and is very clever — and you know our language embodies a proverbial warning as to the difficulty of "beating the Dutch!" Among the framed photographs were several of Deppe, together with a picture of him framed and monument at Pyrmont — my own name being upon it — which at once surprised and pleased me. To go down in stone as one of his devotees is indeed dear to my heart. Fräulein Caland and I had a sympathetic time talking about Deppe and Virgil[2] whom *we* believe to have appropriated Deppe's incomparable method from my own version of it in "Music Study" and in "Deppe Exercises" I printed, and by no means to have improved it but we find it exasperating to think the "Virgil Method" has gone all over the world through the Virgil Clavier whereas in truth it would have been the *"Deppe Method* as developed for the Virgil Clavier." And on the very street where I am staying is one of the Virgil branch schools with a conspicuous girl and sign, "Virgil Piano Teaching School." Fräulein Caland asked me if I might like a card to go to one of his pupil's concerts on Saturday evening. I declined *with* thanks and told her we had enough of Virgil's pupils in New York. The hundreds and hundreds of pupils this man has in his many schools and the very few concert pianists he has turned out is in my opinion a striking proof of the shallowness of his pretentions.

You can't imagine how Berlin has expanded. The old part of the town as I knew it has given up to shops and business and the population is streaming out to Charlottenburg which is no longer a romantic suburb but Berlin itself. . . . We attended a concert and reception at the Reichstag Gebäude. The whole thing was managed by a *nouveau riche* named M. A. Zeichner, who has given nearly all the money for the Wagner monument, the unveiling of which was the occasion of the festival. The original idea of this memorial was that it should be paid for by small subscriptions from music lovers all over Germany and thus be a national tribute, but as the fund came in as slowly as that for the liberty statue did with us in New York, Zeichner, who is a very rich manufacturer of cosmetics, saw an opportunity to make himself famous and offered to give all the money for the statue. He seems to be the Sir Thomas Lipton of Berlin but without the tact and consequently without the popularity of Sir Thomas. After being accepted he next got himself made president of the committee of management and then the Wagner family and the swell portion of the musical fraternity took umbrage and with characteristic German jealousy declared the festival was no real homage to Wagner. Frau Cosima and her brood consequently declined the invitation to be present. The big conductors backed out; neither the emperor nor the crown prince, but only the *second prince* of this brood, "little Prince Eitel" "assisted" and the circle was equally conspicuous by the absence of the long list of high sounding names on the programmes . . . the opening concert and all the preceding occasions though very brilliant and interesting, did not turn out to be all that was expected.

At the first concert the Philharmonic Orchestra at Leipzig [was] conducted by Hans Winterstein . . . you may remember he came to New York a few seasons since, lost a lot of money and then "returned to the spot where he originally fell." The assisting artists were Madame Flaniert from the royal opera in Brussels, Monsieur Delmias, magnificent baritone from the grand opera in Paris, Fräulein Breckenbaukier from the court opera in Coburg, Fräulein Miller from the court opera at Hanover, the very virtuoso Alexander Furedi from Budapest, and my own favorite Schumann-Heink. These artists all did their very best and gave us a truly splendid concert, though a little long, since all had to have an opportunity to display their quality and after it was over began a promenade concert by the orchestra when everybody went into the banquet room for refreshments.

Scores of interesting men were all about, richly decorated with ribbon and orders, medals, crosses, jeweled pins and what — not — impressive to behold: The principal grandés [*sic*] were Prince Friedrich and Count Hochberg — once you remember "Deppe's pupil" and afterward his patron and backer. Our sculptor, Professor Uphues, was decorated like the rest — with a string of glittering medals on his evening coat! I had a warm handshake from Xaver Scharwenka and a little talk with Lessman — now the musical critic of the "Allgemeine Musik Zeitung." Fräulein Caland told me it is impossible to succeed in Berlin unless you have Lessman on your side. She seemed much surprised and pleased to see me. Scharwenka used to teach in Kullak's conservatory when I was studying there. We had the pleasure of Lillie de Hegarmann's company at the concert and I had called her the first thing after arriving and spent most of the day with her. She invited me to stay to luncheon and to dine with her from two to four in the afternoon. She was alone — her husband and children being in Denmark. So she had sent back her Festival tickets not having anyone to go with. On our way we stopped at the Festival office to get Mrs. E's and my tickets for the unveiling next day. Leichauer himself was there and he followed me out to the street and saw Lillie sitting in her carriage. He had met her in Washington so he had sailed up, kissed her hand, and brought Lalo, the music critic of the Paris *Temps* out to the carriage to speak to us. On learning that Lillie had returned her tickets he at once gave her others for the reception of that evening and banquet for the next one. She was terribly in doubt about planning to go without Mr. Hegarmann, but I finally persuaded her to meet us at the Hall that evening and Professor Uphues promised to escort her to her seat. When I said I was going out to Charlottenberg to Professor Uphues to see him and his dolls (puppen as he calls his statues), she also wished to see the puppen and said she would drive over there. This she accordingly did the next morning and found him in a beautiful apartment elegantly furnished and with an immense new studio in process of construction. The Frau Professor and Mrs. Münchhoff were there with the Professor and we had a charming visit and saw all the statues he had there. He is evidently a rich man as well as a very successful one.

<hr />

[1] Elizabeth Caland (1862-1929), Dutch-German piano teacher and music editor who studied piano with Deppe in Berlin and published a manual on Deppe's method.

[2] Almon Kincaid Virgil, founder of the Virgil Clavier School, who patented in 1892 a practice clavier in the form of a small piano having nearly the full compass of the piano. The use of the practice clavier was incorporated into the Virgil method of piano study.

New York November 18th, 1903

My dear Pauline,

Just a year ago today you and I were sailing down New York Harbour at this hour (two S.M.J.L.) I had not *yet* begun to be seasick. It is *lovely* weather, and I almost wish I were aboard the Sequianca again! and returning to the beautiful land of South America! I suppose that President Roosevelt has recognized the secession of Panama from Columbia and the canal will be built. Our papers are all wrangling over it, some are *for,* and some are *against* the President for recognizing Panama, with, what the *Evening Post* calls "most indecent haste!" However, the Republican party is with the President, or he would never have dared do it. Your Aunt Zina, of course, is *down* on the *President,* and is in sympathy with "poor Columbia."

I have been in Paris all summer, at Chatou, a lovely suburban residence where Josephine used to live, at *Malmaison,* after her divorce from Napoleon. I was visiting a former Chicago friend of mine, Mrs. Clarence Eddy, who inherited a fortune from her father and who has lived in Paris for the last eight years. She has a daughter, Mrs. Vogel, who lives in New York, whose son Clifford, a youth of seventeen is a pupil of mine. Mrs. Eddy has a handsome apartment in Paris, and she rented a very charming villa at Chatou for the summer. The places out there are beautifully kept and are gay with flowers. It is not far from St. Germain and Marly-le-roi, a former residence of Louis 14th. . . . Lots of French aristocracy live along the borders of the Seine, and the tall grilled iron gateways with stone lions in front to the *large* estates are very impressive. The French are so awfully exclusive, they *must* have high walls all around their places, so you can only see them through the gates, by glimpses. I saw a good deal of your mother[1] (she looks well) and the children the last fortnight I was in Chatou, and they came out to Mrs. Eddy's twice. . . .

Paris is wonderfully beautiful to look at, though, and I was never weary of visiting the museums and churches. I took Miss Read over with me, and she was boarding in Paris at Rue Vineuse, near the Trocodero. Mrs. Eddy and I used to drive into town every other day through the Bois and then Miss Read and I would go sight seeing. She started for home a month before I did and had a few days in London and Scotland, sailing from Glasgow. I went to Berlin with Mrs. Eddy for the unveiling of Wagner's statue followed by a musical festival which lasted four days. It was magnificent, and it was a great pleasure for me to be in dear old Berlin once more, where I had spent six years of my youth. I picked up many old friends, and made some new ones. Also I spent two days with Lillie de Hegermann delightfully. She was most *cousinly* and cordial, and she invited me to luncheon and to drive, and she went to an evening reception and concert with me, the first night of the festival, in the House of Parliament. She *loves* to be in Berlin, where there is a *court,* and Mrs. de Hegermann is a great favorite of the Emperor. He and the children were away, and Lillie was just going to Denmark to visit Nina. . . . I met Professor Paine and Mrs. Paine in Berlin at the Wagner Festival and you will be pleased to know that our Professor was treated with much honour there. He was the first to be called up to receive a medal and diploma, and his Overture to Oedipus was played and was much applauded. He had a triple recall from the audience. . . .

In Chicago they have been trying to raise seven hundred and fifty thousand dollars to build Theodore a concert hall of *his own* for the orchestra to endow it. So far they have got $400,000, but *there* the fund sticks. Your Uncle Norman is doubtful of success. If the money is not forthcoming the orchestra will be disbanded at the end of the season as the same men cannot *keep on* paying the annual deficit all the time. It will be a terrible shame if all your Uncle's effort and sacrifice to establish a first class orchestra permanently should come to naught. The rich men *will not* come up to the scratch, although the *general public* does all in its power, and fully appreciates Thomas. Your Aunt Rose is writing a book about her garden in Felsengarten, with Kodak illustrations, and she is much absorbed in it. She hopes to get it out for the Christmas sales. . . .

Mrs. Eddy has invited me to return and spend next year with her, and I *may* do so. I am very busy with my class and am President of the Women's Philharmonic Society which your Aunt Zina started. We give concerts twice a month. I am going to continue my Piano Conversations for the Board of Education after Christmas, in the Public School building. The Blancs are in town, and Edith says they have lots of money! . . . Mrs. Prince is very delicate with heart disease. Gerda Dalliba is living under my care now, up here, as she has *at last* broken away from her mother and father who are at St. Albans. Zina joins me in much love. Tell Arthur I got my letter.

Amy

---

[1] Kate Fay Stone.

The American Years

New York March 17, 1905

Dearest Mudkins,

. . . I have been more *rushed* than ever lately, as Rose came on from Boston last Friday and she is comfortably domiciled at Hector's apartment, No. 123 East 24th Street. When she first came it almost made me cry to look at her, she had such a grief-stricken and desolate expression! I went down there to dine on Wednesday evening, however; that time she was handsomely dressed, and had a more cheerful expression. You never saw anything *like* the way her rich Chicago friends fixed her out in clothes! She only had to buy a hat and a wrap! She had many beautiful memorials to show me, in the way of testimonials from different cities to Theodore's memory, bound in black moire antique, and decorated with hand painting on the edges of the leaves. I suppose she has written you about the simple little burial at Mt. Auburn, with only Kate and Mrs. Gardner besides the Thomas children and the clergyman (Mr. King) at the grave. As the coffin was being lowered into the grave, the clock struck *twelve,* Rose said! That was curious, wasn't it? Theodore was buried just at noon as it happened. I asked Rose if it was not an *awful* moment to *her,* but she said, to my surprise, that she felt it "was the *right and proper thing to do*" and that "she felt that *Theodore* wasn't there *any more* and his body was his cast off shell only!" I suppose it must have been a relief to get the thing *done.* I am glad Rose is in New York at this cheerful time of year when spring is coming, and I am confident she will come up under the gaiety of the atmosphere of this city.

Norman came up to see me early yesterday afternoon, and of course I was downtown and *missed him.* I returned towards six o'clock and found a card from him in which he said that Mr. Paderewski had invited him and me to dine with themselves in their Manhattan Hotel, where Norman was also stopping! You can imagine my "amazement and surprise." It was a quarter to six and I only had one hour to dress and get down there, and this when the city is going through a strike with the cars and you never know how long it will take you to catch one! I had great luck in dressing, however, and my *hair* went up all right, in a jiffy! I wore my black lace dress and gold balls. Paddy and his wife and *her* son, Gorky, met us at the entrance and we took a carriage and drove to Delmonico's, where we had a private room, and round table set for five. I had the bliss of being taken in to dinner by our host, and I sat on his right hand. Madame Paderewski was very sweet, *this* time. She is a quiet person and talks but little, but is attentive and polite to her guests. I was delighted that she did *not* talk, as it gave Normie and Paderewski a chance. Her son was a modest and unassuming young fellow, dark in complexion and with black hair, but resembling his mother. He has lived in Chicago for two years, and is going back there. The conversation turned mostly on Theodore, so we were *all*

71

rather serious. Paderewski spoke of him with *deep feeling* and said he "*never* could be replaced as the leader of the orchestra!" Paddy is not so *handsome* as formerly, as he wears his hair combed straight back and it does not tumble about his head in careless and graceful profusion as it used to. I am afraid he is losing his vanity. However, he is just as fascinating, notwithstanding. Madame Paderewski has been suffering with rheumatism for three months, and she is quite lame from it. She was looking for an electric *bath* place here, but said she could not find one in New York. I think he must be anxious about her health.

After dinner they took us to the concert of the Boston Symphony at Carnegie Hall, where we had a *fine* box. Paderewski sat in a corner, in order to conceal himself from the gaze of the audience. It seemed so queer to be going to a concert *with him!* I *had* to sit *in front,* so all I could do was to look around and exchange an occasional *smile,* which I *much* regretted, as I should have preferred to be at his side! I was obliged to be very circumspect on account of Madame Paderewski, as she is so jealous of him, but I think I conducted myself with *prudence!* After the concert was over, at which Kreisler was the soloist, the Paderewski's were claimed by Gericke and Adamo[w]ski, and Norman and I took our leave and went home. He expects to leave for Chicago tomorrow afternoon. I had but little chance to talk to Normie, but the Arithmograph is not *yet* in the market, I gathered. . . .

Are you coming on to New York? The weather is lovely now. . . . My pupils . . . take up my afternoon. We have a concert for Madame Bridice Blye on Wednesday at the Women's Philharmonic and I have thirty tickets to sell! It *is* a *task.*

With best love as ever from your devoted

Amy

New York May 31, 1905

Dearest Zie,

I got your letter, and was sorry to hear you are leaving before another fortnight has elapsed, as I don't believe you will find you have accomplished very much on your book in that space of time, and you might give Rose and the children the pleasure of your company that much longer! I got back from Cambridge a week ago Tuesday night, after a very pleasant little visit. . . . Cambridge was looking its very best, and the lilacs and zinias were in full bloom, as well as the fruit trees. I went to the wedding of Sallie Lawrence, Pauline's friend, and a daughter of Bishop Lawrence. The place where they live is so well adapted to a wedding, as everybody could stream out onto the lawn after congratulating the bride. Very few Cambridge people were asked, and it was mostly a Boston crowd. . . . Edith and Dick called on me Sunday and she announced to Kate that they were coming over in the evening to sing hymns with her! They carried out their word, and sure enough, they appeared with their prayer books at eight o'clock promptly, and we sang hymns vigorously! It seems they have a passion for them. Dick has a good voice, and he enjoys singing on the last note and showing it off. Sheffield was there, too, and *he* likes to sing. I opine that Edith will now be friendly to Kate and the long desired association with the Longfellows will thus be brought about. Norman turned up on Saturday morning and remained over Sunday at Kate's house and we had a pleasant little family reunion with *him*. We went to church Sunday morning, and in the afternoon he went to Mt. Auburn, and joined us at the country club, in Watertown, some distance beyond Mt. Auburn. It is one of those large and pleasant old houses, with lots of land about it and a rolling surface. The house is on a hill, so you have an extended view. Will came up with us, as well as Kate and the girls, and we all set on the broad piazza and had tea and toast. Also, Will's sister, Mrs. Kendall, came over from Walpole. When we returned home we found Sheffield, who had come to Cambridge on a trip, and he had been waiting for us nearly two hours. He stayed to tea and spent the evening, and it was very pleasant to see him again and reminded us of old times. Kate was very sweet about my *birthday* which *I* had entirely forgotten, and when I came out of my room she welcomed me with, "Many Happy Returns," and gave me a box of candy, some lace undersleeves, and the children gave me a pair of scissors. So I fared very well. . . .

Monday evening she invited the Paines to dinner, and they enjoyed it hugely. Professor Paine is looking better than I expected and he told lots of funny stories at dinner. Mrs. Paine was quite gorgeous in a new hair front, and a handsome black silk, with point lace collar and trimming. She also wore a diamond pin and ring! I never saw her so fine! I wore my grey suit with the pink. Kate wore an exquisite black lace, and the girls were charming, of course. Will was handsome and hospitable, and the dinner was a *great success!* . . . On the way home I stopped at Sander's Theatre to hear Henry James lecture on Balzac. I went down and shook hands with him and said a few words to him. He has changed so, you would never know him, and is quite English in his manner, but he remembered us all perfectly. I told him I had thought him and Chicago one of the funniest combinations in the world, to which he replied, "It is a *good* place!" quite as if he had enjoyed himself very much there, and made the stereotyped compliments, and said we had all followed his career as a writer in his *"delightful* novels," with interest and he said with his little choppy English accent, "So kind of you, so kind of you!" After that we parted, with a loose grasp of the hand, and he turned to some grey haired big wigs who were waiting for him. I reminded him that it was many a long year since he and I had been in the town of Cambridge together, and said I must shake hands to celebrate the event.

He gives the lecture again here today, at the Women's Political League. I did not have time to go to the Peirces', but Mr. Peirce said Helen was in Barnstable, he thought. Helen had a splendid time in Europe, and went all round London with the guide book by herself as Gertrude Ellis was ill. I called on Mrs. McKenzie and on Miss Emma Cary on the way home from the lecture. Miss Cary was in bed with a broken ankle . . . Mrs. McKenzie looked well, and she spent Tuesday morning with me. I played a lot of pieces to her, and she was very much surprised apparently at my playing, and exclaimed, "You have made *immense* progress, and you have evidently studied Paderewski." She is a sweet creature and is as devoted to music as ever. I managed to get to Agassiz Museum and look at those glass flowers. Norman and Will and I went together on Sunday. They *are* wonderful. . . .

Ever since my return I have been overwhelmed with people. . . . Now, I must close and go to see Lily so Good bye, with much love to Rose and the children and yourself.

Fondly,

Amy

New York August 11th, 1906

My Dearest Pauline,

. . . We have had the hottest summer, (thunder storms every day, etc. the thunder is roaring now!) and I have been in New York till now. I lock my door and sit in my room in as *near* a state of nature as possible, and in that way manage to bear it very well. We have had quite a little family reunion of late, as your Aunt Lily and Harry Wilmerding have been in town, also Madeline Smith and her mother, and Uncle Norman will be here next week on business. I have not seen your Aunt Lily look so pretty since her marriage as she does this summer! She is as *fresh* as a daisy, and has a *beautiful colour!* She has been up in Maine (near Mt. Desert at *Manset,* the most beautiful place she ever saw, she says) which she doats on, and was also at Roses place in Bethlehem New Hampshire for a visit. I expect to go to Felsengarten next month. On the 18th of August I shall take the boat for Edgartown, on Martha's Vineyard, where I shall stay at the country house of my friends from Washington, General and Mrs. Allen. I visited them in Washington at Christmas time, and it was on my return New Years' Eve, that I found your letter awaiting me, with *lots* of others. It was curious that I had been *haunted by you* for some weeks, and by my trip to

South America, so it seemed like an answer to my thoughts! I have not seen any of *your* family for over a year, but am planning to spend a few days at Fishers Island. . . . Were you not shocked at the deaths of James Peirce, Professor Thayer and Professor Paine? Cambridge will never seem the same again without *them!* I shall miss Paine awfully when I go there. Bertie Peirce is now United States Minister to *Norway,* and he and his wife arrived in Christrania on August 6th. Your Aunt Zina is having a delightful summer in Minneapolis, whither she went to visit Harvey Smith and Edith. Harvey is doing very well in the cement business, and he has an automobile now, and takes your Aunt Zina out on beautiful rides in the evenings. He has two little sons. Laura Sanford gave Madeline a very nice luncheon at her pretty home in Staten Island. I was asked also, and we enjoyed it very much! Her little boy is five years old and is named Richard. I believe I have told you all the family news, and hope you will return the compliment and tell me all about yourself and Arthur. . . . Give my love to Arthur, and my kind remembrances to all my friends and with *lots* to *yourself*

I am,

Your Aunt Amy

New York October 8, 1907

Dearest Zie,

I had thought to have written to thank you for your letter and check before, but this is the first moment I have had to do so. I feel very badly to have you send back the royalty for the book as you are jointly entitled to it, as I have always tried to convince you. But you are so proud and so generous, you always give me back *everything* I give you! You are a natural-born *queen!* and ought to have a realm, and it is too bad you have not one. It is true, that at the present moment I *am* in need of money, as I always am at this time of year, when I have been *spending* all summer, and *making nothing,* and some things *have* to be paid for immediately. My furs, for instance, *had* to be got out of quod, as I shall need them in another week. Then my green hat had to be made over, and I hardly had *shoes* to my feet. So I have replenished these articles out of the money. . . . I am having a new suit made at Arnold's of black gibeline cloth (the new cloth), skirt and jacket. This I am getting on tick, but shall pay for it in installments. I *had* to have a nice tailored suit, as I go out constantly, and my old ones were too shabby. On the street one *must* be presentable. I shall now look very fine, with my new suit, new hat, new furs, and new shoes, and nobody will suspect that I am not rich, or, in fact, that I am exceedingly *poor!* I only regret that you are not equally accoutered for the winter, but if your *readings* are successful, perhaps you *will* be!

I am glad you did not take the Wheeler house, if it would make you miserable, for happiness is the first desirable item. I suppose you would not enjoy working under a *man!* It seems as if you ought to have got a salary for your services, as board and room are not *all* one requires. I really think that boarding suits you better now, than housekeeping, you have got so out of the way of it, I remember it was a fearful effort to you *here,* that *last* year in our flat, small as our family was! What a dismal time we had there the last two years! Whenever I pass the street I say to myself, "Thank heaven we are not there anymore!" I had Laura come over on Wednesday, and the whole day was given up to her, and to signing Norman's *deed,* which I mailed to him. I hope he won't have to sell his stable lot right away, for the horrible typewriter, which, like a monster, has devoured one piece of his property after another! I sometimes fear you and I will end where poor Fran Senkrah is, at the Barnabas House. . . .

My record for the [Women's] Philharmonic this week is as follows: Saturday morning I went down to Steinway's to select the pianos; Monday I went down to the rooms of the Society to see them put in place on stage. The rooms were not ready, and so I went to Steinway's again to countermand them. Tuesday afternoon I went again to the rooms to meet the pianos. Stayed there till nearly five before they arrived. Rushed home and dressed and had dinner, and went back to the rooms for the meeting of the Piano Department. Evening *brilliant* success, large attendance, everybody delighted. Thursday evening went to the reunion of the Vocal Department. This morning (Friday) went to the Council at half past nine, and did not leave till two o'clock. Next Tuesday evening will be an adjourned meeting of the whole society, to decide about changing the name. Must be there. Next Friday morning Directors' meeting of the Piano Department, at ten! Besides all this, I have been running and writing incessantly for the last fortnight to get the programme arranged for Tuesday evening. I never saw a Club in such a continued state of activity as this one, and there seems *no let-up* to it! Mrs. Donington has left for good, apparently, and I am very sorry. Mrs. Coe appeared much better at the meeting of the Council this morning, and I feel much more encouraged about her. I looked *again* in the trunk for my report, enlightened by your letter. Found my report. . . . It was great luck, for I got it just in time to read it at the council in the morning, Mrs. Coe having been inexorable. I was on the point of writing it all over, and had borrowed the programs of Miss Read for the purpose. I wore my black satin, with the white hat (your last creation) on Tuesday evening. They all said I looked stunning! They went beautifully together. The program was *fine.* Hattie Scholder is a wonder, and Brooke sang divinely and looked ideal in his dress suit, while Jennie Dalton was handsome, and sang well, too.

I opened with an address on the Club, and they applauded it enthusiastically. I wish you had been there to see your Society go marching on. Best love to Rose and all the family. I will acknowledge her letter and check next week, tell her. Josie Bates has just got home and spent the afternoon with her. She inquired after you. With much love to yourself, and hoping you will not need the check you sent me, I am forever

Your loving,

Amy

Cambridge July 14, 1908

Dearest Zie,

Your letter is just received and what a *terrible* blow you had! I think Norman did *very wrong,* and no doubt will repent of going to such extremes, later on. He was so angry and wrought up he hardly knew what he was doing, as he wondered you were willfully rushing onto the rocks, and that he would have to pay the damages when you had spent all your money. I am glad you fought it out with him *to the death* and that you will have no more to do with each other, for now *you* will have *peace,* and you will be *off his mind.* He says you go *directly* against his advice *every time,* and your selling that furniture for one hundred and seventy-five dollars after he had it appraised at four hundred and had two dealers bidding against each other for it, drove Norman perfectly wild! He thinks you have no idea of the value of money and that you deliberately pitch it out the window. I tried to convince him to the contrary, and told him I thought you were very prudent about your money, and that you had more money in the bank than *I* had! You always *did,* you know, when we lived together, and I used to be often surprised that you had a reserve sum for occasions. I *still* have the twelve dollars in mind I owe you, and mean to pay it when I can, but the house rent failing me since the first of May has almost beggared me! I should have come out *very well* this year but for that, as you can see, by my managing to carry along this summer without it. Norman has not sent me my check for fifty dollars this month, either, and it is now the *14th!* . . . I am going to get into writing again, as Presser, the editor of Etude[1] has ordered an article on Liszt, and has actually sent me a check for twenty dollars for it. (It appeared in the July number.) He is closer than the bark on the tree, and has badgered me for a long time for articles, but I *would not* write without being paid, and he has *had* to come to it, as he really *wanted* me to write for his paper, which is now a big journal of music, and has a subscription list of one hundred thousand subscribers. Presser always persists in giving me the subject, and does not realize that I *could* choose *my own!* He won't print anything except what he orders. Now he wants me to write an article on "Tausig As I Knew Him," of 2500 words, at four cents per word. I took so *few* lessons from Tausig, I have no facts to relate of him which I have not put in my book. If I could have got the time to visit Mr. Parsons in Garden City and Joseffy in Tarrytown before I left New York, I might have got something from them, as they were both pupils in Tausig's class for a long time. Mrs. Watson also studied with Tausig. . . .

I am now enjoying *Kate's* . . . hospitality. . . . The girls [do] seem to have beaux and lovers, to burn, [however,] and are great belles. Amy[2] has just been visiting the Lorings at Prides' Crossing, near Beverly, where there are two young men, Caleb and Gus. They are millionnaires and swells, and Gus has offered himself twice to Amy, who has refused him. He told her that if she would marry him he would give her a house on Commonwealth Avenue, an automobile, and all the pretty clothes she wanted! . . . She has another lover, Reginald Sweet, of Yonkers who is madly in love with her. He is charming, and very gifted in music, of which he intends to make a profession. Kate says he has been to the house nearly every day this winter and that he *fits into* the family like no one else! Kate just doats [sic] on him, especially on account of his being named *Reginald,* and his beautiful playing! He composed an operetta for the Pudding which was given here and conductor Muck[3] came out from Boston to hear it! Although Sweet has just graduated from Harvard he is going to rush on this week to spend Friday with Amy, and he sent her a handsome pair of sleeve buttons on her birthday. She is a heartless little flirt, though, and has no idea of tying herself up to him for four years while he studies music in Europe! Reginald is twenty-four and his father is well off. . . . He called on me in New York because he said he had read my book long ago, and had always wanted to know me. He has the most beautiful *manners* and I was much taken with him. Kate is looking forward to his coming with so much pleasure, I trust it will give her an oiling! She would like Reginald for a son-in-law very much, I think. Margaret is also popular with men, and has just been to Lexington to visit one of her beaux, named Godkin, whose family invited her! . . . Kate and the girls will go to Fishers Island on Saturday.

With best love,

Amy

P.S. I read my paper at the New York Music Teachers' Convention July 1st and it was a success, they said. I heard a wonderful new pianiste . . . English, named Adele Verne. She made a great sensation! Her playing is *immense!* She is put in the first rank by Paderewski.

[1] *The Etude,* a prominent musical magazine, published by Presser in Philadelphia in America in 1883-1957, to which Amy Fay often contributed articles.

[2] Amy Fay Stone, Amy Fay's niece, daughter of Kate Fay Stone, who became a well known actress with the stage name Amy Faystone.

[3] Karl Muck (1859-1940), German conductor who directed the Boston Symphony Orchestra in 1912-22.

August 19, 1908

Dearest Zie,

I was glad to receive a letter from you which sounded more cheerful than the *last* one! . . . This morning I got a picture card with the town where Safonoff lives on it, and as near as I can make out, it is called Kishowodok or Kirlowodok, Caucasus. There are mountains, they have rounded backs but no *peaks* like ours. They are like Fairfield Hill in St. Albans. A magnificent hotel and park are in the foreground but Safonoff's house is hidden behind the woods on a hill to the left. I wish I could see it, as I read in an article by an American pupil of his (a man) that Safonoff is a very rich man. His wife is a daughter of the count, and her father is a high functionary there. The marriage is perfectly happy, and I heard Safonoff say once that he and his wife did not belong in the category of the mismated. "I am always very much travelling, but we are like lovers, *absolutely,* when we are together, and we have had *ten* children! Two daughters died," he said. Now he has three sons and five daughters. I am going to send you his letter to read and please re-mail to me, as I want to keep it. Safonoff is a *charmer,* you know! He has so much *heart* and is so *accessible!* Entirely different from Theodore in *that* respect, but just as much of genius as conductor. He has the polished manners of a courtier, too. I gave him a copy of my book to read on the steamer, as we were getting to be very good friends.

It is now more than three weeks I have been Rose's guest at lovely Felsengarten, and I am enjoying the perfect rest and quiet and the beauty of it very much, and it is doing my health a great deal of good. I was really in poor condition and very thin when I came. . . . Rose is pretty well, but has bad headaches very frequently, when she is really sick, while they last. She wears herself out, I think, with her everlasting work. Never is she idle for five minutes, and she works like a man in the *garden.* . . . Rose is writing a biography of Theodore now among other things, and it is a *hard* task, sifting out all his letters and papers. I translate German for her. Madeline is here, and is very busy helping Miss Foster with her newly started tea room, to which Rose contributed a hundred dollars. It is a cunning little square building of one room and a small kitchen this side of the Post Office. . . . We had Margaret Stone for a fortnight also, and *she* is *lovely* and so graceful! The Neighborly Club is continued, and was entertained last Saturday by Mrs. George Gleason most delightfully. She sent her automobile for us, and the club was taken all over the farm first. . . .

Best love,

Amy

New York December 23, 1908

Dearest Mudkins,

Merry Christmas! I have been meaning to write this three weeks, but my day is so cut up with pupils and the evenings with concerts I have put it off from day to day. . . . Last night I went to the first of Sam Franko's beautiful concerts of old music, at Mendelssohn Hall, and luckily I was free from rheumatism so I could enjoy it uninterruptedly. It was an *exquisite* program, two cantatas of Bach's gems, as everything he ever wrote was, and *not long.* Also a concert by Handel for orchestra, and more . . . short pieces by Cannabich, Gavotte and Pavane. Franko had an orchestra, a chorus, and good solo singers. The concert concluded with one of Bach's wonderful chorales, so *solemn* and deeply *religious!* It is *amazing, his depths* of *pure spirituality.* I think he is the equal of *Jesus Christ,* in this! Where do you suppose Bach ever got his nature from? It was the development of the thirty years' war (so says Paine) which produced most frightful sufferings and made the people *pour out* supplications for help from *heaven! Poor things!* They had no other hope! I have been steeping myself in biographies of Bach, in order to talk it up in my Piano Conversations, and he was certainly one of the most extraordinary men that was ever produced, not only in his prodigious art, but in his every day *character.* Sam Franko's concerts are really the most *artistic* ones that are given in New York, and it is a delicious *rest* to listen to the old music after all the modern tumultuousness we have to hear so continually in the larger orchestral concerts.

We have now *five* orchestras here, the Philharmonic, Boston, Areno, Volpé, and Franko, besides. The Russian orchestra, under Modest Altschuler, has developed tremendously, and is now admirable. I forgot Walter Damrosch, who gives concerts on Sunday afternoons, and who also has a body of picked men. He and his brother,

Frank Damrosch, are always in the papers! One or other or both together, are always giving concerts! Areno has risen from the Cooper Institute, to Carnegie, with his "People's Concerts." Walter and Frank are like the poor, we have them always with us! I rarely go to their concerts, though Mrs. Flagler has tried to get me into Walter's orchestral association, to help raise money for him, and subscribe twenty-five dollars per year, *myself!* I have declined the sweet privilege! . . . The Manuscript Society has put my name down as one of its directors, although I rarely go there. The Women's Philharmonic is going on so well, I suppose they want me to give them a boost, and a large slice of my time! I have no mind to work for men, however, which is always a thankless task! We had a very brilliant concert at our club on Wednesday evening, with Kaltenborn as violinist, Miss Niebuhr as singer, and Gurickx's pupil, Mme. Pardo, as pianist. She played brilliantly, and scored a success! Isn't it a funny turn of the wheel that *I* should be bringing out Gurickx's pupil at this late hour of the day? I am so glad she has made her debut at last, for she has been tormenting me to get her a piano firm and engagements ever since she came over, nearly two years ago! She got ill and went back to Brussels last year for eight months. Gurickx's rich father-in-law, M. Gens-de-bien, died last summer,so his wife must have come into the fortune. The old man was rich and of a distinguished family.

I enclose a notice of Rivé-King,[1] who now has replaced Bloomfield-Zeisler[2] as a teacher in the Bush Conservatory. You will perceive that many students come to her and I am sure she could send you boarders, as musical students from the west are often *well off!* I think it would be a good thing if you invited Rivé-King to come to luncheon some day, and let her get acquainted with your boarding house. She is warmhearted and full of good sense, and it is delightful to hear her talk about Theodore Thomas, as she played with him so *many* times, and was with him on that great Pacific tour. He even played her waltz for orchestra once, "Blooming Meadows," I think it was at Brighton Beach, so he must have thought a good deal of her. I had a very pleasant meeting with Rivé-King at Oswego, New York in May, when Florence Paine got me an engagement to give a Piano Conversation at the musical club. Rivé-King gave a concert the next night, so I stayed over to hear her, and we had a long talk afterwards and renewed our old friendship. Since her husband's death she has had rather a hard time to make a living, and she was very happy to get the place at Bushes in Chicago. With your proximity to that conservatory it seems as if your houses should be *full.* . . .

As ever your devoted sister,

A. F.

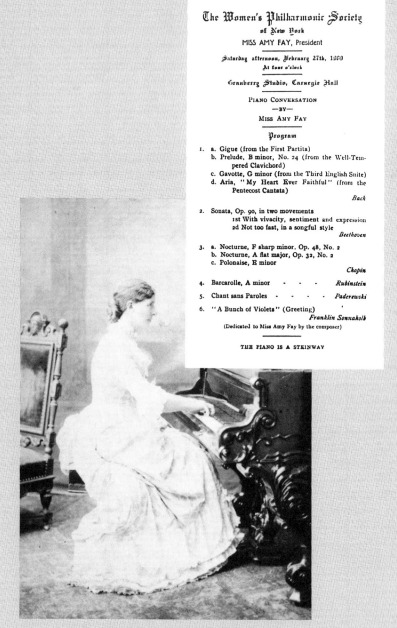

Amy Fay at piano, date unknown

[1] Julie Rivé-King (1857-1937), American pianist, teacher, and composer and one time student of Liszt. She appeared as soloist with Thomas and Seidl and introduced many new works to the United States.

[2] Fannie Bloomfield-Zeisler (1863-1927), an American pianist of Austrian origin and a student of Ziehn, Wolfsohn, and Leschetizky. Widely acclaimed as a pianist following her return to the United States in 1883 following five years of study with Leschetizky.

New York March 1, 1909

Dearest Zie,

. . . Rose and Mrs. Birch have left, and will start from Philadelphia (where Rose went to visit the Hermann Thomases) *today*. I gave a grand reception for them on Monday, which was a howling success. Safonoff came, and made himself most charming to everybody, as he is a thorough man of the world, and that wonderful English pianist, Adele Verne, played. At the end, my little pupil, Lemuel Goldstein (the postman's son) played, and he brought the house down! He was too cunning for anything, and as *cocksure* as my pupils *always are,* when L put them on show! They *never* fail to do their best. Thursday evening Mrs. Birch invited Miss Verne and myself to the Waldorf to dinner and to go to the theatre afterwards, to see Mrs. Hodgeson Burnett's play, "The Dawn of Tomorrow." It is a capital play, and we enjoyed it very much. I gave a Piano Conversation at the Club[1] Saturday and had quite an ovation and Safonoff came to hear the *Bach* numbers, dear man! Had no time for the rest. I thought it a tremendous compliment; the club was *taken down!* I have so *much* to do this week, and have not a *moment,* so must close with *lots of love.*

Your affectionate sister,

Amy

[1] Women's Philharmonic Society.

Amy Fay

New York June 12, 1909

Dearest Zie,

Norman sailed on Thursday on La Provence for Paris, but I did not see him to say good-bye, as he barely got here in time to go aboard, and wrote me a hasty line from the ship. Mme. Loudrillon has moved, and her present address is 1000 rue de Longchamp. I do not believe he would go there, though, as I proposed it to him on a former trip, and I am awfully grieved to hear that you are feeling so miserable and so out of spirits, but moving is always a dreadful ordeal, and no doubt you were not equal to it. I must say, it makes me anxious that you are entirely alone, and I don't know *what* would become of you if anything should happen to you. It is *all wrong,* and you ought to have returned to New York, where I could be in charge of you, at least. Nobody should live in a solitary manner, and *boarding,* even, is better than having *no one* to speak to! I don't think you can stand it better than anyone else, and if you cut loose from your family you ought to get a *chum* as I did in Miss Read. . . .

I thank God for every *day* I live, *now,* and do not want to live with the *worms* as long as I can escape it! Besides, I think life gets more interesting with every year and it is a pity we have to lose our good looks as we grow older! Were it not for that, we would have a better time than ever! Just now I am interested in the *aeroplane* (and whether Lowell will get an answer from *Mars*), and I want to see *it* through. I think it the most wonderful of all the inventions, and I want to see if the north pole will ever be reached by the dirigible balloon! They are going to try the experiment 'ere long. . . . With much love and with an exhortation to cheer up and not to take life so hard, as it is a fleeting thing and with a thousand thanks for the pin, I am, as ever, your devoted sister

Amy

New York June 13, 1909

Dearest Zie,

Your *beautiful* gift was sent from Tiffany's last week, and I was *much* impressed, and thank you for it a *thousand* times! . . . I am always *delighted* when anybody gives me anything, if it be only *worth having!* I must say, I despise a *useless* present, and have never cared for *picture cards,* to which most people attach great significance!

I have had to *learn* to cultivate the picture card habit! It is wonderful how much pleasure they give! But people always tell me "it is the *thought* which pleases them!" I think it *is* nice to get one from *rare and unexpected* people, such as Paderewski and Gurickx, *par exemple*, from whom I received some last year! *That* was flattering! Also, Safonoff sent me one from the Caucasus last summer of his country home. He *is* such a *charmer!* I am hardly reconciled *yet* to his loss! His rich women friends took steam *right after him* and have gone to London, where he has some concerts to conduct! Mrs. Hyde and Mrs. Loomis sailed this month. Mrs. Loomis is simply daft over him, and he often ran in after rehearsals to see her, as she lives only a block from Carnegie Hall. Her husband is Henry Loomis of Burlington, Vermont, a very rich man, but she is a New Yorker. . . . At Mrs. Hyde's party he took me in his arms and kissed me before everybody, and he put me in my carriage, waiting for me till I came downstairs, at the hall door, which was a surprise, as he was the guest of the evening!

Well, I took up the cudgel for him twice in the papers, when he was attacked, so he appreciated *that,* as there was a cabal against Safonoff of Mahler's friends, who were determined to get the Philharmonic and reorganize it on a money basis for Mahler, and they succeeded in shaking Safonoff out of the saddle. My article in the *Tribune* did have an influence, however, and turned the critics in Safonoff's favour for the final concerts. They had all been perfectly *nasty* to him all winter. I wrote a personal letter to Krehbiel[1], and he changed his tune immediately. It was a pity I did not do it earlier in the fray, but Mrs. George R. Sheldon, Mrs. Samuel Untermeyer, and Schelling kept so dark about their plans till they got the money they were after, that the Mahler conspiracy came in the nature of a surprise. I doubt if Safonoff was aware of it himself, but he would have been too proud to say so, if he *were.* As he said to me once: "I never seek positions; they always seek me!" But, as you say, "this is the devil's own world!" How often I have laughed in quoting you on that to people!

I am expecting to leave for Felsengarten the first week in July, as Emily Canfield will leave before that. Poor Emily! Rose writes me she is in a most precarious state of health and her operation, whatever it was, was very severe. Rose has been nursing and feeding her up, but she is in wretched condition. . . . I have not heard from Normie since he sailed. On Friday evening I dined at Mrs. King's and met Mrs. Loring there. The dinner was *deliciously* cooked. It is a long time since I saw Mrs. Loring, she has been traveling abroad two years. She has aged a good deal but seems well. Mrs. King is much happier as a widow, and is looking for *No. 2!* She frankly avows it! . . . Good bye with much love.

Amy

---

[1] Henry Edward Krehbiel (1854-1923), music critic for the *New York Tribune* in 1880-1923.

Amy Fay

Dearest Zie,

Your long, delightful letter was much enjoyed by us all, and seemed like your old self *waking up again!* . . . I was much interested in your newspaper clippings, and you have unearthed several geniuses! The *"Rhapsody"* was beautiful and original too. Did you send me the picture of *Nijinski,* the wonderful Russian dancer, or did *I* cut it out of *Rose's* Chicago paper to send to *you?* I forget about it! Norman wrote what a sensation the Russian actors and dancers have been making in Paris! I saw yesterday that Safonoff is to conduct a musical festival in England in October at Newcastle on Tyne. Wish I were going to be there! He said he should be in Dresden to take a cure in August, so I suppose that is where he is now! I am sorry you never get to Ravinia Park concerts, for I think that concert hall out there is so *charming* for summer, and I want you to see it. Then you can get an excellent dinner in the beer garden, and it is in the open air, like Germany! You and Mrs. Case ought to go out there by *train* on a "bat" sometime. It is too far by trolley, *I* think, although I did it with Norman.

I *don't* play those things Lhevinne did, although I heard *him* play them. He is Safonoff's pupil, you know. I *never* miss his concerts, as I consider him second only to Paderewski! His touch reminds me of Tausig's, with its wonderful sparkle and brilliancy, like *diamonds,* in the "Blue Danube" finale, and also in the final octave passage in the Liszt Sonata, which he carries off with a *bravura* I have never seen equalled! His father-in-law told me that Lhevinne never stops practicing a thing till he has entirely mastered it, no matter *how long* it takes him, and that is characteristic of his playing, that he always is in *magnificent practice,* I think. His wife, on the other hand, also a pupil of Safonoff's and a wonderful pianist, gets tired of her pieces and loses interest after a time. She met Lhevinne in Safonoff's studio, and she said that Safonoff opposed her marriage for a long time, as he thought it would interfere with her career as an artist, which it *has done.* She is always in the shadow of her husband. I was not so much struck with the Debussy piece Paderewski played, but I have heard a good many of Debussy's compositions, but never learned one of them myself. I sent Laura Hoffman his "Jardins sous la pluie" just before I left New York, which is said to be Debussy's *best,* and she is going to study it. She has not been playing at all lately because she was hurrying to finish a translation from the French for Funk and Wagnall, of "The House of the Soul," by *Wagner,* author of the "Simple Life." Laura was to get a hundred and fifty dollars for her work. The book was just finished and published, and she gave me a copy of it before I left New York! "Translation, by Mrs. Laura Sanford Hoffman." She says all the French she ever studied was what *I* taught her at Mrs. Merrill's! It was interrupted by Madeline's advent, your remember! I made Laura study Mendorff and write exercises, which I corrected with the key. After her marriage her father-in-law made her translate from German into French when she spent the summer in Stockbridge, which she enjoyed doing very much.

I believe I did not write you that Laura invited me and my pupils one afternoon in July and we had music and refreshments. She did not play at all but Lucy Greenberg and Lemuel Goldstein did, and she was *much* impressed! Lemuel is twelve, and is my *latest* prodigy! He played at the reception I gave for Rose in February, when *Mrs. Birch* was there, also Lily's Chicago friend, Louise Gortner. *Miss Adele Verne* played, and Safonoff came, but I did not have Lemuel play till after Safonoff left and *Miss Verne requested* me to *let him*. Afterwards I regretted I did not have Safonoff hear Lemuel, as he made such a hit! Everybody in the room was a conoisseur and a *shout* went up when he finished! Mr. Knopf and his family were there among others. I should have liked Safonoff to hear a specimen of my teaching, as he is much a great teacher himself. He is so generous and sympathetic and *so discriminating.* You hear that discrimination of his in the very *tone* of his voice somehow! He is *all perception,* and has such a masterful way with him, and *breadth of vision!* I never saw his equal in this regard, and that is what made Safonoff so attractive and *satisfactory* to me! I always felt that he would feel *exactly as I did* about *music.* One thing was so nice and so unusual about him, and that is, that he felt an interest in other people's achievements. You know I sent him a program of a recital I had at the Women's Philharmonic in the studio (Granberry) Carnegie Hall, one Saturday afternoon, and Safonoff came for the first part of the program, as *busy* as he was! He wrote me a complimentary letter afterwards, too. Oliver Danton has gone over to study with him this summer. Do you remember Danton? Stanfield was so stuck on him for a while, and helped him with his concert in Mendelssohn Hall, of which I was one of the patronesses when we were in 56th Street. Afterwards they had a quarrel, and now they do not speak! Danton went abroad for while. . . .

Last night we went to the Glessner's to supper, and they sent their automobile after us and brought us home — always Rose's style of travel with her friends, you know. At the last minute Rose gave up going, however, because her throat was very bad. . . . The Glessners always have a family supper on Sunday evenings, and there was quite a gathering of them last evening. The fireplaces, mantles and tables were dressed with *quantities* of the most beautiful flowers, and were a *sight* to be seen! . . . My paper is full and it is time for dinner so I will close. Rose and Val join me in much love, and I remain, as ever, your devoted sister.

Amy Fay

Amy Fay

New York February 7, 1910

Dearest Cater,

Well, well, well. What a *surprise.* I declare, I don't know *when* I have been struck of a heap as I was to hear of *Pauline's* having a *baby!* It was the very last thing that would have entered my mind! I always think of her and of Laura Sanford Hoffman together, somehow, as they both have the same kind of fascination, and I had just got the announcement of Laura's second marriage to Mr. Basil Scott on Monday morning! She was married quietly at home, and they left for New Orleans for their wedding tour. Mrs. Sanford sent out the cards after their departure and I was not asked to witness the ceremony. I know nothing of the bridegroom except that he is an *athlete,* lives in Staten Island, and the *beach* in the summer seems to have brought him and Laura into intimacy. I hear he is "the kind of man who looks well in a bathing suit," so I imagine he has a very handsome figure! Laura wrote me on Sunday saying they were to be joined in wedlock the next day! I am not surprised in *her* case, as I have been expecting she would get engaged for some time. This man is more likely to suit her than the elegant and scholarly Walter Hoffman, I think. . . . Arthur is a proud and happy father, I expect! For my part, I think *girls* bring more life and happiness into a household than *boys* do! A boy goes out into the world, whereas a girl *brings her* world into the family. However, there is no reason why the *next* child should not be a boy! . . .

Did you hear Busoni's *second* recital? I thought him *prodigious* in the Chopin Préludes and Liszt *Sonata.* The *last* was simply *sublime!* He went *deeper* into it than Paderewski or Lhevinne, even! I went to see him in the green room, and he kissed my hand quite devoutly and said he should make it a point to have an interview with me when he gets time. I felt much flattered, as he had such enormous success at this concert. He will go on till May. He had to leave next day, February 6, but when he *returns,* he will have three or four days, and then he will write me and make a special appointment to see me, he said. He received a magnificent wreath at this concert, and it was placed on the stage in front of the piano. I looked at the card on it with my opera glass, and on it was "To *Busoni,* from *Paderewski!*" Wasn't that charming in *Paddy* to do by telegraph? None of the papers spoke of it, of course! I have heard Paderewski speak of Busoni with great admiration, and he is the only pianist he considers his own level, I fancy! Even *he* cannot cram Carnegie Hall as Paderewski does, even at half the price for tickets! Wonderful, isn't it?

I wish you were here to go to Mahler's concerts with me! He is a *great* conductor, and has much sense of *rhythm* as Theodore had. Mahler is most *dramatic* and *brilliant* (only 42 years old!) but he has not the *depth* of *feeling* Safonoff had, and does not get the audience off its head as Safonoff did! Never have I seen a conductor get the ovations *he* did! . . .

I gave a musicale the other day and both Edith and Katie Blanc came. I asked about thirty-five guests, and opened the doors between my room and the parlour which makes a nice *suite.* Tell Pauline I think she may consider her baby is her valentine! It was on the eve of Valentine's Day! *I* sent a valentine to my friend Mr. Bushnell, for the first time in I don't know *how many years!* It was a little white Cupid of China, sitting on a gilt heart box, which was filled with peppermints wrapped in pink paper (awfully cunning!) and his wings were tied with pink satin ribbon! I bought it at Purcell's confectionary store. It just fitted in your little square box. I have not heard yet how he liked it! He gave me such a beautiful dinner on my birthday last year as a surprise! I went to South Norwalk to see Laura this week, and found her looking very well and nicely dressed. She seemed more cheerful than usual. . . . Well, it is *late,* and I must *go to bed!* I tried to have Amy[1] visit me, but she has not time to come, I am sorry to say! How is your rheumatism? *Mine* has been *very bad,* but Zina's prescription helped me. Homeopathy is wonderful if you hit the right remedy. Best love and congratulations from

Your affectionate sister,

Amy

---

[1] Amy Faystone, Amy's actress niece.

May 30, 1910

Dearest Cater,

How *are you all?* It is so long since I have written, I fear you have entirely forgotten my existence, but if my money had not given out after going out west I would have stopped over in Cambridge to see you. Although my club raised some money to send me to the Cincinnati Festival, I ran on to Chicago to see Zina and the hundred dollars did not more than cover the expenses to and from Cincinnati, and I had to spend about forty dollars *additional* out of *my own pocky!* Hence, *beggary!* I *did* long to go to Cambridge when my trunk was *once packed,* for it was such a *bother* and I took such a *lot* of clothes along, which I did not put on my back. I was on the go every moment and was mostly in my spring suit! I thought it would be great fun to run on to Boston from Albany, instead of coming tamely home! Tell my nieces that I was much pleased with the charming letters they wrote me when I sent the hatpins! . . .

Today is Decoration Day and the weather is perfect and my studio so quiet and pleasant, no tiresome pupils to bother me, and it is really quite a privilege to write once more. I have now lived in New York for twenty years and have such a nice circle of friends and acquaintances that I am in a whirl all the while, and experience the greatest difficulty in getting time to write or practice. The long tranquil days of the past are myth! I have learned Liszt's Mephisto Waltz, which I attacked last summer, before Busoni came over, and have been practicing all winter. I consider it one of the most difficult things I ever have played, and will study it six months or a year *more* before I play it in public. I had it in mind for many years, in fact since I heard Liszt play it himself in Weimar, but hated to *begin* the tussle with it! I think, though, that I will give a great interpretation of it eventually, as I consider it one of Liszt's very *greatest* works. Busoni played his one arrangement, which he filled with sky rockets, but left out absolutely all Liszt's greatest moments in it. Liszt would turn over in his grave if he heard Busoni's arrangement! I was *amazed* at Busoni's *want of taste,* and of course the music stores are selling his arrangement and it is supplanting the *real thing!* But enough of that!

I wish you could have been at the Festival,[1] which was simply *perfectly magnificent.* I don't know *when* I have enjoyed anything so much as Rose and Norman and I had such pleasant little family meetings at our meals in the Grand Hotel. Rose was treated like a princess, and no doubt she told you how she was given the seat of honor between the president and the governor! The calm and tranquil way in which she walks over the heads of the swells everywhere fills me with admiration mingled with awe! But she was just the same as a *child,* when she conquered Edith Longfellow, who was the swellest girl in *Cambridge,* you remember! Wasn't it delightful that Theodore's statue is such a success and really looks *like him?* It was taken at about forty years of age as we first knew him, and before he began to grow stout. The statue was so *well placed,* at the end of the foyer, but *well out* from the wall so that all the people came *towards* him, and swirled around the statue and down the other side. It gave the exact impression that he was giving a concert, surrounded by one of those big audiences he so often had, and it was particularly appropriate. The artist reproduced perfectly his power and force of personality, and the eye is *very* striking! It was certainly *inspiring* to see Theodore *standing there on his pedestal,* with the world at his feet, as he was in his *prime* that summer when you and Peggy were in Chicago and we were all so crazy over Theodore. In a sense, it was as if he had come to life again, and I think Rose was very happy over it. Probably Walter Damrosch will never be easy now till he gets *his* friends to erect a bronze statue to *him,* as he tries to imitate Theodore in everything as closely as possible and wants everyone to believe that *he* is the *"one and only."*

The American Years

Taft made such a beautiful dedicatory speech and what *pleased me* was the concluding sentence, in which he declared the statue to be a "fitting tribute to *the greatest musical leader we ever had in this country.*" He did not say "one" of the greatest, as he easily *might* have done! The Chicago orchestra, one hundred strong, and trained up to the *top notch,* played superbly, and Stock is a *very* talented conductor. But *Safonoff* is the only conductor who has the same kind of magnetism and fascination that Theodore had, for me! He has made Berlin his home this winter and is overwhelmed with engagements for *next* year, wherever he has conducted! He conducted two concerts in Rome, for instance, and next year they want six! I heard that he is much pleased about it. The work I enjoyed *most* at the festival was Pierné's *Children's Crusade.* Seven hundred children sang in the chorus, picked voices, and they knew their parts so perfectly that they sang without book. There was a steadiness and *power* in what they did which was overwhelming. They were supplemented by an adult chorus, so that *twelve hundred singers* gave the work, in *all,* and it was a *lovely* sight, as the women singers were dressed in white (the men in black) and *filled* the enormous stage like an army! I am quite in the mood to read Charles Auchester again and revive the memory of the description of an English Musical Festival under Mendelssohn's leadership, which had a tremendous effect on me as a girl.

Yesterday I went to hear a pupil of Joseffy play with orchestra, a young Italian named Pasquale Tallorico who is a protégé of Charles E. Bushnell from Philadelphia, who gave me a dinner on my birthday one year ago. Bushnell's a Standard Oil man, is rich and a widower about fifty years old, without children. He is connected with many of the most exclusive families in Philadelphia, but is a lover of music and dotes on Tallarico who is nineteen years old and a very poetic and gifted fellow. We have a new orchestra which I never heard of till *yesterday!* It is called the *"Men's Orchestra"* and is conducted by Volpé. It seems to be a lot of fellows who play different instruments who get together on Sunday afternoons and give concerts in a small hall in 55th Street near Sixth Avenue about a block from Zina's and my flat in 56th Street where you once made me a little visit. Joseffy was standing in the doorway, and he looked very little changed, though he must be sixty years old now! . . . When I see him, it is like an old ghost out of the past! I took two of *my* pupils along, Lucy Greenberg, aged fourteen, and Lemuel Goldstein, twelve. They both play well and Lucy has just played at the Women's Philharmonic and made a sensation! I am going to bring her out next winter. Joseffy's pupil played the Weber Concertstück beautifully.

I found Zina looking very well and she has a very cute little flat on the ground floor, and a nice little maid to wait on her. I think she is not *extremely* well fixed, and hope she will *stay put!* As for Norman, he was in excellent spirits and is a pet of Mrs. Hugh Birch round the corner and her charming daughter Helen, and he is well fixed, too. Do write and tell me all about Pauline's baby and the girls! . . .

Amy Fay

With best love to all including *Mousie* I am

Your affectionate sister,

Amy

---

[1] Cincinnati May Music Festival, formally organized in 1873. Theodore Thomas was its conductor from its inception until 1904.

New York November 1, 1910

Dearest Normie,

. . . Rose is leaving tomorrow for Chicago, however, and *she* will post you up on the family news of this section! I gave a party for her last evening, at which I had Lucy Greenberg play Mozart's concerto in D minor and Weber's "Perpetual Motion." Only musical connoisseurs were invited, and I think they were astounded at her *performance!* Zina heard her as a child of *nine* and I was thinking of Zina all the evening and wishing she could hear *Lucy, now,* as she is a veritable *virtuosa* at fifteen! Particularly in this *beautiful* work of Mozart, and I am so stuck on Mozart anyway! There is *nothing* more distinguished in style than he is, and Deppe was perfectly right about him way back in the *seventies* and his predictions are about to come true, for I perceive by the signs of the times that Mozart is about to become the rage *instrumentally.* The new French pianist, Bouchard, has put Mozart's little Sonata in C major on his first program, which I have taught to Laura Sanford, Lucy Greenberg, and Lemuel Goldstein, as little children, and they say "what *he* makes of it is *amazing!*" Bouchard has not yet played, but he is the leading French pianist of the younger school. He is announced for a piano recital on November 11th at *Mendelssohn* Hall, I am happy to say, so, for *once,* we won't have to go to that great barn of a Carnegie!

I went to hear Hofmann on Saturday afternoon and he played a *prodigious* program, and most remarkably! He has gained very much the last three years, and is more emotional than he was. You will enjoy his *Beethoven* playing, and the lost groschen *Rondo* is a *tour de force,* the like of which will not soon be heard again! Hofmann's interpretation of it is the very opposite of d'Albert's, for he makes it wonderfully *gay*, whereas d'Albert gave it a very serious cast, especially the last

92

part, which he piled up tremendously, in the minor mode. That *Rondo* should be tackled only by artists of the *first rank,* but, *no matter,* Kate has learned it, along with the D minor sonata of Chopin and various other little trifles, such as the chromatique étude in F minor, by Liszt! You may recall Paderewski's and de Pachmann's wonderful playing of *this etude!* This evening is Mahler's first concert with the Philharmonic Orchestra, and I am really curious to see what the size of the audience hall will be! They give us sixteen concerts for six dollars this year, up among the gallery gods, where I sit! Great efforts have been made by the management to boom Mahler, but, with all his genius as a conductor he is so self-centered, I do not believe he will get the *hold* on our public that Safonoff had! I have a new violinist friend in whom I am interested, Mr. Doage Fredericks, a Dane and scholar of Gaye, who came to this country in July, and was presented to me by a music publisher here. I have not yet heard Fredericks play, but he has such a brilliant and fascinating personality, it seems as if he *must* be very talented! He *says he* is, and I am taking his word for it. We are going to study the Sibelius violin concerto together. It is a long and formidable work, which it requires nearly an hour to play through. Thirty-nine pages! I have been practicing the accompaniment the last two months and it is very somber and interesting. It seems to express the rocks and the pines and the trackless ocean! I am curious to see how it will work out.

Last night I had here only people who understand music; Mr. and Mrs. Knopf, Mr. and Mrs. Gergen (Mrs. Eddy's daughter), Mr. Stuart, Mr. Shieb, a talented pupil of mine, Miss Bates, Miss Read, Mrs. Leonardos Williams and her sister, Miss Carpenter, etc. Mrs. Williams used to be Miss Nina Rathbone of Grand Rapids, Michigan, who went abroad and studied Wagnerian operas and became a successful prima donna. She was under contract at Berne, where she met her husband, a rich New Yorker of a good family, and married him. This settled her career and she broke her contract and returned to this country, and they live in in the next street (92nd) near the river, where they have bought a handsome house. Mrs. Williams wants to keep up her artistic affiliations, and she gives the most *delightful* dinner parties, at which she combines professional talent and her fashionable friends in a way that no one else has done that I know of! She has been good enough to take *me* into her "innermost *inner,*" much to my profit and pleasure, for I have never been at any house which is pleasanter! I must take you there sometime, for she really *is* a *personality,* a typical Brünhilde and Valkyrie. She is very tall, blonde, and imposing, and you see at a glance that she is *somebody!* Her husband is a quiet but cultivated man, with *cash to burn,* apparently! Tell Zina Mr. Knopf enjoyed *hugely* last night and he entirely appreciated the Mozart concerto! He is so *musical,* and so is Mr. Francis Stuart, the singing teacher, who always backs me *up* and frequently *divides* his pupils with mine! He says I make them so much more musical when I give them piano lessons, that it makes it easier for him! Last night, after hearing Lucy, Stuart exclaimed, "Well, you *are a great teacher!*" He said it was so *amazing,* the power and brilliancy and *freedom* which I give my pupils. My Burlington pupil, Eugene Toyner, has given eight piano recitals this summer. He is entirely different from Laura Sanford and Lucy, but plays exquisitely, and is full of *expression*. Well, I expect you have had enough of *music* for today, so I will close this letter, with much love, from

Sister Amy

P.S. I saw Mary Perkins and she and Bessie are going to Egypt in a week. Best love to Mudkins and please send her this letter. Also give my love to Helen Birch. How is she progressing with her *compositions?*

New York November 25, 1910

Dearest Cater,

. . . Has Margaret kept up her Brahms Sonata of late? Eugene Toyner would like to hear her play it, and I would like him to, also, as it is rarely played. He would be glad to call, if invited and lives in Boston on Huntington Avenue, No. 204 with his mother and brother. Eugene has given two recitals in Lowell and two in Roxbury of late, and his manager, Mrs. Dunwell, is looking after him nicely. I want him to finish up Liszt's "*St. Francis walking on the waves,*" which he has a talent for playing, I think. He is not enough of a worker, though, and will never strain his views! He *half* learns loads of pieces, and was always at him to *complete what he began*. I have no doubt he will run and get the Brahms Sonata as soon as he hears Margaret play it, and will read it a few times. To really *study it* would be quite a different matter! But he is certainly very *musical* in his conception. . . .

Yesterday afternoon I was invited to a reception to *Bonci* and his wife (now one of the *great* stars of the opera) by the E. Francis Hydes of No. 36 West 58th Street. Mr. Hyde is a rich banker here who came from Poultney, Vermont where he played the organ as a youth he told me! The Hydes have no children which is a pity as they are *both* rich and charming people. They were friends of Thomas and Safonoff and Mr. Hyde was for years President of the Philharmonic orchestra here. Carnegie is his successor as president. Bonci is now giving song recitals with *immense* success and is going on tour in them. He is a jolly little man, quite simple and unpretentious in manner, and one would never *dream* he is such a wonderful artist and actor! I asked him how he liked giving song recitals compared with opera? He replied that he *liked it,* but that it is *much harder!* Bonci has mastered the pronunciation of English very well. . . .

On Sunday afternoon I went to hear Scharwenka play his new concerto (the 4th) with Mahler and the Philharmonic orchestra. I must say I was *charmed,* both with the composition and with Scharwenka's rendering of it, which was *masterly!* I had no idea he had such a perfect technic. It was *awfully* difficult to play, and the Tarantella movement at the close went like lightening. His *scale* was wonderful! I suppose you heard it with the Boston Symphony Orchestra? My respect for Scharwenka *went up* a hundred per cent! He gives his first recital here on Saturday and it is too bad that Hofmann plays the same afternoon. I hate to miss Hofmann, as he gives extraordinary programs always. Laura Sanford came to see me yesterday for the first time in ages! She is now Mrs. Basil Scott and still lives in Staten Island. She seems very much in love, and has grown very *thin.* . . . Well, here is a pupil, so I must stop writing. . . .

With much love to all, as ever,

Your devoted sister,

Amy

New York April 12, 1911

Dearest Cater,

. . . I am just *crazy* to go abroad this summer, and I *ought* to be on hand for the grand celebration of Liszt's centenary, which will be at Heidelberg in August, I believe. There will be a gathering of the clans among the famous musicians. Busoni will be there and I should suppose Paderewski and perhaps Safonoff might be. Safonoff has an engagement to conduct six orchestral concerts in Rome in *June,* at the Exposition. My former pupil, Nora Smith, is living in Rome now, and it would be so nice to go there with *her* as a guide. Miss Read has engaged her passage on the Venezia for July 1st and I would give anything to accompany her! I see no prospect of my being able to do so, however, and keep asking my brain how I could earn five hundred dollars the next two months! With my playing and my writing, it seems

95

a pity I can't *make it pay!* I could write another book if only I could get across the big pond and have some experiences worth describing! Norman has been in New York a good deal this season working up his new "working capital company." He is gradually edging it along but it is slow to get consolidated. I do feel much sympathy for poor Normie, and wish he *could* have a streak of good luck, for a change. He is so heroic and uncomplaining! I *do think* he had such a *tough time* with that typewriter business, and to think it resulted in nothing but the entire loss of his fortune, after such *effort* was really harrowing! If *I* were *the Lord,* I should take pity on him! It is lucky he had that long stay in Paris, which was the only pleasant feature of the typewriter! . . . My paper is full but I will write again in a day or two, as I have a lot more to say! Give my love to Will and to Margaret and Amy. I had a card from d'Indy congratulating me on Val's wedding, which he must have seen in the Paris *Herald.* The musical journals say that d'Indy has been ill. Good-bye with best love from

Amy Fay

New York May 25, 1911

Dearest Rose,

My birthday has come and gone most uneventfully and you would never suspect I was the author of the *Book of the Age.*[1] "It *has been* hot, and *now* is cool, yet saw I never the righteous forsaken, nor the sick, begging their bread! But I see *everyday* a woman who is begging to go to Europe, but she don't get there." Her first name begins with *A* and her last name with *F.* Have you any idea whom I mean? If not, guess again! *We* are having a water famine *here,* also, and it won't rain till the moon changes. *Next* month it will rain all the time. So, cheer up! I was just thinking the other day that *you* must be feeding on *nice, juicy* asparagus, as I was chewing on some dry old hay stalks down here, and *sure enough,* I was *right* in my guess! *Clever Amy!* But I never knew *you* to get discouraged over your *garden* before, and you must need a change! Why didn't you go to Europe with your friends, the Birches, and join Kate and her family in their wild Parisian revels? I read that Paris is at its *loveliest, now.* The whole world must be over there! Miss Read has taken her passage for the first of July on the *Venezia!* I am *consumed* with envy and jealousy, in consequence! You see I am getting so old, I am afraid I won't be able to strump around much longer! My life line is shortening and my legs are very stiff! I *would* like to be at the Liszt centennial in Heidelberg, in October. What fun it would be to tell Richard Strauss how I puzzled over his handwriting last summer in Felsengarten!

He and Nikisch are both going to conduct. I wonder if Paderewski will be there! Paddy was foolish enough to add another movement to his symphony, and it made it an *hour and a half* performing in Berlin like the *other* big modern composers! It does not seem to have been a success. He will hate *Berlin* more than ever and it *does* seem to be his *Waterloo!* He vowed he *never* would play there again in consequence of the roasting he got there early in his career. But he *should play* there, and reinstate himself, for probably the Berliners would *now* succumb to him as *pianist,* like the rest of the world! He certainly can *play piano! . . .*

Tomorrow I have an interesting invitation to an operatic wedding breakfast, much to my surprise! It is that of Mr. William Wade Henshaw and Miss Mabel Clyde. Mr. Henshaw is one of the leading Wagnerian singers (very fine) at the Metropolitan Opera House, and Miss Clyde is a daughter of Mr. and Mrs. William Pancoat Clyde of the Clyde Steamship Company, said to be *immensely rich!* They live at No. 1 West 51st Street (Fifth Avenue) and the hour fixed for the breakfast is half after *twelve* so I am looking forward to something very *swell!* Mr. Henshaw was invited to be the guest of honour at our Women's Philharmonic one evening in the spring, by a Miss Egan of Elgin, Illinois (picked up by me at the MTNA), one of our *new members,* who is an old friend of his! Mr. Henshaw arrived late and brought his fiancée with him. He is a handsome man, tall and large, with an imposing personality. Miss Clyde was not either youthful or pretty, but was extremely clever and sympathetic, and I took a decided liking to her, though I knew nothing of her having such a lot of money. I asked if she were musical, and whether she could play Mr. Henshaw's accompaniments? "Oh, no!" she exclaimed, "I think Mr. Henshaw would *run away* if he heard me *attempt the piano!*" "Well," I said, "you will have to *adore* him and be absolutely *wrapped up* in his career. That is the way *all* wives of these big artists do." This seemed to be a new thought to Miss Clyde and she turned to Mr. Henshaw and said "Look here! Is it *true* what Miss Fay says that I have got to *worship you* and all that sort of thing?" He *smiled* benignly but did not commit himself. This is Mr. Henshaw's second marriage, as he is a widower and his wife left a little girl, who is about ten years old. . . . I was intending to go down to MacMillan's for a copy of my *book,* to present to Mr. Henshaw as a wedding present, but I am so hard up, I don't think I will! . . .

Mr. Henshaw . . . declares he has followed my life for *years back,* and knows *"all about me."* In short, he thinks I am *great, grand,* and *glorious,* and it is undoubtedly *his* wish that I be present at his wedding! *Funny,* isn't it? You never *heard* anyone go on as he did about my "nobility of character!" I didn't know *myself,* I was *so noble,* and I'll bet *you didn't* either! We make *strange* discoveries sometimes!

To change the subject, wasn't it a *tragedy,* Mahler's death! Nothing could have been more unexpected by *me,* when I last saw him conduct the Berlioz symphony with such brilliance and aplomb! I little *dreamed* he was laying down his baton for the *last time!* And now we are to have a new conductor, Joseph Stransky, a young Bohemian, instead of *Safonoff,* as I had fondly hoped! They might as well have engaged *Spiering,* who did *splendidly,* when Mahler fell ill, *just as good* as *Mahler,* in fact, *I* thought! Finck eulogizes Mahler, while Krehbiel is dreadfully severe on him, which means that these two critics are quarreling as you and Annie Kelly did over cold tea! Mahler serves as bone of contention. The new Public Library was opened *at last* on Thursday, with due pageant, and all of New York's four hundred, including your humble servant, marched into it. It is a *great* thing for the city. I shall hope to be with you later in beautiful Felsengarten, as usual, though Zina is urging me to come to Chicago as are also my pupils. The little article I wrote for the *Etude* which you advised me to *send* finds favour with the musicians and I have had many compliments.

With best love, as ever,

Amy

---

[1] A reference to *Music Study in Germany.*

New York June 14, 1911

Dearest Cater,

A thousand thanks for your *delightful* letter from Sevilla, which was *most interesting* and made my mouth water to *"go along"* as Thomas used to say ("you like to go along?") Do you remember his saying that? I was simply *flabergasted* at the generosity of your offering to pay my passage *to and from,* and it seems an *awful lot* of money for you to give out of hand, and you had better *consider well,* for I should hate to put you out of pocket or inconvenience you financially, notwithstanding my eagerness to be at the Liszt Centennial. My heart is set on it because I am *67 years* old and don't dare trust to the *future* any more, at *my* age! *"Do it now,"* is my motto, and take *no chances!* The centennial is to be in October, and at *Prague* I heard a few days ago, and not Heidelberg, which was a mistake. I thought it queer at the time when the *Etude* printed it, as Liszt had no affiliations with Heidelberg but he *was* a *Hungarian,* and spent a large portion of his time in Prague every year and there is a Liszt Museum there, to which he gave his decorations and presents he received on his tours. Prague is a beautiful and romantic looking city, I am told, and very few Americans have been there compared with the rest of Europe, so Americans are very well treated there, a young man told me. Liszt was born on October 22nd, 1811, in Raiding, Hungary, so I suppose the *date* of the month will be celebrated although it is still so far off, that the musical papers have hardly begun to write

98

it up. Nikisch and Richard Strauss will conduct but I have heard no further particulars. Miss Reed has engaged passage on the Venezia for Italy July 1st and is urging me *continually* to sail with *her,* and that is what I should *prefer* to do, if I have the luck to get the money! I am putting faith in my *luck,* which is often very *good,* and hope it won't go back on me. Possibly as *you* have made me an offer somebody *else* may hear of it and do likewise! I know *Rose* would have given me the money if she had not just put eight hundred dollars into an automobile, which she has been devoting herself to learn to run! . . .

Norman has been buzzing about considerably on business this winter and he comes to New York every few weeks. He and Henry Fay have many consultations together about a new printing press invention he is thinking of booning. I suppose you know that Henry has become a Christian Scientist and is now completely changed and is as genial as can be and ready to talk and be agreeable to everybody, Normie says! It must be a great improvement for every time I saw him at Woods Hole a few years ago he completely ignored my presence! Norman says Henry expressed amazement himself at the way his wife has put up with his boorishness all these years! He said he *wondered* how she had endured it! Zina seems to take life easily and philosophically and does not exert herself specially. Lily has gone on a visit to her son in Cambridge and spends her time mostly with her *husband* (who is better) this spring. . . . I must catch this mail as the French steamer goes tomorrow, so must break off this letter, but will continue it *presently.* Give *lots* of *love* to the *girls* and Mousie! I hope you will try *Aix* as Norman did for rheumatism. In haste

Your ever grateful and affectionate sister,

Amy

New York July 1st, 1911

Dearest Cater,

Miss Read and I are sailing for Italy today on the "*Venezia,*" which seems a long voyage! We shall go to Rome, and I will write you as soon as we reach the other side. We shall make a flying visit through the leading Italian cities, and then go to Switzerland. I shall have my letters addressed care of the American Express Co., wherever we stop. My former pupil, Nora Smith, lives in Rome and has been studying music there for two years. She is overjoyed at my coming, and will be an excellent *guide.* Am just in the hurry of final *packing,* but am taking as little as *possible!*

Amy Fay

With best love, and hoping soon to see you, believe me.

Your affectionate sister,

Amy Fay

Lake Como August 11, 1911

Dearest Cater,

Your letter and prompt check arrived yesterday, for both of which I thank you a *thousand times!* I did not want to *hurry* you about the check, which was why I wrote you I had a fund for the time, to *bridge over.* We leave here tomorrow for Switzerland, stopping first at Lugano, on our way to Lucerne, where I have an old professional acquaintance, Mr. Louis Lombard, who has invited us to an orchestral event in honor of Gabriel Fauré and afterwards to dinner. Louis Lombard was in his youth a piano teacher in Buffalo whose acquaintance I made at the old M.T.N.A. (Music Teachers National Association) when I lived in Chicago. I met him subsequently in New York at a dinner given by Mrs. Eddy at the Marie Antoinette Hotel when she and Eddy were going to Paris to live. Louis Lombard married a widow who had four children, but also some *money!* He is a born financier, and managed her money so well that he greatly increased it. Since then he has made a great fortune of his own through successful investments. They say everything he touches turns to gold! At all events, he bought the finest palace in Lombardy, where he was *born.* Here he lives on Lake Lugano in a white marble palace, where he gives concerts solely by invitation on Sunday afternoons at four, with his own orchestra of musicians hired from the Milan orchestra, and in his own private concert hall. Isn't that swell? Louis Lombard has some talent himself, as a composer. He now has four children of his own, making eight with his wife's four children, in the family. I gave Ethel Camp a letter to Mr. Lombard, and she and her husband, Emil Hugli, have a chocolate factory or something in Lugano and go there once a year. She has sung at his concerts and had a brilliant success! She has studied ever since she was married with a good teacher in Berne and seems to have become a fine artist. I believe I wrote you how she went on the stage and sang the role of Ortrud in Lohengrin there. I think it was wonderful she could do it! I am very anxious to see Mr. Lombard's place which Mrs. Eddy used to be *enthusiastic* about, and I think it was that which fired her ambition to build a villa on the Seine herself! I am going to write to Madame Loudrillon immediately and see if she can tell me all about Mrs. Eddy's death, of which I know nothing but the mere fact. . . .

We have had a delightful week *here* and I only wish you could have borne us company. Although it is hot we have a little *breeze* from the water, which is very refreshing, and this hotel is perfect. It has been thoroughly renovated, and is well furnished and comfortable, the meals are excellent, and life is arranged for the open air. All of our meals are eaten in the pergala of the gardens in front of the hotel. We sit out of doors and read, and in the evenings the moonlight on the waters is enchanting. This is the most delightful place to *read,* and there are books and newspapers in plenty, and quite a good upright piano, on which Miss Read and I play when we feel disposed. We have nice rooms, third floor front, adjoining, with balcony in front and we can get up and go there any time in the night and see the view and the moonlight on the lake, which is like a big river winding through these mountain ranges on both sides, which turn all colors at sunset! The hotel is right *on* the water. You can take the lift and go up on the roof of the house, where it is lovely to sit mornings or at night, with a beautiful view, back of the hotel as well as in front of it. There are pleasant walks and excursions one can make, and the little steamboats touch here several times per day and you can make a trip up and down the lake in them for a small sum. We crossed over to Bellagio yesterday and went through the grounds of one of the fine villas over there which one can do for a franc. We could see three lakes from one spot up there. It is quite a climb up to the tower, though. The shops over there are full of fascinating trifles, and it is hard to resist spending your last penny on them! They are cheap too!

Day before yesterday we walked over the beautiful estate here, which belonged to the Princess Carlotta of Saxe-Meininger, now dead. It is the property of the Duke now, and he only occupies it in April and May, which is the season here. The garden is beautiful and of considerable extent. It was full of all kinds of exotic plants and trees and interested me very much, it was so entirely different from anything *we* have at home. It had such a princely look, too! They say the rhododendrons there are a sight in May! A great *bank* of them went up the hill. We saw the original of Canova's "Cupid and Psyche" in the art room, *most exquisite* and in marble instead of the usual plaster cast. There was a collection of all varieties of cactus, funny looking plants, and there were some tree ferns imported from Africa in a gorge which they call "The Trout." The gardeners were working away, and the grounds are kept up all the year for the sake of the two months the duke is there. You pay a franc to go in there and the caretaker speaks English and shows you around. We went at five in the afternoon and as we were the last party for the day he gave us a good deal of time and we saw the place very thoroughly. The ride back in the evening from Bellagio on the boat was delightful. This climate agrees with me and I feel well here. . . .

I have been reading a novel called "*In the Branch*," by Pierre Coulevain, a French woman, which interested me very much. I wonder if Will has read it? It was advertized to have gone through thirty-five editions. Miss Read took it out of the public library in New York and she lent it to me. It was in the English translation. In the steamer was another book of hers called "American Nobility" and I did not read it but the scene is laid in New York, I believe. It was a new name to me. Do you know anything about this writer?[1] She seems *original*.

You know I think one can have more variety if one goes to a good boarding house than to a hotel, because you pick up acquaintances, and often very pleasant ones. Almost *all* the charming men I have met in the course of my life were in boarding houses, even Burgess and Forsyth, both of them "*swells*." If it had not been for Zina's boarding house I very much doubt if Rose or Lily ever would have found *their* husbands! When I was in Berlin at the Holtzendorffs boarding house Miss Johnston met *Mr. Sloane* there and cut *me* out, and eventually married him, you remember! Last winter I sat at the table with nine young men at Mrs. Franks' boarding house, awfully nice fellows, every one of them. That is where agreeable men are, in boarding houses! If the girls want to have a nice flirtation you had better try one of those boarding houses, as Burgess told me. He said he was tired of going to his room in a hotel and not having a soul to speak to and I will never forget how pleased he was to talk to Zina and me at the Holtzendorffs. Even our fastidious *brother* liked to go to Sandi's boarding house in Chicago where I found all the women as daft over Norman as we used to be over Forsyth. . . .

I will forward you Zina's letter to me. Give my love to Will and the girls, and with much love to yourself, I am

Your affectionate sister,

Amy

---

[1] Pierre de Coulevain was the pseudonym of Madame Favre de Coulevain.

Paris August 13th 1911

Dearest Cater,

Your letter of August 7th and the check reached me here in Paris, after I sent to Brussels to have my mail forwarded, which will account for my tardy acknowledgement of the same! I only got to Paris last Thursday and was in a hotel the first two nights, so did not get a chance to write till I was installed at the pension of Madame Loudrillon. She lives at 100 rue de Longchamps, you may remember. I was so grateful to you for your prompt sending of the money, although it seems as if I were a *robber* to take so much! I cannot sufficiently express my gratitude for the opportunities you have given me this summer to see parts of Europe which I have for *years* had a longing to see, and Italy and Switzerland opened new vistas to my gaze. I am determined to write something after I get home and try for a magazine to print it, as I have had such an interesting trip and seen so *much*! I was to have sailed September 2nd with Miss Read, but concluded it would be a mistake not to stay a little longer, as I was very anxious to see Madame Loudrillon and try to find another publisher of her translation of my book, as Dujavic, the one she gave it to before, has gone into bankruptcy, and the book is out of print. As this is Liszt's centennial year, and concerts will be given in many cities in his honour the week of his birthday, October 22nd, it is a particularly good time for my book to reappear, as Liszt's name will be in the papers everywhere. The festival in *Heidelberg* will take place as I wrote you, but there will be another in Prague. Miss Read sent me a program of the *Heidelberg fête* she got in a German music store, and the festival lasts for five days, with the most distinguished artists and conductors. Among those who will play piano are St. Saëns and Edward Rioler of Paris. Dr. Philipp Wolfrum and Richard Strauss will be *conductors*. Busoni will play the concerto in A major with orchestra, and the *"Totentanz"* (Dance of Death paraphrase of Dies Irae for piano and orchestra) with which he made such a sensation in America last year. Arthur Friedheim will represent the *German* pianists and will play some of the great solo works of Liszt for piano. The only *woman* pianist will be Fran Frieda Kwast-Hoddap of Berlin, who will play the Concerto pathétique with her husband James Kwast, for two pianos! The men are so busy showing *themselves off*, you may depend they will not let the women in! It is ever so. Fortunately they are obliged to have women singers!

Liszt's oratorio of Christus will be performed at the opening concert, Sunday, October 22nd, and on Monday his two symphonies, the "Dante," and the "Faust" ones will be played. Tuesday will be a piano and song recital, Friedheim pianist, and Ernst von Possart of Berlin and Madame Charles Cahier, court opera singer of Vienna, will be the singers. Edouard Rioler of Paris will play the two Franziskus Paula pieces, and *"Feux Follets,"* and Sixth Rhapsody. Madame Charles Cahier will sing four songs. There will be a second concert on Tuesday in the evening, with an immense orchestra and Symphonic Poem, "Ce qu'on entend sur les montagnes" (after Victor Hugo) will be performed. *Richard Strauss* will conduct. On *this* program *Busoni* will appear. It will close with the "Tasso" symphonic poem. Wednesday morning the concert will open with the 129th Psalm for Baritone and organ, which will be sung by Theodore Harrison of New York (whomever *he* may be!) Five songs will be sung by Madame Louise Debogis-Genf. Saint-Saëns will play "Danse macabre" (symphonic poem after H. Casalis) and *"Au bord d'une source"* also a transcription of Glinka's "*Techerkomas Marsch*" from Russlan and Ludmilla. At the first concert Wednesday evening, October 25th Longfellow's "*Bells of Strasbourg*" for Baritone, mixed chorus, Orchestra and Organ will be given, Theodore Harrison of New York as "*Lucifer.*" Fritz Hirt of Heidelberg will play some violin pieces with organ accompaniment. "*Hymn of a Child at its Awakening*" (Victor Hugo) will be sung by a chorus of women, with harp, piano and organ, solo singer Miss Martha Fickler, of Heidelberg. "*Chorus of Angels*" from *Faust* for mixed choir, with harp, piano and organ will be sung. Court singer, Hans Taenzler from Carlsruhe, will sing songs from Schiller's *Wilhelm Tell*, with orchestral accompaniment, and the concert will close with "*Gaudeamus igitur,*" *Humoreske* for Orchestra and chorus, Wolfrum conductor. You will perceive by the above that a very thorough idea of Liszt in all his greatest works will be given in his festival of five days, and I am glad this *tardy* justice to him as a *composer* will be done. His day has been long in coming!

I was *delighted* to meet *Will* at the American Express office here, and have had *two* pleasant evening calls from him, and day before yesterday we *tried* to take a boat ride on the Seine, but the boats were crowded and we could not get seated *either* way, so we got discouraged, and are going to try again this afternoon. We went to see Balzac's house, and where Benjamin Franklin lived and "put up his first thunder storm." I was glad to see this interesting old part of Paris. I have not done anything of any account since I came here as Madame Loudrillon and I have been running round after a publisher. We have hopes of one now, but are not yet sure. I took her to drive in the Bois after our excursions . . . I am thinking of sailing on the Holland American steamer "Nordham" on September 23rd but am not *fully decided*. I have engaged a berth, but *may* put off sailing till a week later. Wish we were going on the same ship! Sunday I shall take a cup of tea at Miss Bullett's, which is the only wild excitement in sight at this present writing! Paris has been pretty hot in the day time, but cools off after dark. The city is *crowded* with people, and the dogs around here *bark all the time* including *Madame Loudrillon's pet dog*, which is rather trying to my nerves! That is the *worst* with *dogs*. They *will bark*! . . . With best love to the girls and yourself.

As ever,

Amy

Lucerne August 23rd 1911

Dearest Cater,

It seems quite jolly, our little correspondence every few days, and quite as if we were having a conversation! I *did so* wish for you on *Monday* evening when I went to an orchestral concert in the Rue-Saal here, conducted by Furnagallis, with Isaye as solo violinist and a young singer from Boston, Miss Evelyn Parnell. *She* was very *bad*, however! Isaye played the concerto in G minor by Bruch and the old Mendelssohn concerto we have heard *"all* the big" violinists play, till it hangs to every hair of our heads! As an encore to the latter he played Saint-Saëns *"Havanaise."* Well, Isaye was simply *immense*, and better than ever! I never heard anything so magnificent as it was! His technic was *dazzling* and his *tone* and *depths* of expression surpass all the other violinists. The public was crazy over him and the orchestra beside itself. I had not heard Isaye for *years* but he really *is greater* than *ever*! He must look to his laurels, with Kathleen Pardou in the field, for she, although only twenty years old, is a genius of the first rank. She plays with the Boston Symphony orchestra next season, at its *first* concert, and then goes on tour with it! She is a Canada girl, and was born in Ontario, but studied at the Moscow Conservatory with Anerperg, who also taught *Zimbalist* whom Mrs. Dalliba was so wild over! Saint-Saëns' *"Havanaise"* is a difficult and fascinating composition and had chromatic thirds and sixths in it which were as *smooth as glass* under Isaye's wonderful fingers! It was fun to hear him do them! The way he whipped up the tempo of the finale of the Mendelssohn was fun to hear, and the orchestra had to strain every nerve to keep up with him! Furnagallis is a good conductor, though, and between them he and Isaye carried it off, *haut la main*! The orchestra broke out into such tremendous applause that Isaye suddenly turned the tables on them by whirling round and applauding the orchestra, clapping his hands enthusiastically! This produced a laugh from the public, and it was nice in Isaye. I wonder if he will go over to America again sometime!

I met César Thomson, his rival, at Lugano, when Miss Read and I attended the concert Louis Lombard invited us to. Thomson and Gabriel Fauré were both there, and Fauré was guest of honour and also at the dinner with us. He is a very poetic personality and I was charmed with him. Both he and Thomson have a striking and attractive appearance. The concert was at four P.M. and we took the train up there and then walked through a beautiful avenue of trees to the palace, where we were met by servants in livery, who conducted us to the concert hall, adjacent. The orchestra from Milan furnished the players, and Mr. Lombard was conductor except for Fauré's work, which Fauré conducted himself. The audience was entirely by invitation, people from Lugano, and everybody was charmingly attired. I never saw so many pretty hats in town! Mrs. Lombard and her guests sat in a box upstairs at the back of the hall. . . . An article in a Boston magazine giving the particulars (written by Jon Mitchell Chaffie, whomever *he* may be!) Mrs. Lombard sent me! Dinner was served at half-past seven and was very delicious, of course! I told Miss Read I never expected to have such a combination *again* as the concert, and two artists of the first rank, and dinner in a *palace*! Mrs. Lombard asked me to come up again on Monday and Tuesday afternoons to some rehearsals, and we were asked to remain for dinner on Monday, also. So we became very good friends with them all. Mrs. Lombard has two grown daughters, pretty girls, by her first husband, who were there also. Miss Read preceded me to Lucerne, as I stopped at *Rodi Fiesso* two days, to visit Madame Cappiani, an old friend of mine. She left on Sunday for Mannheim. I am to join her in a few days in Holland.

New York November 18, 1911

Dearest Mudkins,

Your letter of November 1st is at hand and I will try to answer it *now* as I have been breathlessly *busy*. I have had *no* time for letters! For some reason I have to go out nearly every evening and don't get to bed before one o'clock very much, as things are *hectic* in New York! . . . On Monday evening I gave a Piano Conversation by request before Wesley Weymann's *Pi Tau Kappa* Club, which was gotten up by himself and his pupils before he went abroad to study. It meets regularly at the house of Reverend Howard Duffield, 49 Fifth Avenue (near 12th Street). Miss Sara Dunn, the step sister of *Natalie* and Wesley's guardian angel you may remember (like Aunt Amelia to Grandpapa), is wrapped up in *Wesley* and looks after all his affairs while he is away! She is a regular contributor of musical articles to the *Sun* as Henderson's[1] assistant, and also to *Town and Country*, which has a larger circulation among the swells, as it has illustrations of the beautiful country houses of the *rich*, and of their *estates*, in it. Natalie will give me some very flattering notices, therefore. She writes well. Wesley has been studying with Leschetizky and others for two years and is now concertizing abroad. He came back this summer and gave a piano recital, mostly of MacDowell's work, some weeks ago, in New York, which Miss Read and I attended. It was in a private home just opposite our former flat in West 56th Street. . . . They were awfully polite to me at Wesley's club and treated me with distinguished consideration. The parlours were crowded, and after the concert was over great pleasure was expressed by those present. People always *love* the talk I give about the pieces and they *never* get *enough* of *that*. No matter *how much* I say, *they* invariably say I "don't talk *half enough*." I gave a little talk on Liszt at the Women's Philharmonic in celebration of his centennial, and now I am asked where I go to repeat the talk on Liszt. I played his *Ave Maria* and *Loreley*. I am to give a talk on Liszt November 28th at the *Fraternal Association of Musicians* which is a men's affair. They expect to make a conspicuous occasion of it, and are inviting Huneker[2] and Hagby, etc. All the leading musicians will be invited. As I said, I gave a recital *Monday* evening; *Tuesday* evening I had a business meeting of the Council for the

Women's Philharmonic, *Wednesday* evening I stayed at home, *Thursday* evening I went to the concert of the Philharmonic Orchestra, with its new conductor, Stransky. *Friday* evening I went to an exquisite piano recital of a Leschetizky pupil, Miss Monica Dailie, a new young lady pianist, and *Saturday* evening we had the "*Informal*" of the Women's Philharmonic at which Lucy Greenberg was the pianist, so I had to prepare *her* to play. You see I have been out every night but one this week! Lucy did play *magnificently* last night, and she made a great impression. Two of Mr. Stuart's pupils sang *finely*, a man and a woman, and he was there, himself. . . . My hand is all right again and was not injured by my fall, so I think it was a bruise, and *not* a tendon, although it got such a *wrench* I had a terrible fright over it. I feared it would be stiff for life! Everybody on board ship was much *exercised* over it, as I played a great deal for them before my fall. I think *sprains* are nearly incurable. Miss Bates says that Mary Perkins and Bessie are back from Europe again and they have been to all sorts of places, like Turkey, for instance. They visited Ernest Schelling and his wife in *their* beautiful home near Geneva, Switzerland, and Paderewski was there for three days, before he and his wife sailed for South America and Mary and Bessie saw *them*. Paderewski is *devoted* to Schelling, it seems! They are uneasy about Paderewski's *health*, as he has not been well. He gave ninety-seven concerts in South America. He must be very fond of Bessie, as he gave her a *beautiful* portrait of himself some years ago, which I saw at Mary's house. I think it was a pencil drawing by an artist. Bessie has visited him at Morges. Mrs. Schelling was Bessie's friend, Miss Draper, you remember!

It was Paderewski's influence which saw Stransky to New York, I imagine, as conductor of the Philharmonic Orchestra, as Paderewski declared he was the coming conductor! Stransky is a Bohemian and only thirty-eight years old. He has money and ambition and is good looking. He is very good in Wagner, but seems a novice in Beethoven. The first night I thought him very talented, but he did not show up well the second concert in César Franck's symphony in D minor, and he bored me dreadfully. I don't know how Stransky will ultimately prove, but after Safonoff and Mahler, he is a decided *come down*. He is better than *Walter Damrosch*, though, and he conducted Liszt's *Tasso* superbly and beat *Walter* all to pieces on it! I was delighted to hear that *Walter and Frank* were *both* at the concert, in a box near the stage! Walter had just had "*Tasso*" at his Sunday concert! Stransky certainly has *climax* and *fire*, but he has not all those *intermediate shades* of tone between *forte* and *piano*, though he doubtless will improve with experience. It was a sensation to see "*Theodore Thomas* orchestra" advertized to give a concert on December 13th and I hope the people will turn out well for it. I don't feel nice about Stock's program. He begins with Beethoven's overture to Coriolanus and it seems to me we have just had that from some orchestra, then he plays Strauss's Don Juan, and we have just had *that*, also! The *soloist* is a *violinist* (Spalding) and Brahms' 2nd Symphony will close the program. Either a singer or a pianist would give more variety in an orchestral concert, in *my* humble opinion, but I suppose Stock has his reasons for his selection. There is nothing undignified in a *Philharmonic* concert. Still, severity can be *overdone!* Normie is dusting around and has sold quite a number of the boxes to people like Carnegie and Gary, and he has taken one himself, where I expect to sit. He said he thought he would invite Mrs. George Sheldon to sit in his box! Mrs. Sheldon is going to give a reception for Stransky. Dr. Horgett told me a good story about Safonoff, and he said Safonoff declared to *him* that there was only *one thing* he would like to do in *America*, and *that was*, he "would like to take the *Theodore Thomas orchestra* and conduct it on a tour through Europe!" Safonoff went out to hear Theodore's orchestra just after Theodore's death, and he was immensely impressed with it. He had some friends in Chicago who invited him, thinking that Safonoff might be chosen to succeed Theodore as conductor. Safonoff received an invitation to conduct the Philharmonic Orchestra this year, but he refused to accept an engagement for one year only. Now that Pulitzer has just died and left half a million to the Philharmonic Orchestra in his *will*, it is to be regretted that Safonoff declined to come! I have *never* got over *his loss!*

Last week's Musical Courier gave the description of Liszt's centennials in Europe. The one in *Budapest* was *the one to go to*, and was magnificent! All the gang *I* knew was there, and it just *broke my heart* that *I* was *not present*. It was the greatest *pity* I could not manage to be there, but I ought to have arranged for it before I went to Europe, as I was at the *end* of my wardrobe and had not money to buy some new dresses for Paris! I would not have gone unless *handsomely dressed* to *such* an occasion. But it *was too bad* and a great opportunity was lost for me. . . .

With best love,

Amy

---

[1] William James Henderson, music critic of the *New York Times* in 1887-1902 and of the *New York Sun* from 1902 to 1937.

[2] James Gibbons Huneker, New York music critic who was associated with the *Sun* (1900-12, 1919-21) and *Times* (1912-19).

York December 15, 1911

Dearest Lak,

Your charming letter gave me such pleasure and I have been waiting from day to day to get the time to answer it, but I am overwhelmed with engagements continually and get very *tired*. . . . I was so mad when I was in Brussels! Gurickx was most anxious to devote one day to me, but his wife was so jealous she would not permit him to carry out his scheme so all he could do was to invite me to dinner at the Hotel Royale, and I saw him only a little over two hours! They have been married *twenty years* and have a grown daughter, and I have seen him now for the *second* time only! I thought she was too *mean* for anything! But Gurickx was a fool to tell her anything about it that I was in town. He could have managed perfectly well if he had not been so frank and open. He is more charming than ever and is considered to have made a most successful career! His wife is young (compared with him) about forty-two and charming and rich, and the daughter of one of the most aristocratic families in Brussels. She was Mademoiselle Gens-de-Briens. Gurickx is Professor in the Royal Conservatory, and he has taken a beautiful new house in the centre of the aristocratic quarter of the city, No. 55 Boulevard de Saint Michel as they are going to present their daughter *Germaine*, a beautiful girl of nineteen, in society this year. The little boy, Jean-Marie, is eight years old, and is the apple of Gurickx's eye evidently! His face softens when he speaks of him. The family were all at the seashore so I did not see them. . . . Mary Perkins and Bessie have got back from their perennial year in Europe. *I* have not yet seen them, but Josie Bates *has*, and she told me they had been to strange weird places, such as Turkey, and had a most interesting time. They are intimate friends of the Paderewskis and saw them *three whole days* before they sailed for South America on his last tour. They were at Schellings' country house in Switzerland together. Ernest Schelling is a splendid pianist, a pupil of Paderewski and a special favorite of his. He was from Philadelphia but married Miss Draper, a very rich girl, and friend of Bessie Perkins. So Bessie had the soft soap on Paddy! He gave her a most beautiful pencil sketch of himself when she visited him in Morges once, and I *envy* her *dreadfully!* Mary and I are now very good friends again so I shall see her *in time* and hear the news!

The Theodore Thomas orchestra gave a magnificent concert here on Wednesday P.M., Mr. Stock conducting. Norman was much wrought up and he sold twenty-eight boxes for it, taking one himself, in which I sat and helped him to do honour to Mrs. Andrew D. White, wife of the former minister to Berlin and now president of Cornell. I found her a very intelligent and charming woman. We have had such a *lot* of orchestral and all sorts of concerts the past week that Carnegie Hall was not crowded, but they had a good house. Stock was on his mettle and so was the orchestra and the concert was superb. It was a gathering of old times in the audience and many were there who had formerly seen Theodore's baton wave! Many musicians came, and the new conductor of the Philharmonic, Stransky, sat in the box next to me. Hector and Marie Thomas occupied the centre box opposite the stage, with their party. The town got quite a shaking up! The orchestra will give two concerts here in February with the Toronto Mendelssohn chorus.

Amy Fay

I was invited last Monday evening to be guest of honour of the MacDowell Club and of Kurt Schindler, conductor, of its chorus at the performance of Liszt's oratorio of St. Elizabeth. I sat in the box with Mona Bagby, Rudolph Schirmer, Zimbalist the famous violinist, and Alma Gluck of the Metropolitan Opera Company. It was a brilliant occasion and splendid performance! Best love to Madeline and to your dear self from

Amy

New York January 25, 1912

Dearest Mudkins,

. . . I *am* so *interested* about your *book*, and I *do hope* you *will* get it before the public. With Morowitz to back it financially it seems to me it *ought* to be printed *anyway*, whether the reader considers it good, bad, or indifferent! After all, the *public* is the only true judge, and you never *will* know the worth of your book until the public has had an opportunity to *read* it! I should not be *set up* or *cast down* by the opinion of any *one* reader. You may recall the "London Times" said *my book* was a "*chronicle of small* beer," the *only* bad notice it ever had! But if *that* critic had had the reading of it before it was printed, it *never would have come out!* I have always expected Mr. George Smalley wrote that notice, as he was so disagreeable and domineering to Lily and me when we called and presented a letter of introduction, I forget from *whom!* He *froze us out* in less than five minutes, and that in spite of the fact that we were *both young and handsome* and *well dressed* at that period of *Norman's* prosperity! Get out into the *ocean*, say I, and then find out if you can *swim!*. . . Lucy's concert came off last evening and was a brilliant success, but the expenses mounted up so I'm afraid she won't clear the hundred dollars I hoped for. I sold a good many tickets and my friends responded very generally, but I should have had *patronesses* to help me. I consulted with Mary Perkins and Bessie about patronesses, as they are so executive. *They* thought patronesses were "out of date," and that people would take the tickets just the same for the asking. . . . After the concert was over we had quite a reception and then I went to the Drawing Room Club by Evelyn Mellen's invitation *also in the Waldorf!* I got to bed after two o'clock and had a good supper there! Josie Bates sent two dollars and came to the concert. Very nice of her!

I have no news to relate, as I have done *nothing* but teach Lucy and write letters

110

for *days!* Thank heaven it is all over now, and I can once more practice a little myself!
. . . Best love to you all.

Your devoted sister,

Amy

February 21, 1912

[from a letter to Rose]

Volpé is a Bohemian and is a very fine conductor. He has created an orchestra
of his own, collected from good theatre players, about seventy-five young fellows,
with whom Volpé rehearses every Sunday morning. The men *enjoy* good music (after
the *theatre* ragtime) beyond *anything*, and they *play* with an ardour and impetuosity
that is most contagious! The program was unusual and *very* beautiful, and Spalding
was soloist. He played an exquisite concerto by Bach, with such a *ravishing* orchestral
accompaniment, especially in the *second* movement *Adagio*, where the *solo* violin
takes the *melody*, and all the double basses, *in unison*, march along at its side and
touch off the notes, *over* it, *under* it, and *around* and *about* it, like discreet men
of the world, who know *what* to say, and don't say *too much* or *too little!* It *was
so interesting* and done with such *elegance* by Bach! What a *gift* he had! Such a
sense of *ease and mastery!* The program opened with Mozart's splendid Symphony
in E flat major which I have not heard since very early Theodore years! It has the
Menuet I used to play that Pychowski taught me when I went to Geneveo, at
seventeen. Pretty thing! Mozart is *going* to be the rage soon, you mark my
words! Musicians are just waking up to him, and Deppe's prophecies will come
true. He said "Mozart composed *twenty* piano concertos, and *nine* of them are
masterpieces, but they are never played!" Grieg's *"Lyric Suite"* was another piece
Volpe had on the program last night and the *Nocturne* in *that* was a *"poet's
dream."* The *March of the Dwarfs* followed it, and was encored. I went into the
green room soon after the concert with Mr. Bushnell to congratulate Volpe, who
was in high spirits over the success of the concert. He was *delighted* I was there,
he said, and asked me to *back* him up (the orchestra needs money, of course!) I
assured him I would toot his horn all I could! He presented me to Mr. Spalding,
an attractive youth, with very talented, large, flashing eyes! The name "Miss Fay"

did not seem to convey anything to his mind and he looked *bored*. I went to the other side of the room to speak with Mr. Benoist, when Spalding *came* to suddenly *rushed over*, and exclaimed, "I did not know it was Miss *"Amy"* Fay I was addressing" (in the manner *you* say people exclaim, Oh, Mrs. *"Theodore"* Thomas!"). We then had a sympathetic little talk. He said he had heard a *great deal about me*, and I said I had been reading *about him* in the Musical Courier long before his return from his studies abroad. (He certainly plays beautifully but is not such a big genius as Mischa Elman and Kathleen Pardou, who are both about Spalding's age.) . . .

Mr. Stransky is coming out *strong* and is gaining here. Paderewski's good opinion of him is being justified. Stransky has a remarkable gift in arranging his programs, which are very new and original, and always have some interesting novelty on them, so that you hate to miss a concert. Stransky has *force and good sense* and the men of the orchestra have become very fond of him. The orchestra has gained immensely in fire and virtuosity and plays very much like the Boston Symphony one. Stransky is very dramatic and always rises to a climax. He has both grandeur and delicacy of conception. Miss Read and I subscribed for sixteen concerts, and we go every Thursday evening and enjoy them, with the balcony all to ourselves. There is *no crowd*, as for the *Boston* nights. . . .

I went to a big evening party at the grand white marble mansion of Mrs. Samuel Thorne February 10th, which is corner of Fifth Avenue and 73rd Street. I saw Carnegie and his wife there, and *multi-millionaires galore*, puffing themselves out over their shirt fronts, like pouter pigeons! Paul Crevatt was *one*. I met Mrs. George B. Loring, (mirabile dictu!), *Mr. Edward H. Blanc* and wife! This is the very first time I ever have met *Blanc* in society, which shows how *absolutely far apart* our spheres are! *He* has grown *stouter*, and I have grown *thinner!* . . .

New York February 29, 1912

Dearest Mudkins,

. . . This week I am up to my ears in engagements, last night and the night before the Chicago orchestra concerts, with the Toronto Mendelssohn Chorus, magnificent! The orchestra is simply beyond anything, and as for little *Stock,*[1] he was *compressed fire!* He was evidently on the ragged edge of his nerve, he is *busting* with ambition! He is a *splendid* conductor, though! It was triumph for *Theodore*, this glorious orchestra bringing him back to the world and causing him to speak again to his New York public with *"tongues of angels."* Coming as it did on top of Rose's book,[2] which is exciting *wide* interest, the orchestra seems to set its seal upon his life work! The hall was *packed* with New York's finest people and it was a gorgeous and fashionable audience. Norman had a box, and filled it with sympathetic friends. I invited Nora Smith's artist friend and teacher, Mr. Luigi Gulli, who has just arrived from *Rome* with her, and is looking for engagements to play in public. He is a fine pianist and cultivated man. Nora *adores* him, it is evident, and works for him, tooth and nail, after the manner of women in love! . . . She also has another friend from Rome (painter) who came over with Nora to see New York. They are stopping at the Hotel Lucerne in Amsterdam Avenue 79th Street. Gulli has taken a room outside where he can have his piano and practice all he likes. I think Nora will return to the west ultimately.

Saturday evening is my annual reception from the Women's Philharmonic in the Chapter Room, Carnegie Hall. The club is taking a great interest in it this time and is making a great effort. Our orchestra is to play, Martina Johnstone conductor. She will play a solo accompanied by the orchestra. She is a beautiful artist but I don't know if you ever heard of her? She is a Swede and was brought over by Gilmore and travelled with him. I have no business to be writing this letter as I have *loads* to do and must close with best love and congratulations on your *birthday*. May you have *Many Happy Returns*.

Your devoted sister,

Amy

---

[1] Frederick Stock, conductor of the Chicago Symphony in those years.
[2] Rose Fay Thomas' *Memoirs*, published in New York in 1911 by Moffat, Yard & Company.

New York March 2, 1912

Dearest Mudkins,

How are you getting on with your Donoghue article? I *hope* you have *stuck to it* and got it done! Rose has a new book of essays all ready for the printer and has even selected *four* designs for the book cover. Such is *her* celebrity in book writing. It tires her soul, however, that the *Thomas* biography sells so slowly, as the first edition is not yet exhausted, but it is such a *large*, expensive book, I am not surprised! The same is true of Lillie de Hegermann's book, which I made Lucy Greenberg give me for a Christmas present, and it costs $3.50. That is too much for the average pocket-book! I found Lillie's book extremely entertaining, but think it would require a knowledge of the French people and their language to make it widely appreciated. It is not a book for the masses! . . .

I have been going out a *great deal* lately, and it has been forced upon me. I am constantly being invited to be guest of honour by musical clubs, etc. Last Monday I was guest of honour at the *Chiropean* Club of Brooklyn, which celebrated its seventeenth birthday, and is the largest club there. It numbers *three hundred*, and the Brooklyn aristocracy belongs to it. The meeting was in the Porch Gallery, which is a large club house, and everything was done *in style!* An elaborate luncheon was given, and I sat at the right hand of the president, Mrs. McIntosh. . . . After the luncheon a very attractive musical programme was rendered by Mr. and Mrs. Woodman of Brooklyn. *He*, composer-pianist, and *she*, singer. *Both* were talented and they gave great pleasure, also a young girl violinist who played with Dr. Woodman one movement of his sonata for violin and piano. Very good. His songs were *all* pretty, and his wife sang them *beautifully!* After the music came speeches, and the installation of officers for the following year. Four of the members spoke and the speeches were very witty and amusing and there was much laughter and applause. The exercises concluded with a hymn to the Chiropean Club which was sung all standing, and was composed by Dr. Woodman. After this, punch and teas were served, also ices and then we went home. I got back by subway at half-past six, ate a hearty dinner, and went with Miss Read to the Philharmonic Society (orchestra) concert. Stransky was a decided genius for arranging interesting and novel programmes, and I hate to miss a concert. He is a fine conductor and is popular here although he is a novice compared with Safonoff and Thomas. I felt dreadfully sorry at the change of name in the Theodore Thomas orchestra, and you will see that it will be abolished altogether before long as *founder* of it. They will find the new name too long and cumbersome! Probably Stock's friends were at the bottom of it! They are making a sad mistake! I have kept this since Monday intending to write another sheet but must send it off now. Your *splendid* one arrived on Tuesday for which my best thanks. With much love, as ever.

Your devoted sister,

Amy Fay

The American Years

New York April 3, 1912

Dearest Rose,

Your letter containing the check for forty dollars reached me all right, and I hope by this time you are safe in Chicago after your last jaunt to Florida. . . . I don't envy you your task of breaking up in Chicago and can't help regretting that splendid city is to know our family no more! New York is expanding *every minute* and is really a *huge* menagerie of all kinds of people! It really frightens me sometimes when one really *takes it in!* I am curious to note the impression it will make on *Zina* after her long absence! The enormous skyscrapers really *darken* the air, and hang over one with threatening mien. Opposite the corner where Roger Peet's store stands which Zina will recall, the most stupendous skyscraper we have *yet* towers aloft. When it is filled with people what will become of humanity, for there is a constant *river* of human beings *pouring* through Broadway *now* in the vicinity of West 33rd Street! It is fortunate aeroplanes have arrived, for we shall require them for transportation! . . . Norman's book[1] is out but I have not yet *seen it.* Mr. Bushnell wrote me it had a flattering review in the *Sun,* with Normie's picture, so it must have made a mark!

---

[1] Norman's book *Big Business and Government* was published in 1912.

April 5, 1912

Last night I went to a concert at Carnegie Hall to hear a young cellist named Paulo Gruppe, at the request of his mother, who is the wife of a New York painter, and who is trying to manage her son, or *assist* in making his career a success. He appeared jointly with Madame Jomelli, the French singer who was with Chaminade in this country. The program was a song a cello recital, of which Jomelli had the lion's share. She sang *lots* of songs, and *all kinds of songs*, including one *lovely* tragic one of *her own* composition called "J'ai pleure en rêve," which was jointly encored enthusiastically. Another exquisite little song, which delighted my ear was a cradle song by *Mozart*, which I never heard before. The song which took the public by storm, however was Hood's "Song of the Shirt," although it was a very ugly setting by Sydney Homer, and it must have been on account of the words it was so frantically

115

applauded. Debussy and Gabriel Fauré were on the program, with lovely French songs. I think Jomelli is well worth hearing, and she is on her way to Chicago *today*. She was loaded with magnificent flowers which she had the good taste to carry to the grand piano and lay on its lid. Some, in pots, stood around it on the floor. It made a *lovely mass* of *colour* right in the centre of the stage. After the concert I went to speak to the artists, and a new departure was taken when the people went onto the *stage*, where the artists received them, as if a reception room, instead of our being jounced in the stuffy greenroom. The main body of the hall was in shadow as the electric lights were turned out but the *stage* was all *light* and *colour* with the flowers and palms. It was really a *capital* idea, and Jomelli, in her superb *gown*, was like a big flower, *herself*. She was in *despair how* to dispose of the beautiful *floral* tributes, as they were going to Chicago by the next train. I did not stay to see what became of them! Probably she distributed them among friends. There was *one* tree of red Japanese roses, the *prettiest* thing you *ever* saw, quite tall in a pot, and with red gauze bows tied in its branches. One lady said to Jomelli's husband, "you can *keep* the plants in *this basket* as we bought them with roots!" Oh yes, replied the melifluous husband, "we shall *keep* the *plants*, of *course!*" In the same breath he whispered an aside to another person, on the left, *"Help yourself to the flowers!"* "We are going to Chicago, and *can't* take them along." He was also Jomelli's accompanist. Well, I must hence to church, so good-bye.

With love from

Amy Fay

New York April 21, 1912

Dearest Mudkins,

I have been wanting to write you for *ages*, but *could not* get at it somehow! First, I want to thank you for the pretty *Easter card*, with the double association of Willie Huntington and yourself, with the sweet peas and the lamb! The poor little beast *has* a most tragic and sentimental expression, as you say!

Life is evidently not what it ought to be for the lambskin, and perhaps he forsees the butcher's knife! I did not send out any cards on Easter, although I bought some lovely ones, but may get them off yet! You know I have no talent for doing things up and mailing them, it always seems such a piece of work, although it *isn't!* I am always surprised at *your* energy about doing the proper thing at the *right time!* Now I will wager you have sent something to *Laura* for her birthday this month, whereas I have done *nothing at all!* To be sure *I* have been dreadfully *down hearted* over my finances and worried to death, as Norman suddenly stopped my allowance two months ago of fifty dollars a month, declaring he must give it to the Wildermings *instead*, and he could not help *them and me!* At the same time he announced there would be *no March dividend* from the estate, as usual! Well, that was a *double facer*, as you may well surmise, and I was at my wit's end *where* the money was coming from to pay *my* board and expenses! Luckily I had saved a hundred dollars, and was feeling unusually *flush* for *me!* I took that for my board and room! Then I prayed to the Lord to send me some *jobs* by which I could earn some money! Strange to say, my prayers were answered and I got various small sums for unexpected lessons, and one or two little articles ordered by the "Etude," etc. I have got through two months and am *ahead* for *this* month's board till May! Rose sent me a check *yesterday* for fifty dollars, but I hope to get along without using it, and will *not* use it unless in *extremity*. She is always so generous! I forgot to say that a tardy *dividened did* come finally, but not so large as usual. Still it tided me over, as it amounted to $108.00 dollars. I shall *keep on* praying to the Lord for jobs! I owed $65.00 to Arnold and Constable, and $40.00 to Mrs. Lemmon. . . . The *Etude* had written me for an obituary of W.S.B. Mathews, a Chicago musician who used to be very spiteful to me! (of *all* people!) and I may get two or three dollars out of that. Amusing, isn't it? If I chose I could *now* pay off all the mean things he used to write about *my playing* but I *shan't!* It would never have occurred to me that I might make a little money out of *Mathew's* death, nor would it ever have occurred to him!

All this week New York has been *crushed* under the *Titanic horror!* Was there *ever* anything so *dreadful!* The poor Arthur Ryersons! Their case was particularly sad, as they were going home for the funeral of one of their sons, and now Arthur Ryerson has perished! Mrs. Ryerson and her two daughters and one son are here at the Hotel St. Regis. Norman called on them but did not see them. They sent word they would be here several days as they were getting their mourning to wear. This morning, at St. Agnes Church in 92nd St. the clergyman *Dr. Bellinger* offered a special prayer for two children, with their nurse, who had been rescued from the *Titanic* and were *in the Church!* It seemed like a *miracle!* There has been such a *rush* for the *newspapers*, it must have been a bonanza for *them!* . . . The *men* behaved *splendidly* on the *Titanic*, didn't they? I was proud of our countrymen! By another week the sensation will be over and forgotton. In *New York* things *don't last long!* There is too much doing! Norman had thirteen friends and acquaintances on board, and among them was your former boarder Mr. Kent, of Buffalo! *He* went down, as no doubt you observed! Frank Millet the artist, too! I was so sorry that *he* perished! . . . I was quite blue over Burgesses death, by the way, which you sent me news of, and I did not realize how much I cared for him! I very much *regret*

Amy Fay

I did not write and describe to him Val's wedding a year ago, as I was on the point of doing, it would have interested him so much! I am *surprised you* did not answer his letter, as you were always *devoted* to him! He *was* a charmer, as you say, and I never shall forget his pretty laugh! It was a pity he dropped out of our lives altogether. After all, one does not replace the old loves. When I saw Gurickx last fall I found him *more* attractive than ever! He is the quintessence of *elegance* now! He always *was so intelligent* in conversation! Gurickx is *all art!* I have had some lovely letters from him lately, *full* of affection and appreciation. He writes a *charming* letter, so caressing! . . . This afternoon, Miss Read, Madeline, and I went to Gussie Cotthow's farewell concert, at Belasco's Theatre. Gussie is engaged to a young Californian singer named Mr. Gerot, whom she first met when she was *thirteen* years old on a concert tour! Since then she has met him *twice* more. They will be married in June and will go abroad to live for several years, till *he* has made his reputation as a *singer*. Gussie has just returned from a tremendous tour way out to Vancouver! Her mother is with her. She plays beautifully and is *very pretty*. Gussie and Fanny Bloomfield have "done" *Europe* thoroughly and carried off the honours everywhere! By the way, have you heard Backhaus? *He* is the miracle of the *present* and I was *never* so taken by surprise as I was by *that* young man, who is only twenty-seven years old! His *virtuosity* is simply *staggering* and absolutely *consummate*. But his *conception* keeps *fully pace with it*, and his performance of Beethoven's thirty-two Variations in C minor, which I used to play, was a revelation! I never would have believed what he could make of them, if I had not *heard it!* The composition is a more colossal work than I had any idea of! It was like making Beethoven's acquaintance *all over again* to hear Backhaus play these variations, and finding him *miles higher* as a *mountain peak of genius* than I *ever* had conceived him, *much* as I have studied Beethoven! I thought I knew my Beethoven, too! Paderewski, Josef Hofmann and d'Albert do not *approach* Backhaus in *this particular* composition of Beethoven! The *enormous energy* he put into it is *overwhelming* in its effect. As for the great *Etudes* of Chopin, such as the "Winter Wind" and the C minor "Revolutionary Etude" (so called) the way Backhaus' left hand seethes through the difficulties of *those* and *drives them before him* with unerring sureness, rapidity, and indescribable *splendour*, take your breath away! He certainly is a *Titan*, and endlessly fascinating! I went in to speak to him at a concert of the Boston Symphony (in the green room) the day before his recital and found him a blonde young man like a Swede, with large blue eyes, light hair, and calm and tranquil expression. I said to Backhaus, "I am coming to your concert tomorrow to hear you play *Debussy*, I am curious to hear what you will make out of *him*. "So," replied he, "then you are *not* interested in my Beethoven?" *"No"* said I, "I have heard you play the Kreutzer Sonata and I *know* you can play *Beethoven*." Backhaus did not trouble himself to speak *further!* But he got his revenge the next day when he bowled me completely over with thirty-two Variations. I met him on the street and he seemed to emanate light as he walked, with his tranquil smile, and his fair hair blowing back under his hat! Anybody so sure of himself I *never* saw! Impossible to feaze him! Good-bye now with *best love*, from

Your devoted sister,

Amy

New York May 12, 1912

Dearest Mudkins,

By this time I suppose you feel quite settled in your new abode, although I should think you would miss your friends and your *church* on the north side, not to mention home comforts! However, you were ever a gypsy, as I maintain, and must have an entire change once in so often! I hope you are now near enough to be able to visit *Addie Wilkes* once in a while. Others of my friends are on the south side, such as Fannie Bloomfield-Zeisler, Mrs. Leonard (my pupil) and *Mrs. Young*, wife of the professor. You met the *last two*, you remember, that day at Lyon and Healy's. Rose made her little visit and departed for Felsengarten last Monday. . . . Rose perfectly *hates* New York and declares that the noise here *drives her crazy*, so I don't think the idea of her making her *home* here is a very practical one! While she was with the Hector Thomases she was all very well, but as soon as she came to stay with *me* she was cross as sticks, and as *testy* as Theodore! I really was *surprised* at the way she acted, and cannot say that I enjoyed her visit in consequence. Probably she was tired out with moving. On the contrary, I was *very pleased* when she seated herself in a taxi to drive to the railroad! . . .

I gave a little evening for Madeline and invited fourteen people, but only *seven* came! Rose was here, and my old pupil Nora Smith and her teacher, Signor Luigi Gulli, recently arrived from *Rome*, were the principal guests, together with a Mrs. Nisbet, with whom Nora was staying. She is an attractive young woman, wife of Dr. Nisbet (formerly from Chicago) and has an attractive home in an apartment house near the Museum of Natural History, on that park at 68th Street. I went to Gulli's studio when I was in Rome and heard him play there. He is a fine artist, about the age of Consolo, of whom he was a friend in boyhood. Nora is *devoted* to Gulli, and is doing all in her power to get him *started*, which is not an easy matter at this

119

season of the year. Gulli looks much more like an American than he does an Italian, and he speaks English fluently, which is a good thing. . . . Mrs. Nisbet invited Rose and me down to her house to hear Gulli play on her Steinway *grand*, a fine *new* one, and we had a very charming afternoon there. Norman and the Hector Thomases came and Normie enjoyed Gulli's *Brahms* playing *immensely!*

We had the parade of the twenty thousand suffragettes a week ago last Saturday, and I wanted Rose to go with me to witness it, as I had one of the finest windows offered me right opposite the Public Library on 42nd Street and Fifth Avenue. She could not be persuaded to go, and so I went alone. I sat in a nice armchair right in the window and saw the whole show to the *greatest* advantage as we were in the second story only. It was really a *lovely sight* and *quite impressive*. The procession was largely comprised of young and pretty women, charmingly attired in white, with colored scarfs of silk in orange, blue, green, and purple, and with jaunty little straw hats, carrying banners or gay little flags. Their skirts were short, and their little feet were dainty shod, in white shoes or black, and they stepped out with such *grace* and *airiness* of movement! They had been instructed to be *dignified* in their demeanor and to keep their eyes looking *straight* before them, which they did. Consequently there was a sense of perfect *propriety* in the demeanor of the suffragettes. No flirting or ogling of the men as they passed swiftly along. Mrs. Oliver Belmont was the star and attracted all eyes as she marched along in solitary grandeur, like a marshall between two battalions and was arrayed in a white cloth with a white straw hat. Mrs. Nathan was another prominent suffragette, who marched by herself in a similar way. The Public Library was *crowded* with people, and they lined the avenue all along the route. The *men* were *intensely* interested spectators and were more inclined *for*, than *against!* The parade really made a great moral affect, and I think achieved a *victory*. The march was from Washington Park to Carnegie Hall, which was beautifully decorated with flowers, and *there* the *speeches* were made. I was awfully sorry Rose did not go and take some Kodak views of the procession to put in her album as it was a *national event*. . . .

Rose would not remain for the annual dinner of the "*Hopkinsfolk*," two days after her departure, which I tried to persuade her to put in an appearance at, and neither would Lily or Madeline stay! It seemed *too bad* when they were right here on the *spot*, and could so easily have done so! As for *Norman*, he of course, had a dinner engagement *he* could not break, so *he* did not come either! I was very sorry as such a family gathering will not occur again among the *Fays*! I was the sole representative of our branch but I was also hostess of the occasion and was determined to exert myself and *make* them have a good time! I *did so*, and the result was *most gratifying!* . . .

The season is now over and my labours over the Womens Philharmonic will have a lull. I almost forgot to write you about the President's Reception, which took place in the evening of March 2nd at our dear Chapter Room. After the troubles I had all winter through Mrs. Hunsicker with the club I did not expect much, and so I sent out seventy-five invitations to my *personal friends*. I asked most of the nice men I know, and almost *all* of them *came*. I had a *beautiful new* pink satin dress for the occasion, and had my hair dressed by Lebeau, the fine French hair dresser I discovered this winter. He is a perfect *artist* and does hair better than anybody I ever had! They all said I "never looked so well" as I did that night! In fact, they *raved* so over my appearance that it quite *cheered* me up in my old age! It shows the power of *dress* in renovating one! Our orchestra, which is now under the direction of Martina Johnstone (and is playing *admirably*), was to play, and Gulli was to be pianist, his first public appearance! When I reached the hall, it was *crowded*, much to my surprise, and with a very swell audience. . . . Mrs. Roberts made a very handsome speech and presented me with a handsome gold lorgnette on behalf of the Club. It was bought at Tiffany's and will be a most *useful* possession. I have long wished for one. I also received *four bouquets*. . . . Altogether the reception was a tremendous success and was a surprise to my enemy, Mrs. Hunsicker, I fancy! She was not there, but her henchman, Katherine Smith, was! So she heard about it! Although no longer a member of the club, however, Mrs. Hunsicker has not ceased to stir up dissension in it under the rose! She consorts with Mrs. Evans and others of the club.

Best love,

Amy

New York May 13, 1912

My dear Rose,

. . . I had the Hopkinsfolk dinner here on Tuesday, and it was a *howling success!* They all went home *enthusiastic*, and declared they had the *"best time ever!"* They elected me president, and I accepted the position and will busy myself thinking up things for next year! Mrs. Franks got up a delicious dinner at two dollars per head, the long table was set in her cozy parlour, which we had the monopoly of, and it was as *nice* as it could be! At dessert we had singing by *Caruso* and the sextet from *Lucia* from the Grammophone, which Carrie Franks had placed in the hall, and started for our delectation. It was quite entertaining and a good finale to the dinner. . . . Norman had an engagement, and was not present, much to the general regret. The *only* evening in the week he was engaged, too! I was quite mortified that *none* of my family except myself felt interest to come, when *four* of them were in town so near to the little family festivity, heralded so many weeks in advance, and it *did* seem as if they *might* have been with us had they *cared* to, much as I endeavoured to *smooth over their absence!* I made great exertions, however, to be entertaining, and played a *lot* after we returned to my room the latter part of the evening. They went off in *shrieks of laughter* at my funny stories illustrative of my *pieces*, and I had some new inspirations at the moment. The men lit their cigars and sat back comfortably on the sofa, which I had placed in front of the mantlepiece, and I had the folding doors open into the parlour, and a window open in my bedroom to let in fresh air. We closed the evening by singing *"Like a golden thread, if love,"* and *"The summer day doth fade away"*, from Uncle Henry's carols. It was nearly midnight when the party broke up. They went away *pleased* and *satisfied*. May Camp made candy and almonds for the dinner, and I contributed the *claret* (also *flowers*), so we could drink the health of the "absent ones". Nelson was much missed and the *only* letter read was *his*, from Washington. He spoke of Henry Camp's death, and said he "laid a laurel wreath on Henry's coffin, as he was a gallant officer and it was a *fitting tribute!*" I thought it very nice in Nelson to remember that. . . .

Last night Miss Read and I went to the last reunion of the Manuscript Society, of which I am a member and had a very good time. That was where I wanted to take *you*. Coming home we were with *Musin* the violinist. Tomorrow evening our little orchestra of the Women's Philharmonic gives a concert at the M[a]cDowell Club rooms. So good-bye and "no more" at present from

Your loving sister,

Amy

P.S. Please send this round the family! It will save my writing it all over again.

New York May 30th, 1912

Dearest Mudkins,

. . . It is very gloomy out but the gloom and uncertainty of the weather is in harmonious accord with the unsettled gloom of my soul, for soon I shall have to get out of my charming quarters here which are so admirably adapted to my tastes and needs! My plans are not settled beyond the fact that I shall visit Rose and Felsengarten and then go to Laura's in Saranac. . . . I have considered *Staten Island* somewhat, in case I have to give up *New York for good*, as Marian has such a delightful and spacious house out there, and in consideration of my giving her piano lessons she might be glad to have me board with her at cheap rates. Also she is in a thickly settled part of the Island where I could pick up scholars probably, with her to push me. I have not made any overture to her *as yet*, because I thought it best to wait and see which way the cat will jump, by which I mean Rose and Norman! If Rose decides to live in Boston, I shall not attempt a combination with her. As for Norman, he does not know *himself* what *he* will do, and perhaps he will just keep *writing* and pay his *board and keep* with his *pen*. He says that on account of his age he could not get a position with another man's business, but would *have* to have a business of *his own*. That he *can* ever achieve the *latter* seems *very dubious* to *me*. I don't count on *him* anymore. . . . That typewriter nearly *killed* him in my estimation and he is very excitable now and ought not to have anything to do but spend a comfortable *income*. It is *too bad*, and he has not the reward in his declining years that his generosity and work *merit*. I never can understand *why* he was permitted by Providence to run upon the rocks as he did, and it makes one doubt the guardian angel! I was overjoyed that he has written that brilliant *book*[1] and redeemed his self respect somewhat by *that* unexpected achievement! He has let the world know that he is still *alive and kicking!* . . .

I shall be here till July 8th as I have two or three things to do before I pack up. I have planned a little piano recital for next Wednesday evening which will be a "talk on Liszt," with illustrations from his works on the piano. Mr. Granberry, a successful piano teacher here, who comes from Alabama, has kindly put his pleasant studio at Carnegie Hall at my disposal, so I shall have no expenses except the printing of the tickets, and if I can get a little help from some of the Women's Philharmonic, I *may* make twenty-five dollars or so. We still have a meeting of the Council over which I must preside in June. My gifted boy pupil, Lemuel Goldstein son of the postman, is to play the first movement of the Beethoven concerto in B flat with cadenza, which I played with such success at the Worcester Festival, you remember! He will play the evening of June 7th with orchestral accompaniment at the annual commencement of the Morris High School in the Bronx. He has had one rehearsal of it. A *Mr. Tracy* is conductor. This is a splendid school, with all the modern equipments and has a *large and beautiful* hall, with a double row of gothic windows and a fine stage. It is really impressive, and will be *crowded* on that evening. I am anxious to be present as Lemuel's teacher, for he always gets great applause! Lemuel was *confirmed* last week, and is now fifteen years old. He is a remarkably intellectual mind and can talk with *anybody!* I had to go to the synagogue and see him through the service as the Jews always *insist* upon making you part and parcel of everything.

It was an all day affair and I left the house at half past eight, and did not get home till late in the afternoon. It is the second time I have done this, as another of my Jewish boys was confirmed in the winter. *His* name was Meyer Larkin, and *he* belongs to the old orthodox Jews, while Lemuel belongs to the Reformed Jews. I was quite the guest of honour at *Meyer's* Temple, which is in East 91st Street near Lexington Avenue, while Lemuel's is in the Bronx and is more fashionable as to the congregation, which is made up of a richer class of Jews. The orthodox Jews wear the scarf which Moses prescribed, with the blue border, and the men wear their hats also. When I appeared at Meyer's confirmation my name was announced, and the electric chandelier was turned on. Alas I received a blessing in the special exhortation and prayer! A grand family dinner succeded *both* confirmations, and the rabbi was present at the head of the table! I will describe this more at length another time. Now I must close, with much love, and renewed thanks for your check. . . .

A.F.

---

[1] *Big Business and Government.*

New York June 20, 1912

Dearest Mudkins,

I have had in mind to write to you for a week back, in answer to your *last* letter of good advice and now I will *do so!* . . . I have considered applying to an agency for a position in a music school here, and would like to be in Mr. Granberry's Piano School the best, but he is in Europe now. He caters to the rich class and is very successful with that kind of people, but *my* scholars are always from the poorer ones who can't *pay* what my class of work *ought* to get! My results from an *artistic* standpoint have been *brilliant* this season, and Lemuel Goldstein at fifteen has just played the first movement, with Hummel cadenza, of Beethoven's second concerto (B flat major) at the Morris High School, *with orchestra*, in a big concert, while Lucy Greenberg, in addition to *her own* concert last winter has rehearsed the difficult *Mozart* concerto in D minor with Volpé's orchestra, and came off with flying colors! I hope he will let her play it next winter in one of his Carnegie Hall concerts, as he made

124

a sensation with it in the *rehearsal* at which the guarantor of the orchestra and many musicians were present. Mr. Bushnell and Mr. Pelignan were among them and they congratulated me warmly on my *"talented pupil."* Volpé led the applause himself with repeated "Bravas," and Lucy was *surrounded* when she arose from the piano! Volpé remarked on the *difficulty* of the concerto. I wish you could have heard Lucy *roll off* the big cadenze, with her *impeccable technic!* I invoked the *shades of Deppe* while she was playing it! How *delighted* he would have been with the results of his method in America! This concerto is the one I heard played at the *Mozart* Festival in Salzburg by Essipoff years ago, and she told me, herself, she was *"dreadfully nervous"* about playing it there. As for Lemuel Goldstein, he brought the house down the other night with the Beethoven, and I was taken by surprise myself at the exquisite quality of his tone in that big hall, for he is a fragile boy and has small hands. Every *note* was clear as a bell, as so musical! I got two new pupils the next day from it! I am working up a reputation among the *Jews*, and what I do among *them* seems to be *conspicuous*, somehow! *They appreciate* the *music*, for *one* thing.

Morris High School is in the Bronx and you take the subway to 166th Street. It is a magnificently equipped school of modern construction and has a beautiful great hall, with large stage, grand piano, and a double row of gothic windows around it. In the evening it lights up brilliantly and is a cheerful airy, and attractive place. The concert was given by pupils of the school, and the orchestra was conducted by a very good musician named Mr. Edwin L. Tracy, who is also a teacher of piano, violin, and chorus, all three! He arranged a miscellaneous and very attractive program, on the *popular* order, and I enjoyed the occasion very much. I sat back of the orchestra directly in the centre of the house. The orchestra was on the floor, while the stage was covered with youths and maidens from fifteen to seventeen years of age. They were all facing me, and you can imagine how *pretty* the girls looked in their dainty muslins, with rosy cheeks, bright eyes, and all excited! The chorus was the *"close"* of the occasion, and the young fresh voices rang out delightfully. It was a charming idea, all the young people doing their stunts for each other, and the big audience showering applause! It is the best encouragement for American music that I know of. If you glance at the programme you will see that some of the pupils played their own compositions! Mr. Tracy conducted the orchestra, or played the violin in it while a young violinist conducted *his own piece*, or played piano accompaniments for the singer. In short, he was a *general utility* man! He complimented me on Lemuel's playing after the concert was over. . . .

My own concert took place in the Granberry Studio at Carnegie Hall, on Wednesday Evening, June fifth. Mr. Granberry sailed for Europe the day before, but he offered the studio to me free of charge. My expenses were about eight dollars, for programmes, tickets, hair-dresser, carfare, etc. I took in sixty-five dollars so the little affair paid very well. I had scarcely any assistance, except from Miss Read, who sold seven tickets, and she acted as door-keeper. The studio holds about a hundred and twenty-five people and was *packed*. The audience was very choice, and Nora Smith and Signor Gulli were there, also Dr. Elsenheimer, who is a very good musician. He plays and lectures on music. Mme. Tupin, who writes for the musical journals, and who gives concerts with the Jenks Keyboard and lectures, came, and our Club was well represented. My programme was *"simply exquisite,"* Nora said and I never did myself such *justice*, as I was not a bit nervous, and was in *splendid practice*. I *know* that *every piece* could not *fail* to *please*, and so it *was!* . . . Marian Hadlock was inspired to bring me a great bouquet of roses fresh from her garden, and they were the finishing touch! Dr. Hargett, a fine looking man and friend of mine carried them up and presented them to me. He made an impression and many inquired who he was after the concert. Dr. Hargett was formerly in Chicago, a dental surgeon, he was a worshipper of Theodore Thomas. For eight years he never missed a concert and he had all Thomas's programs bound in a book for preservation. His brother is a fine photographer in Philadelphia, and he made a life-size photograph of Theodore's head and bust which Dr. Hargett has framed and hung in his office here, in 125th Street. When Safonoff was conductor of the Philharmonic orchestra Dr. Hargett invited him to dinner and he spent four hours pouring over the book of programs, which he declared was a *"treasure of Art."* *"Never lose this book!"* said he. Dr. Hargett sent me a check of two dollars for my concert. Mrs. Winthrop, Mrs. Hyde, Mrs. Lanterback, Mrs. Peters, and Mr. Stuart each sent a check for five dollars. Mr. Stuart has always been my friend and patron and has sent me pupils. He is immensely successful and *coins* money every minute he is awake! The Musical Journals were very complimentary, and altogether this concert was a *complete success!* I gave it *really to pay for my board*, for I had got down to *nothing*, and am living on it *now!* . . . I have to attend the Music Teachers' convention here next week. What do you think of Roosevelt now? I see nothing of Norman. Good-bye with much love and congratulations on your *book*[1] being published from

Your affectionate sister,

Amy Fay

---

[1] Reference to MFP's book *Cooperative Housekeeping*.

New York July 3, 1912

Dear Mudkins,

All your letters and enclosed letters are received, for all of which my best thanks!

What a *capital* letter Helen Ellis writes! She surprises me with her brilliant, off-hand style (Extremely *interesting*, too!) I cannot *combine* with other musicians unless they want to combine! Stuart keeps to himself and has only a moderate sized studio in Carnegie Hall, where rents are terrific. He generally sends me a pupil or two every winter, and is very kind in *dividing* his pay with me! Whenever he gets a pupil who is *un*musical he sends them to me, as he says I always *"make them musical,"* and so much easier for *him* to teach! He has done this repeatedly, his pupils pay him four dollars, and he gives me *half*. . . . I went to see Miss Patterson the other night and suggested her adding a piano department to her school. She did not accept, but said she would advertize me to give a lecture next winter. She has been very good in asking me and my pupils to play at her home entertainments, which she gives sytematically. They are always *crowded*, and reporters from the papers are always present and put the reports in. She advertizes everything she does, and *every week*. She says, "You must *keep advertizing all the time*." This I know very well myself, but how *can I*, when my income barely covers my expenses? All of these people who are successful *advertize*, and that is all there is *to it!* What else could they do? None of the piano teachers here compare with me as a teacher! Even Joseffy! I have heard their pupils, and I *know*. I give *both technic* and *conception*. That, they cannot *any of them do!* My pupils *shine out* in their public appearances, and shoot way *beyond* their playing in the *lessons*. They always take *me* by surprise, *much* as I labour over them, and hit the bull's eye every time!

My reputation here is very great now, and if I only could advertize liberally as my *confrères* do, I would have no trouble. For one thing, I made a great mistake to give up *my own* playing in public, as I have done ever since I lived up here. I am now determined to resume my yearly Piano Conversations, and I think I will then get concert engagements in small cities and towns as I used to in Chicago. Also, my playing is now much more *appreciated*, as the public is more advanced. My pupils *love* to hear me play and are always begging me to! Lemuel said that *his father* in speaking of my concert on June 5th, said that my playing "did not sound like *fingers on the keys*, but like *beautiful wave of sound* floating in the air! You did not know *from whence* it *proceeded*." I was very much *delighted* with that for that was the way *Liszt's* playing struck *me*, and forever dwells in my memory! That *floating cloud-like exhibition*, I think I do to some extent imitate it! He is always in my mind, *wonderful being that he was!* Nobody could ever attain to his spirituality, even Paderewski. Perhaps that young Backhaus is a big a genius! He gave me a fearful time with Beethoven's thirty-two variations in C minor, an even absolutely *new* impression of Beethoven himself! It was a *prodigious* performance. If you ever get a chance to hear Backhaus do this, don't *miss it!* As I have familiarized you with the composition it will interest you doubly. Last week we had the usual convention of the New York State Music Teachers' Association here, from 25th to 27th of June, and it was held in Columbia College, which was a splendid place for it. The grounds up there are so attractive now, with big trees and grass, also two fountains, on each side of the entrance portals. The large gilded figure of Alma Mahler seated in the centre is impressive. The program committee did its work very well, and we had some splendid concerts notably Mendelssohn's Oratorio of St. Paul one evening in the Gymnasium, which I greatly enjoyed. . . . The acoustic was perfect and the voices sounded delicious. I always doat on a chorus. It is so delightful to get into a great wave of *voices* and float away with them. Miss Read will tell you about the wonderful young pianist, Cecile Ayeres, who made a sensation with her debut. I missed *that* concert, unluckily! She seems to be an entirely unique personality and a genius! Miss Read said she was tiny, and pretty, and *all alive* and *nerves*, which *took hold* of you. She was really a sensation. There was a very remarkable young girl *cellist* in the last evening concert, a Russian, by the name of Sara Gurowitsch. She was a *virtuosa*, and had a fabulous technic and beautiful touch. We had beautiful singers, both male and female! Bispham played his usual prominent role, both as lecturer and singer. He did his *very best!* Also Marie Rappold, of the Metropolitan Opera Company sang lots of unusual songs, and looked and sang beautifully. I took much pleasure in meeting a lot of familiar old M.T.N.A. faces at this convention. . . . Mrs. Virgil made a splurge with her improved *clavier* and her compositions for children. She is composing a good deal now, but did not play. The pieces were displayed on sale. Her second husband is an inventor and made the new clavier! I am going back tomorrow and expect to go the Bethlehem *Tuesday*. Must close, now, as it is time. Good-bye, with much love.

Amy

Felsengarten
Mount Theodore Thomas, Bethlehem, N.H.

Friday, August 28, 1912

Dearest Mudkins,

For days I have wanted to answer your letter of August 9th but it was impossible! The very day you wrote I gave a concert at Lake Saranac in combination with the Library Association and cleared forty-five dollars over expenses which I divided with the Association. Thus we *each* got $22.50 and I paid my travelling expenses *here* out of that money! I knew I could not sell the tickets alone, so I asked

Laura if there were not some good object the people could be interested in with which I could combine! And she hit upon the Library Association as it was trying to pay off a mortgage and Mrs. Baldwin was at the head of it. She is a very attractive person, wife of Dr. Baldwin (*the* leading physician) and the most influential woman in Saranac Lake. If *she* took hold of a thing, it would be a "go!" Mrs. Baldwin was amenable, so I went ahead, and the *"piano conversation"* was in the *library*, where a hundred chairs were placed. Tickets *fifty cents!* Madeline sold twenty-seven tickets. The place was *packed*, and with a very choice audience, among which were some professional musicians. It was a *smashing success, everybody* was *enthusiastic*, and the *men* enjoyed it beyond anything! They were most *demonstrative* and *smiled* from *ear to ear* when I was *talking!* I certainly have a *hold* on an audience when I *speak*, and the people *sit there* as if they were spellbound! They laugh and break into applause, and *never* want me to stop. They always declare afterwards that they *"never enjoyed* an evening so much in their lives," and invariably add "we wished you would *talk a great deal more!"* Funny isn't it? One of the nurses told Madeline that an old fellow who sat behind her and who *never* had spoken to her *before*, struck her on the shoulder twice and said *"Just look* at *Baldwin! See* what a *good time he is having!"* (*meaning Dr. Baldwin!*) I played the *Moonlight* Sonata *this time*, as I had played the *Pathétique* at the *Sanitorium* a week or two before when I gave a *free* concert to the patients and made them all happy. I sent to MacMillan for some copies of my book and presented one to the Trudeau Sanitorium and the other to the library. I thought it would be a good investment in Lake Saranac, where they have nothing to do *but read!* There are six thousand consumptives there! It *is* a most charming place to visit, in summer! . . .

I took my departure from Saranac on Friday of last week and went to Plattsburg, where I spent the night at the house of our friends the *Bixbys*, who spoke most affectionately and *appreciatively* of *you*. It was *"Merchants' Week"* in Plattsburg, and they were having a gala week of it. Fireworks, automobile parades, floats, decorations, and speakers. The shops were full of *goods* for sale. Governor Dix was the guest of honour and spoke on Friday evening. A small platform with one hundred chairs on it was erected on the green. At eight o'clock he appeared and was escorted to a front seat on it. As Mr. Bixby is editor of the *"Evening Star"* we sat in the best seats, directly behind the governor, much to my surprise! He is a stately, handsome man, blond, with regular features and an exquisite *smile*. His manners are quiet and the *pink* of elegance. His speech was sensible and to the point, but he lacks *authority*, and is a little to reserved in manner. He is not a bit of an egotist and has *no* self assertion. In conversation, however, he is a perfect charmer! He is sincere, simple, and cordial, with serious eyes, and a subtle smile which is fascinating. I took a fancy to him *at once*. Mrs. Bixby knows the governor, and is always at ease in public. She presented me to him as the author of *"Music Study in Germany."* He bent his gaze upon me and gave me a cordial hand pressure (with that *smile*) and said, "Miss Fay, I am *proud* to meet you!" I retorted that *I* felt "*honoured* at meeting *the governor!*" After that we had a charming little talk as we watched the military tactics of the troops in his honour. He had been to inspect the Danemora prison that afternoon, so had it on his mind. He said "our greatest excise is from the sale of *whiskey* and then we find the men in prison who have made *us rich* and *themselves criminals.*" This made him *grieve*, he added, and he could not get it off his mind. It was *so sweet of him*, I thought! My hand is tired and I must finish this letter later! Will close now, with much love. Rose, Lily, and Harry are all here and join me in love to you.

Your affectionate sister,

Amy Fay

September 18, 1912

Dearest Mudkins,

. . . Ever since I came here it seems as if the sun could not make up its mind to shine except for an hour or so, and then the sky clouded over. At night it is *very cold*, and even with my flannel wrapper on I find it hard to keep warm *in bed!* Rose has an open fire in the parlour in the *evening* and also in the dining room off and on, but for the most part I have to wrap up in a shawl or something to avoid taking cold! We shall be leaving soon now, about the 1st of October. I am sure it will be a *beautiful* month just as I take the train for New York! We have had *no hot* weather since I left there, and I have worn a muslim dress only *twice!* I might just as well have left all my thin clothing at home! The trees are now turning and the landscape is becoming more beautiful and brilliant every day! I find it *lonesome*, though, because Rose does not permit tourists to walk out here anymore. It used to cheer me up to see them in their pretty white dresses roving among the woods, and I also liked the exercise of taking them about and explaining things to them. . . . Yesterday we had a delightful dinner made up *partly* from *two* of my former tourists which I culled out, Mr. and Mrs. Erastus Gates! . . . Mr. Gates and his wife live in Pasadena but they come here every summer and travel in their automobile, (from California!) the "*Thomas Flyer*" as the machine is called! . . . I think they are New England people. Erastus is an attractive man about sixty, I should say, one of those Americans for whom the best is *good enough* (like Ellsworth and Burnham) a natural *connoisseur*, particularly about *music*, of which he is an extraordinary judge. I would rather play to *him* than *anybody*, unless *Safonoff!* He has such a sensitive ear, and such an instantaneous comprehension of the *meaning* of a composition! I always feel with Erastus, as I did with Safonoff, that I will be *immediately under-stood*. So it is a great pleasure to play for him. . . . His brother was a highly cultivated and literary professor and president of Amherst College and Rose made a *mark* on him! He has not been out here since the last three years. He was all ready to *propose* and she burst into tears and *slopped* over so, that he was mortified and disappeared from view! She did not give him any encouragement! He was a widower, and in deep grief over the death of his wife, who was an exquisite woman. He wrote a little book about her for private circulation, of which he presented a copy to Rose. The dinner was delicious yesterday, and we even had a bottle of *good champagne!* . . .

Amy Stone[1] is a fascinating little puss and is entirely absorbed in her affairs with the men at present. Margaret is entirely *wrapped up* in her approaching nuptials in November and for the *moment* forgets all about *Amy*, which is a great loss to *Amy!* Their sweet sisterhood is broken in upon by *man*, and Amy declares "Margot don't care a fig for her anymore!" She misses the sisterly affection *very much*. I hope Amy will marry a man who has *money*, for she is ambitious, and love in a cottage would not suit *her* ideas *at all*. I wish *you* were here to go out riding in Roses automobile with us! She drives the car to perfection and it goes *beautifully*. It is an enormous addition to the pleasure of living in this beautiful scenery. We do not take very long rides, but we go out often. Littleton seems a very short distance, and *formerly* it took all day to go over with one horse up those long hills, at a *snail's pace!* Mrs. George Glessner invited us to a dinner last week while Helen Birch and Amy were here, and we had a delightful afternoon there. . . .

You will be surprised to hear that I am actually working on my South American little book, and am *determined* to finish it before I leave here, if possible! I wish I could print it in a *magazine*, as a series of articles, and then it would be *paid for* and I should not be such an *everlasting time* getting a *little* money for it! How did you manage to put the subject of every page at the *top of it*, in *Music Study*? That must have been an *awful* piece of work, but it *does* add very much in reading it, I think! Did you do it in the proofs, or did you have the book type written before sending it to the printer? A young girl from *Boston* who is *temporary* organist at the summer Episcopal church for tourists here, told me she had carried my book about in her pocket, and she made *all her pupils* read it! She was *delighted* to find I was the writer of the letters and said she had "*never enjoyed* a book so *much!*" That is what they *all* say and it is a comfort to think *your time* was *well spent* on it! It was all *your idea* anyway, and without you the letters would have gone into the waste basket, and nobody would ever have heard of *A. Fay!* I would never have known I had talent for letter writing if *you* had not had the discrimination to discover the

Amy Fay

fact! . . . Best love and good-bye from

Amy

---

[1] Amy Fay Stone, Amy Fay's niece, who took the name Amy Faystone as her stagename. She was the daughter of Amy's sister Kate.

New York October 17th, 1912

Dearest Mudkins,

. . . It seems *ages* since I saw you, and this long separation has something *unnatural* about it. Now that all the family has left Chicago I should think you would feel you ought to turn your face towards your once loved New York! It seems strange you ever should have *left it*, especially as you never seemed to mind the hot summer *bakings* when you lived here. There is no question that as a city Chicago is infinitely superior to this over-crowded place, but there are *family* reasons why you should return and you ought not to be so isolated as you are from us all. Rose is now at the Hector Thomases, corner of Park Avenue and 80th Street. . . . Today I dined with Mrs. Grenville Winthrop, and had a very delicious dinner, soup, roast chicken, fried bananas, etc., a new salad I never ate (cream cheese made into balls and inserted in large *green grapes*) with lettuce and mayonnaise sauce, *delicious!* For dessert, ice cream with *hot* chocolate sauce. I don't think I have eaten fried bananas since you left New York and Mrs. Winthrop spoke of that *never* to be forgotten luncheon in 56th Steet when you had them, you may remember. She said she had never forgotten that luncheon and *how nice it was!* She asked about you. Mrs. Winthrop has changed a good deal and is pretty old now, but she is greatly improved because she has now learned *not* to *talk* too much, and is like other people. I think she was *made* to hold her tongue by those brutal nurses when she was insane for several years, and now she has learned self control. Now she talks agreeably and naturally and has lost that *volubility* she formerly had. She is a good friend to me and I have never neglected her. I have gone to see her a good deal, and she appreciates it. Her daughter who married Norton Goddard was left a widow with four little girls and lives on Park Avenue.

I read in today's Sunday Times a notice of Lillie de Hegermann's published letters[1] in Harper's. The Times gave a whole page to them, together with her photograph at twenty-four, and a day or two ago the same picture was in the Sunday *Tribune*

132

with a two column notice. I have only seen two numbers of the Harper's, but think the letters are awfully clever! I suppose *you* have kept track of them, as you do of everything! With all this *advertizing* the book should have a large sale and Lillie should make *some money* out of it! It was I who put her to writing these memoirs the year of the World's Fair in Chicago, when she was at Norman's house. We were talking about my book when I exclaimed, "I wish I had had *your* opportunities, Lillie! *What a book* I could have made out of them! Why don't *you* write a book?" She looked reflective and said, "Why, yes, it is true I have all the letters I wrote to Aunt Maria." Well, that's *splendid*," I said, "go ahead and copy them out and you'll have *your book!*" Lillie at once *caught on*, she is so quick! Sure enough she has *done it!* I think her letters show *close observation* and *infinite tact* in dealing with royalties! She is as clever as Rose is with rich people! That first number at Compiegne where *Theophile Gautier* was her neighbor at dinner, and afterward wrote her that *poem* is *capital*, and the Virginia Reel she danced with Emperor Napoleon, and her singing *"Nelly Bly"* and *"Swannee River"* to him! I enjoyed that number immensely. Until now I have heard nothing said about the book, but these big newspapers will now bring it into notice. Lillie's so accurate, too, in her account of life in a palace, it is really most valuable and instructive to read what she says. The papers make no comments, but just print extracts from the book without saying it is good from a *literary* standpoint. It seems to me they do not appreciate the *cleverness* of it, but I may be mistaken. Lillie has certainly had an amazing career!

You will be pleased to learn that I got nineteen dollars and something from *London* on *Music Study* just about the end of September. *Last* year it was $18.14 so it is a trifle more this year, which is encouraging. I think we got only $47.00 from the New York MacMillan last year, but I forget about it. Perhaps it was fifty! In London it keeps along about the same. People *still* enthuse over it. At the first *"Saturday Informal"* of the Women's Philharmonic last week a pretty woman came up to be presented to me and she said she had read my book. Then she exclaimed impulsively, *"You darling! No one could read that book and not enjoy with you!"* I thought it was so sweet of her, but I forget her name! She exclaimed so *passionately*, I was quite touched by her enthusiasm! At the meeting of the City Federation of Clubs last Friday I met two women, and one of them said, the *other* had just been telling her about my book, how "delightful" it was, and she added, "I am going to buy it and read it immediately!" They asked permission to come and call. We had a very interesting "Informal," as Mrs. Sherwood, (the *first* wife of the pianist Sherwood,) was the pianist and Mary Sherwood (his daughter) who has lately married and is now Mrs. Simmons sang. . . . Mrs. Sherwood played beautifully and her daughter charmed everybody with her singing. Refreshments were served afterward and everybody was happy! It was one of our pleasant reunions.

Katherine Smith has resigned and has gone completely over to Mrs. Hunsicker, taking the orchestra *with her!* I was *much* disgusted, as our orchestra was doing so finely under Martina Johnstone's leadership. She is a *real* artist and inspiring conductor and plays the violin so beautifully herself! But she is under Katherine Smith's thumb and does whatever she says! The orchestra gave one final concert last season in May and it was in the MacDowell Club Hall and was crowded! When I got to my seat you may imagine how mad I was to find Mrs. Hunsicker's name in *large letters* on the front page of the program as the prima donna of our most *brilliant* concert! *My* name was on the *back* of the programme in *small* letters, and *yours* was *omitted altogether,* which is against the constitution! Did you *ever* hear of such colossal cheek in your life? Here is Mrs. Hunsicker entirely *out* of the club and at swordspoints with *me!* But her ambition was fired to sing with the orchestra of the *"Women's Philharmonic Society,"* and she and Katherine Smith and Miss Johnstone the conductor hatched it out between themselves! I would not have gone to the concert if I had been informed of their action. The next thing I knew Katherine resigned from the club! I wrote to Miss Johnstone, but received an insolent reply and *no* information before she sailed for Europe to spend the summer! Such is life! Here we have *laboured* over that orchestra and raised the money to pay the conductor two hundred dollars per year besides the expenses of music and room rent and now they just take French leave and ignore us entirely! Isn't it enough to make a person sick? I suppose Mrs. Hunsicker enjoyed singing with an orchestra so much that she was bound to get a handle over it. She and Katherine are as thick as thieves! Norman called for a moment the other day and looked as well as he used to in Newport! He is going in with Charlie Wetmore and will have an office in Wall Street soon and a *salary!* Write soon and best love from

Amy

---

[1] A reference to *In the Courts of Memory, 1858-1875,* from *Contemporary Letters,* by Amy's cousin Lillie (Greenough) de Hegermann-Lindencrone.

New York December 8, 1912

Dearest Mudkins,

You were an *angel* to send me the Macmillan check just when you did, as I was two weeks in arrears for my board, having just returned from Cambridge, and all I had in the bank was $22.89, although I had a few dollars in my pocketbook! My lessons have tided me over small daily expenses, such as one always has *here*, for you remember in New York *City* one *has to* take out one's pocketbook *every day* for *some* small expenditure, if not a large one! It is impossible for me to pay expenses on $40.00 per month *house rent*, and my *lessons*, almost entirely among the *Jews* who cannot pay high terms. I teach a *great deal* but cannot get even *three* dollars per lesson, as I used to in Chicago without difficulty. Two, or even one dollar is about what the Jews pay, or else *nothing!* You see, I ought to have *advertized* all these years, but have no means of letting the public know *where* I am to be found! The conservatories gobble all the good paying pupils, which are recruited from the *country* at large, and not from *New York City*, by the *constant* sending out, *broadcast* of *circulars*. Look at Miss Patterson! She was smart enough to advertize in the Texas newspapers, and she got *seven* young girls as boarders in her house immediately! But she *had* the capital to do it with! I had *just* money *enough with* Normie's fifty dollars per month, but he has not given me one cent since March and that means a deficit of $450.00 in my pocky! I worried through twelve weeks in Saranac and Bethlehem and saved board that way. Also, Rose was very generous and helped me out with her money from the estate. But now I have to forage around again to live. . . .

Norman's affairs are now beginning to look up, but I see nothing of him, scarcely! He invited Rose and me to dine at restaurant *"Beaux Arts"* (Sixth Avenue and 40th Street) on Thanksgiving Day, and we went to the Philharmonic Concert afterwards, Stransky conductor. I was cheered to see Normie take out a *large wad* of *bank bills* and order a *three dollar* bottle of delicious *claret* for dinner, quite as in the good old Chicago days! He was faultlessly dressed, and looked the New York *howling swell* to perfection! He also made a remark that he was *"going* to give me some money," and I live in hopes it *may* materialize *soon*, or I shall *have* to jog his elbow, which is *not pleasant!* He telegraphed to Ernest Smith in British Columbia to come to New York, which Ernest *did*, and he will now get a good position in the Montana Irrigation Project, which is the scheme or *syndicate* Charlie Wetmore has got Norman into as manager. A very *rich syndicate*, and it owns large tracts of land there. It is just the kind of work for *Ernest*, as he knows Montana *well*, and the dear boy was delighted! The blizzards killed off his sheep, and left him in bad plight last winter. You know Ernest has changed his name to Ernest Norman *Fay*, through the act of the legislature, as he found he was taken for a *crook* when he gave the name of *Smith* in British Columbia! People thought he was travelling under an *alias!* I think it is much nicer, he will be another *Norman Fay!* It seemed to make Normie take a great interest in him and he will push him to the front he says! Ernie has always gone about his own business so quietly and bravely, never asking help from anyone, and he is very *attractive* in *my* estimation. He possesses Papa's large-minded calm. I think he is very sympathetic to Norman and thus *your* old idea of Norman's combining with the *Smith nephews* will *at last* be realized! It was one of your *many good ideas!*

Amy Fay

Rose has taken a *lovely* apartment at 383 Park Avenue, and she is putting her things into it now. She and Norman will live together and combine expenses. He selected it, and it is near 84th Street. Norman's present address is the Harvard Club, 27 West 44th Street. I must close now as I have no time for more, but will continue later and send best love and warmest thanks. In haste. Your loving sister.

Amy

New York December 29, 1912

Dearest Mudkins,

At last I have found a free moment in which to write you, by staying home from church this morning, but as I attended service on Christmas Day it is not very long since I had a *sermon!* I go to St. Agnes close by, as Dr. Vibbert is now *"emeritus,"* which is to be interpreted *"retired,"* and Dr. Morkridge reigns in his stead at Trinity Chapel. I *now* have a delightful minister at St. Agnes, Rev. Dr. Bellinger of Virginia. *He* is a *charmer*, as a *man*, and is also an *extemely interesting preacher*, full of southern warmth and eloquence, combined with university training and intellectuality! I take such pleasure in him that I am, if possible, a greater frequenter of the courts of the *"House of the Lord"* than ever! . . . Mrs. Bellinger is also a southerner and there is a large family of five or six children, I believe! Dr. Bellinger has been a great traveller in Europe and used to make a trip every year, his wife told me, till his family got too large to permit the expense. This gives him an *all round* culture and knowledge of the world, which makes him a delightfully sympathetic companion, like Burgess! He is idolized by his congregation, of course, so it is difficult to get hold of him! I sent him a copy of my book,[1] though, as he rather takes to *me*, and I have a few minutes chat with him *after service* frequently. That is *all I can get!* . . .

Yesterday I went to the funeral of Miss Georgianna Schumann, member of the Women's Philharmonic and I *think* one of *your charter* members. She was an intelligent *German* women and musician and of sympathetic nature. . . . She was in straitened circumstances but managed to keep her little home and *died* there of paralytic stroke on Friday night at four o'clock, without pain. She was buried from the undertaker's right across the street from where she lived Eighth Avenue and 56th Street and had a *beautiful* funeral, *I* thought! I had always imagined that to have funeral services at such a place must be ghastly, but found it quite the contrary! I should quite like to be buried that way *myself!* The room was a good sized one and had a crimson velvet carpet on the floor, which gave it a cheerful aspect, and the walls were simple and in keeping. A bronze panel of mortuary design was at the farther end of it. The room was long and narrow, and the casket was placed on a bier in the centre of it. Chairs were put against the wall on each side, and here sat the friends, only a *few!* The minister was a German Lutheran. He read the prayer in German, but made his discourse in English, a *remarkably* good and appropriate one. Rudolph Schirmer had offered to pay all the expenses of the funeral, but was not present at it. Everything was done in the best of style, simple, but elegant! The casket was black, with silver handles, three on each side, very handsome; it was partly open, and on the foot of it was an exquisite wreath, and large bouquet of lillies of the valley, also sent by Schirmer! . . . As the room was narrow, the friends were brought into close juxtaposition sitting on each side of it, and when the minister, who had evidently been a friend of the deceased, gave us an interesting and intimate talk on *death*, and interwove some pleasant remembrances of Miss Schumann in it, it was all most appropriate and soothing. We were sitting there comfortably together, and dreadful *marble* isolation of death was absent! Miss Schumann had only *one* close friend, also a former member of our club, a Suede or Scandinavian, I forget her name, but she was devoted to her, and was with Miss Schumann when she died and held her hand till the last breath. In fact she thought Miss Schumann *dead*, when she took hold of her hand, but at the touch the warmth and colour returned to her cheek and lips for an instant. I told her that was the marvellous effect of *love*, and she recognized her hand and *responded* to it at the supreme moment! This friend accompanied the body to Woodlawn cemetery, the sole attendant. *I* would have gone but I was going to a magnificent concert given by Isaye and Godowsky at Carnegie Hall and had already bought my ticket!

Godowsky has given two wonderful piano recitals here and his is on the topmost pinnacle of art, but as he is playing the Knabe piano he has had a hard time with the critics, most of whom are affiliated with the Steinway Firm. The consequence is they have written very mean notices about Godowsky, with the result that people were kept away from the concerts. This was a cause of grief to Godowsky and he said he would be very glad if *I* would write something about his playing and put it in the *Musical Courier*. I assured him I would be only *too glad* to help him, but I was sure they would not put the notice in if I did write one, as everything I said would be in direct contradiction to what the critics had said! I was too busy anyhow to attempt it as I was practicing for my own recital at our club.

My concert was a great success by the way. I sent out invitations and Rose and Norman were there, also Mary Perkins and Josie Bates and Mr. and Mrs. Geiger (Mrs. Eddy's daughter) just back from Europe after a two years' absence. I had a beautiful singer to assist me, Mr. Earle Tuckerman, baritone, and it was an awfully pretty programme. Rose was very complimentary for *her*, and exclaimed over my playing, "You played *superbly*, Sister Amy," (and so said they all!). I am reading Lillie de Hegermann's book and think it is very clever and amusing but there is no feeling in it! Just observation! . . . I did not buy *any* Christmas presents but got some myself and also *many* Christmas cards! . . . With best love and a Happy New Year.

As ever,

Amy

---

[1] *Music Study in Germany.*

New York January 22, 1913

Dearest Mudkins,

It seems a hundred years since I had a letter from you and I hope it does not mean that you are under the weather! We are *all* getting very lazy about letter writing as we grow older, owing, I suppose, to lack of interest in life. For myself, I *have* to answer so *many* truck epistles of one sort or another all the while that it exhausts my mental energy entirely! Just now, for instance, we are getting up a card party for the benefit of the Women's Philharmonic Society, which is at a *low ebb*, owing to the many resignations we have had since Mrs. Hunsicker's and Katherine Smith's operations! Had I not *witnessed* it, I never would have believed that *one woman could* blast a prosperous club as Mrs. Hunsicker did *ours*, just out of pure malice and deviltry! She could not have done it, though, if not aided by the treachery of *some* of the *members*, and the *abject cowardice* of *others*, who were afraid to stand up for the rights of the Society.

I went to a very jolly musical reception given for Scharwenka and his wife at the home of Dr. Ernst Eberhard who founded a conservatory in West 85th Street a few blocks down from here. I never knew anything about this conservatory till I was asked to this party a week ago Monday. The guests were *numerous* and were all musicians of one kind or another, mostly teachers of voice or piano or harmony, etc. Mrs. Eberhard and her daughter *received*, and a pretty girl, named *Miss Clover*. Everybody was light hearted and gay, and there was no constraint and no effort, but simplicity and comfort. Plenty of flowers and good music, punch and

138

a good supper. Like the Israelites of old we "ate, drank, and were merry!" I am very fond of Scharwenka and his wife, they are both so genial and good hearted. They entered heartily into the thing and made everybody feel at home. Dr. Eberhard himself has been ill in a sanitorium for a good while and has *died* since the party! His picture and biographical sketch are in the *Musical Courier* today. He was a direct descendant of the old ducal house of Wartenburg and seems to have been a fine man. I have met him at the M.T.N.A. in the old days, I think, as his name seemed so familiar, and everybody at the party seemed to know all about me. It often happens to me now-a-days to meet a lot of musicians and have them come up to me and say "Oh *Amy Fay* how d'ye do! *We all know and love you!*" It is really *quite touching!* I have a different kind of foothold now from what I ever had before and in New York my foot seems to be on my *native hearth*. Everybody is so friendly! They treat me with a sort of affectionate deference wherever I go and seem *so glad* to see me!

Rose and Normie are now installed in their new apartment and they enjoy their new home very much. . . . Mrs. Grenville Winthrop gave a luncheon party for Rose last Wednesday of six. . . . Mrs. Winthrop is now in my neighborhood as she is living in the *Belmont*, a *huge* apartment house on Amsterdam Avenue and 86th Street. It takes up a *whole block*, with its Italian Garden in the court, and contains a thousand flats! I started in good season for Mrs. Winthrop's as I supposed, but when I got half way there, happening to glance at a clock in a shop window, I found I was forty minutes ahead of time! I had forgotten to set my watch back which had been gaining ten minutes per day for several days! I did not want to walk back to my house, so spent as much time as I could gazing at the shop window. *Still* I had twenty minutes to wait, so I was inspired to go down into the subway and buy a ticket, and set down on a *bench* till four minutes of one when I emerged and walked a half block to Mrs. Winthrop's, arriving on the stroke of the clock! Rose, on the other hand came up on the trolley and was twenty minutes *late*, owing to a blockade on the track. I was in a *state of mind*, fearing she had *forgotten* the invitation altogether. We finally sat down to the table without her and then she appeared, much to my relief! We were the last to take our leave when it was time to go home and I was looking forward to an exchange of news on the way, but Rose was in such a tearing hurry she would not wait for me one second as I had my gloves and coat to put on, but rushed off as fast as she could go, without explanations. It was rather awkward for *me!* . . .

I don't go to see her and Norman very often, the temperature is too frigid there (in a *moral sense*) for *me!* Norman was more like his old self and limbered out some the night I ran in there and staid to dinner, after Mrs. Goddard's reception a fortnight ago. I think Rose has a jealous nature, and if she has a *man at all*, she *owns him*. It was so with Theodore Thomas, and I have always felt that if she had *wanted* to, she could have got me the engagement to play with him that time. I am convinced she did not care to have him take an interest in *me!* Now Rose has *Norman*, and

THE WOMEN'S PHILHARMONIC SOCIETY OF NEW YORK

MRS. MELUSINA FAY PEIRCE, Founder
MISS AMY FAY, President

Studio 839
Carnegie Hall

Saturday Afternoon
March 22, 1913, 4 o'clock

PROGRAM

ARTISTS

MISS ELENORE ALTMAN, Pianist — *Pupil of*
MRS. LOUISE C. BODEMANN, Soprano *Stojowski,*

Paderewski friend of pupil

PIANO—
Sonata, B flat minor . . . . . Chopin
Grave. Scherzo. Marche Funebre. Presto
MISS ELENORE ALTMAN

VOCAL—
Birthday Song . . . . . Woodman
Fairy Pipers . . . . . Brewer
Ah! Love but a day . . . (Mrs) Beach
MRS. LOUISE C. BODEMANN

PIANO—
Legend, Op. 8, No. 1 . . . Stojowski
Un Moment Musical . . . Paderewski
Polonaise, E major . . . . Liszt
MISS ELENORE ALTMAN

VOCAL—
Niemand hat's geschen . . . Loewe
Wenn die Rosen bluchen . . Reichardt
Vergebliches Staendchen . . Brahms
MRS. LOUISE C. BODEMANN

THE PIANO IS A STEINWAY

Mrs Lillian Obynden, accompanist.
(John Marble's sister.)

CONCERT
OF THE
ORCHESTRA
OF THE
WOMEN'S PHILHARMONIC SOCIETY

MRS. MELUSINA FAY PEIRCE, Founder
MISS AMY FAY, President
MADELINE HOBART EDDY, Conductor
LOIS HUNTINGTON, Concertmeister
assisted by
KARL FORMES, Baritone

PROGRAM

PART I

1. Overture, Egmont . . . . . Beethoven
2. Songs—(a) "Im Meiner Heimath" . . Hildach
   (b) "Auf Wiedersehen" . . . Liebe
   (c) "Mein Madel Hat 'Nen Rosenmunds" . Brahms
   KARL FORMES
3. (a) Solveig's Song . . . . Grieg
   (b) To Spring . . . . . Grieg
4. Piano Solos—(a) "On Quiet Woodland Path" Richard Strauss
   (b) Impromptu, A flat major . . Chopin
   MISS AMY FAY
5. String Orchestra—(a) Vision . . Rheinberger
   (b) Tarantelle . . . Madeline Eddy

PART II

1. Surprise Symphony, G Major . . . Haydn
   Adagio Cantabile; Vivace assai
   Andante
   Menuetto
   Allegro di molto
2. Aria from Macbeth—Pietà Rispetto Onore . Delibes
   KARL FORMES
3. Meditation from Thais . . . Massenet
   (by request)
   MISS HUNTINGTON and Orchestra
4. Piano Solos—(a) Ave Maria . . . Liszt
   (b) Die Loreley . . . Liszt
   MISS AMY FAY
5. (a) Cavatina . . . . . Raff
   (b) Barcarolle from Tales of Hoffmann . Offenbach

STEINWAY PIANO USED

Subscriptions are solicited for the support and enlarging of the orchestra

---

ORCHESTRA

VIOLINS
Cornelia Blaine
Leila Cannes
Laura Clark
Ada Heinemann
Idalian Van Heyer Hennen
Minnie Herzog
Lois Huntington
Margaret Krauss
Amy Robie
Elisabeth Ruddell
Martha Mayer Thompson

VIOLAS
Elsie Radler
Melinda Rockwool

CELLOS
Florence Brooks
Marie Eddy
Gertrude Wolf

BASS
Juliette Mousson

FLUTE
Gussie Blucher

CLARINET
Elsa DuBois

TRUMPET
Katharine Femen

DRUMS
Anna Fricke

PIANO
Frances Eddy

140

I shall never have any comfort out of *him*, you will see! He *did* give me fifty dollars this month though, for which I was devoutly thankful. I don't know what I should have done without it! He has not been to see me *once* since last winter! . . . I have *more* to say, but must close for today.

With much love, as ever,

Amy

Feb/March 1913

[fragment of letter to Zina]

. . . I want you to represent our club as *Founder* of it, at the Federation meeting. You will enjoy Miss Egan, for she has a rare gift of making friends among the *best people, wherever* she goes! I was *surprised* to see how she got on in New York City, as she came from a western town, and had *no* social backing whatever! But people like her and take to her, somehow. She belonged to the Women's Philharmonic at my suggestion, and was so courageous and *loyal* to me all through the war with Mrs. Hunsicker when all the members were such cowards and afraid to stand up against Mrs. Hunsicker! I never could have fought the battle to a successful finish but for Miss Egan's championship, and I shall always be grateful to her for it! She is an "Irish Catholic," too! but you can't down her, and she has the warm Irish heart! She has a talent for dress, and always gets herself up effectively, although she teaches music, and is not rich! Miss Egan has *very good taste!* I miss her very much, and she has been in Mexico all winter with her brother and has only *recently returned* home. Her address is Miss Anna Egan, 525 Chicago Street, Elgin, Illinois. I am anxious you should meet her and let her tell you all about our club battles last year, in which she took such a decided stand! I think you will like her as much as you do Mrs. Case. . . .

New York November 27, 1913

My Beloved Little Madeline,

Your *two nice* letters have remained unanswered *so long* that I am almost ashamed to allude to them, but I will try to make up for my negligence *now*. The truth is I have a large class of twelve pupils this year, and you will perceive at a glance what *loads* of time it takes to teach them! Especially with *my* thorough methods and disregard of the *clock!* Then I am back again as president of the Women's Philharmonic in spite of my resignation last June, for they *will have it so*, although I have been president for ten years! I *had* to resume office! This is also a great tax on my time, attending business meetings, arranging programs and reorganizing our little Women's Orchestra, etc. Added to this are the encessant *social* demands, and *concerts galore*, which I *must attend*. This year it is unprecedented, as *most* of the great *world* pianists are here at *once*, and are giving recitals every day or two! Paderewski, Hofmann, Backhaus, Carreño, Bauer, Mme. Cornelia Rider-Possart, *all* are trying to outdo each other. *All* of them *magnificent.*

I went to hear Mme. Rider-Possart yesterday. She lives in Berlin, but is an American by birth. She is a very beautiful woman, perhaps thirty years old, with a superb, statuesque figure and dark hair, almost *black*. She was attired in an exquisite white satin dress, the new kind, which looks *heavy* like cloth. I don't know if "*charmeuse*" is the technical name for it or not! I actually do not know yet what *charmeuse* is! It *seems* as if it ought to be a *thin* material! But this new satin makes up beautifully for *winter wear*, as there is more body to it. It is like cloth, with a satin finish. Mme. Possart's *corsage* was of white lace, with short sleeves, and as she has a beautiful *neck, arms* and *hands,* she looked *lovely* in it! She has vivid brunette colouring, and "the *rich blood mantels her cheek*," as the novelist would say! I wish *Laura* could have seen her, for *she* would have *revelled* in her beauty! Mme. Possart is a splendid pianist and she gave a very interesting recital. Many of *my old* pieces were in it, and some *new ones!* She has a *beautiful* touch and a thoroughly schooled style and *masters* everything she plays. I enjoy her playing very much, and it *is* a pleasure to see a *beautiful woman* on the stage, instead of the *eternal* black coat men! We have not had one since *Carreño.* She, by the way, is failing in health, and looked very *ill* the last time I heard her. One of her Berlin pupils informed me that Carreño *has heart disease* and is in a serious condition. She appeared with the Philharmonic Orchestra under Stransky as leader, a short time ago, and when I went into the artists' room to congratulate her on her *splendid* performance of the Tchaikowsky concerto, she did *not smile once*, but looked really *tragic* and *ill!* She might be on the brink of *death*, for aught I know! She embraced, and *kissed me* on *both cheeks!* The critics were very severe on her piano recital which followed shortly after, and said they marked a "sad change in her playing." Now she is announcing another recital for December 9th. She has *one son*, besides two daughters at home, a very talented youth but a "ne'er-do-well," although he has a fine *voice*, and talent as a violinist. He is a burden and care to his mother, instead of being a help and support to her.

I have been to three recitals of Paderewski, and *that idol still* remains on his *throne, unapproachably* great! The beautiful *red gold* has *gone out* of his *hair, utterly,* and left it somewhat *grizzled*, although still plentiful. It is *such a pity*, as it takes all the *brightness* out of his stage appearance! He cuts his hair shorter, and the golden locks do not *fly back*, as he *walks!* Still, he is a *commanding* artistic personality and the public goes mad over him greater than ever! I went in to the green room to congratulate him on his triumph and was received with effusion both by Paderewski and by Mme. Paderewski. Rose gave them a fine dinner on Thanksgiving Day to which *I* was invited, and Paderewski was at the head of the table on Rose's *right*, while his wife was at the *foot* of it, with your Uncle Norman. The other guests were Mr. and Mrs. *Finck* (critic of the *Evening Post*), Mr. Krammer who was formerly first violin (concert-meister) in Theodore's orchestra and is now occupying the same post in the Philharmonic in New York, Mme. Paderewski's son, *Gorski* (by her first husband) sat on my right, and Amy Stone was opposite *him* on the other side of the table. Gorski is a good looking chap and looked about twenty-eight years old, and very like his mother. I was on the left of Paderewski, round the corner of the table and wore my pink satin, décolletée, of course! Paddy was *devoted* to me the *entire evening*, even *after dinner* he lit a cigaret for me and *resumed* conversation! And what do you suppose we were talking about? You would *never* guess, so I may as well tell you, it was about the Old Testament! We went through *Moses*, and *David and Goliath*, and *Solomon*, and the *ten commandments* and *Proverbs!* He began by saying he was a Catholic and that he *enjoyed* that religion because it was the religion of his ancestors. I asked him if he believed in the *"Resurrection of the Body"* as set forth by the *creed?* He said he *did not*, as the body decomposed after death. He added that nobody had ever asked him *that* question before! I then eulogized *Moses* as the writer of the ten commandments, but Paddy did not think he *was* the *author* of them, but that he had got them from the Egyptians in Egypt. He has *no* great opinion of *Moses! Goliath*, he *admired*, and said he was a *"fine, big fellow*, who wanted somebody to fight with him." That *"mean little David"* accepted his challenge, and then "like *all* those Jewish boys of the time, who could *throw stones*, he hit Goliath in the temple and *killed him!"* But *that* was *no good square fight at all*," reiterated Paddy. He felt utter *disgust* for David, therefore! Solomon he regards as an amusing cynic and man of the world, and said he was a "funny fellow." He said there was *"no love"* in the *Jewish religion. "Only law."* *I* said that "love was brought in by *Jesus Christ*," to which Paddy assented. When we had reached this point the signal was given to rise from the table and adjourn to the drawing room, after having first drunk to the health of Paderewski and his wife in champagne. Rose's dinner was *delicious* and a *great success!* She had *two cooks* having got in a *second one* to reinforce her own, and the consequence was, *nothing* was overdone or spoiled from nervousness or getting rattled on the part of the *girl!* Mme. Paderewski looked a perfect *beauty*, in a beautiful silk white, with black lace trimming, low neck, and some very fine *real white* lace, which softened her shoulders. Her face was like a *cameo*, with perfectly regular features, and her hair (*very abundant*) fell in *heavy bands* on each side of it, and was of *raven blackness!* She certainly was *exquisite*, and I could well conceive how Paderewski had become infatuated with her. She is rather *petite* in stature, and her neck is handsome. Paderewski is her opposite in every particular and is *six feet* in heighth! He is a most formidable apparition when he enters a drawing room, and seems to *fill* the whole *room completely!*

In the center of the table was the superb silver centre piece for fruit presented to Theodore by Paderewski, of boat-like shape and filled with fruits of different varieties. Everybody seemed to enjoy the evening, and conversation flowed *gaily along*, without *effort*. I forgot to say that prior to our long talk on *religion* and the *Bible*, Paderewski and I had a discussion about the comparative merits of *Beethoven and Wagner*, in which Mr. Finck took part! *Paddy* is the most *brilliant talker* and more *wholly spontaneous* than *any* I *ever* have talked with, but perhaps it is because I am sympathetic to him, as *Rose* says *she* "has *nothing* in common with Paderewski," and that they have "nothing to say to each other." This is incomprehensible to *me!* I went down to see Rose beforehand, and told her to *be sure* to put Paderewski *next to me*, if she wanted him to *enjoy* himself! "Don't you worry! He'll have a good time!" replied Rose! On thinking it over I guess she concluded it would be good policy to follow my advice, so you will perceive that I was felicitously placed, round the corner to his right, at table! So was Paderewski! He did his duty faithfully to Rose for a quarter of an hour and then turned to me, while Mr. Finck was a good talker to Rose. Like all writers for the papers, Mr. Finck is well up on the current topics of the day. Norman divided himself between Mrs. Finck on his left, and Mme. Paderewski on his right, assisted by Mr. Krammer, the concertmeister. Amy Stone talked to Gorski across the table, and as she looked as *pretty as a peach*, in *white*, *Gorski* was in luck! Mme. Paderewski is very fond of Norman, so *she* was all right! It turned out a *beautifully* arranged dinner. After dinner Mme. Paderewski produced *her own* bundle of cigarettes, very long and delicate and presented them to the company. Paderewski lighted *mine* for me! He told some amusing anecdotes at table for the benefit of the company. Once he discovered when on the stage that his *white suspenders* were hanging down *behind*, and he had to bow and to retreat to the artists' room in that condition. Wasn't that *funny*? Another time his valet forgot to pack Paddy's white waistcoat, and he went out and bought another. It was too short in front, though all right when he played. As soon as he rose from the piano it *shot up!* There was a gap between it and his trousers.

Paddys' third Recital took place on Saturday afternoon, and he was in his very best form, and at the *top notch* of his powers. The program was *perfect*, and his *vast* audience was *entranced* with delight! I went to say a word to him in the green room where I found Rose and Norman coming out of the door. The hall was just one *roaring mob shouting bravos*, and Steinway's men had to come and roll away the grand piano, while the lights were turned out on the stage, after Paderewski had played five encores! He was in a most joyous mood and entirely satisfied with himself! This is his last appearance prior to his departure for the west *today*, going first to St. Louis then Detroit, Cleveland, Chicago, etc.! He will return in *March* after going to the Pacific Coast, but will spend *Christmas* in *Boston*, where he has a lot of cronies, *Adamo[w]skis*, etc. Paderewski played *two* sonatas at this last concert, Beethoven's in D minor, Op. 31, No. 2, and Schumann's *enormously difficult* and *collossal* one in F sharp minor. This work he gave a *wonderful* interpretation of, and it is considered the *touchstone* of achievement by the great virtuosi. For one of his closing *encore* pieces he played the familiar Prelude in A flat by Chopin, with the *bell tone* in the *bass*, *expressly for me* (he said afterwards) as he had heard me say that I liked it. I myself had forgotten having spoken of it, so it was very sweet in Paderewski! It does affect me more than anything he plays, and I can't bear to hear anybody *else* play it! . . .

As ever your affectionate,

Amy

New York January 7, 1914

My dearest Fanny,

. . . I think from your acounts of Malden that you have hit upon a very pleasant place, and perhaps you will enjoy life more there. The people of New England are so up to date and well read, they know what is doing in the world. It is a great thing to belong to a musical club, too! I *always* do, wherever I may be, and it seems almost like a family tie, you get so used to your *clubites!* Our Women's Philharmonic got a bad setback through that horrid Mrs. Hunsicker of Weehauken, who tried to get possession of the presidency and run me out! She could not *do it*, but she has created endless discord in the club until *I* got *her out*, finally but with dreadful slaughter! Many members resigned, preferring giving up their membership to remaining in the club while Mrs. Hunsicker was in it! Nobody *liked her* but *all* were afraid of her, she was such a bully! That treacherous Katherine Smith went over to Mrs. Hunsicker, horse, foot and dragons, and carried off our orchestra with her, of which she was *chairman!* This after all the time and money we had spent getting the orchestra started and putting in such a fine violinist as Martina Johnstone as conductor! We paid *her* two hundred dollars per year as conductor! I met Katherine Smith the other night at Carnegie Hall, and she had the cheek to say to me, "Oh, Miss Fay, you don't *know* what *beautiful* work the orchestra is doing under Martina this winter! We are very anxious to have you come and hear us play!" I think I see myself going to hear the orchestra, after the shabby way they have treated us! I shall say, "If you want *my ears*, you must stay in *my club*! I don't propose to give them to you for *nothing!*" Miss Smith was dazzled by Mrs. Hunsicker's automobile and good clothes, and she thought there would be *"millions in it,"* but I have yet to hear that Mrs. Hunsicker has given the orchestra *one cent!* They must have got beautifully taken in by *her!* She wanted to *sing herself*, at the concerts of our orchestra, and that was what she was aiming for! She managed to get herself on the program, too, at the very last concert *we* gave at the MacDowell Club Rooms, before the orchestra decamped for good! It made me *so mad!* Well, she is gone, now, which is one comfort! This year we are trying a different plan, and that is to have the club in the evening at private homes of the members! I had the last meeting in this house, and it was just like a party, with lovely music, and passed off beautifully. I had a *fine punch* with a *stick in it*, and delicious sandwiches and cake for refreshments. Many *men* came and made it very pleasant and everyone was in evening dress. The next meeting will take place a week from tonight at Miss Elizabeth K. Patterson's, and she is a capital entertainer! My former pupil, Eugene Toyner, will play five pieces, and he plays *well!*

We have organized a new orchestra, under Miss Madeline Eddy, who is a daughter of the Reverend Layton Eddy (Episcopal minister) and has much energy and character. She has *some principle*, I am glad to say, and will not behave as Miss Johnstone did to us! We are going to give a concert soon for the benefit of the orchestra. . . .

I am now getting up a program of American composers, and am going to give one of my Piano Conversations here as soon as I am ready! Probably towards March or April, and I think it will make a hit! I shall begin with MacDowell's Sea Pieces, then I will play Country Scenes, by Professor J. K. Paine, formerly of Harvard, and then I shall conclude with Jerome Hopkins' *"Wind Demon,"* "Addio," and Mermaid's *"Rhapsody at Sunrise,"* which is an awfully pretty piece! I shall talk a lot about each composer and tell anecdotes, etc. which will amuse and entertain the audience! On Monday I lunched at the Holland House with Mme. Fanny Bloomfield-Zeisler from Chicago, who gave a splendid piano recital on Saturday here. Three ladies besides myself were invited, one of them a gifted young pianist from Hungary, Mme. Yolando Mero! One lady, a *Mrs. White*, said such a pleasant thing of my *book!* She said, "When one has read *that book*, it becomes a part of one!" I was much pleased at this remark! It had so much *heart* in it! I am *delighted* your children have begun to learn music! I have twelve pupils at present. . . . Do write me occasionally and let me hear about *you all!* With much love, I am your affectionate

Aunt Amy

The American Years

New York February 15, 1914

Dearest Mudkins,

. . . I omitted to tell you of *another* sad death, that of Evelyn Mellen, who has been suffering from heart disease for about a year and growing steadily *worse*. She passed away shortly after New Years quietly and peacefully. . . . I think her death was a relief to her family as she had been ill a year and there was no prospect of recovery. I felt I lost my best friend in Evelyn, as her home was always open to me and she was so generous of her hospitality. We always had fun together when I went there to call and she always kept me to lunch and dinner. She gave a handsome reception to *Rose* the first winter she was here, and Rose returned it by inviting her daughter to a luncheon. Evelyn Junior is now a handsome woman and has learned how to *dress* and do her hair! You remember how you used to worry over her appearance! She has *entirely changed* since going abroad to study the violin.

Jennie Pierce is looking older than she did formerly. Father Ritchie has not been in good health since the shock of Miss Brooks' death and has resigned his parish of St. Ignatius's Church. *He* was nearly killed by automobile a year ago and has never recovered from the shock. I saw in the Chicago Musical Leader the deaths of Emil Liebling and Mr. Perkins the *same day*, and also that of Phelps, the singing teacher! Mrs. Watson died last fall, at the hospital of an operation. I was dreadfully afraid the Nihilists would shoot Paderewski, but he is returning here to give his next concert of March 7th at Carnegie Hall. I hope he will escape all dangers to his life! He was dreadfully *nervous* about himself, but has shaken it off the papers say!

I entertained the Women's Philharmonic here again last Tuesday evening, and it really was a *delightful* party everybody said. I wish I could afford to have it once a month, as I understand how to entertain, and the house is very attractive and pretty. We had three artists on the program. They were Madame Schnelock, *violinist*, a fine contralto singer, whose name escapes me, and Lemuel Goldstein, pianist, *my* very talented pupil! He fascinates everybody, just as Laura Sanford used to with her playing! He is very poetic and has much technic also, and he always *makes his mark* when he plays in public! After the music we had a good punch, sandwiches and cake, all *very nicely made*, and people ate, drank, and were merry! Norman was in Cleveland on a business trip, so could not come, but Rose came and also brought Katherine Wilmerding, the *first visit* Katherine has made *me* all winter! I presented the guests to Rose and she was quite a *star!* I have a very agreeable Irishman, a journalist and correspondent for the Irish papers, named Mr. Heppenstall. He is *good looking* and is my neighbor at the table. I invited *him* to come, and I presented him to my niece, and she had a very good time! He wants me to tell Amy Faystone that a play by his friend *Springer* is to be put on by the

147

Iowa New Yorkers

HOTEL ASTOR
February 27th, 1914
TWO O'CLOCK

MRS. JAMES S. CLARKSON, PRESIDENT
MISS MARGARET H. READ, CHAIRMAN OF THE DAY

PIANO CONVERSATION
BY
MISS AMY FAY

Programme

"If Amy Fay had not chosen to be the superb pianist she is, she might have struck thirteen in literature."

ELBERT HUBBARD.

I.	(a)	GIGUE - - - - - - - -	
	(b)	PRELUDE, B MINOR - (Well tempered Clavichord)	
	(c)	GAVOTTE, G MINOR - - - - -	- Bach
	(d)	MENUET - - - - - - -	
II.		ADAGIO AND FINALE (Sonate Pathétique) - - -	Beethoven
III.	(a)	ROMANCE, "Long Years Have Passed" - -	Rubinstein
	(b)	ETUDE, E FLAT MINOR, No. 6 - - - -	Chopin
IV.	(a)	NOCTURNE, F SHARP MINOR	
	(b)	NOCTURNE, A FLAT MAJOR	- Chopin
	(c)	POLONAISE, E FLAT MINOR	
V.		GONDOLIERA - - - - - - - -	- Liszt

STEINWAY PIANO USED

148

Castle Square Co. the week after next. Mr. Springer is going on to Boston and he would like to meet Amy, at Mr. Heppenstall's suggestion, so she must be on the look out for him. How is she progressing in her *art*, by the way?

Last Sunday I heard my old friend *Sloane* give a lecture on the Balkan problem at the Methodist Episcopal Church on east 86th Street and Madison Avenue at ten in the morning. Well, it was a *masterly* lecture and *most interesting*. His wife was not there. I spoke to him for a moment afterwards and he was *very cordial*. I was elected last year into the Authors' Guild when Sloane, Gehlett, Burgess and Edwin Starkham (a poet) were the committee, but did not *accept* as the dues are ten dollars per year! *Too bad*. Good-bye with much love from

Your affectionate sister,

Amy

P.S. I have been invited to give a Piano Conversation on February 29th by the "*Iowa Club*" here, and shall do so. It will meet at *Hotel Astor*. It is a Woman's Club. Give my love to everybody!

New York March 12, 1914

Dearest Mudkins,

It is ages and ages since your last letter, and I am getting uneasy at not hearing from you. I should have sent you a letter before, but have been dreadfully busy, and go out so much in the evening, it seems impossible to write any but the most *urgent notes* which *have to be answered all the while*. The last I heard from you was that you were in Brookline organizing *Co-op*, so you seem to have returned to your muttons, so to speak. I am curious to learn the result of your labour. Helen is an energetic and *direct* little body, and would, I should think, be a valuable ally. Your associations always seem to have a life of their own, and they endure and produce *results* even after you retire from them, which is encouraging!

We had a meeting of the Women's Philharmonic this week, at the house of *Mrs. Lusk* who was formerly Clementine Tetedoux and a pupil of Madame Cappiani, I *think* one of *our scholarship* pupils, although she denies it. I *think I recall* that Madame Cappiani gave me this information when I visited her in Switzerland, but

Mrs. Lusk was very sensitive about it when I spoke of it to her. She was a *free* pupil of Cappiani, and that I know by *her own* admission. At all events, she is a beautiful woman and she has developed into a *lovely* singer. She became the second wife of Dr. Theodore Lusk, the skin specialist, and they have a beautiful little boy baby. They live near Morningside Park, in full sight of the cathedral. Mrs. Lusk has always been a good member of our Society and this winter she is particularly active. She is chairman of the programme committee and this is the second time she has entertained the club at her own home, and when you consider what a lot of *sandwiches and punch* have to be provided, you will appreciate the *work* it is! This last meeting was an *ideal* one, to *my* thinking, and was just the *kind* of things to my taste, for a club like ours. Mrs. Lusk had made the occasion in honour of Mr. Homer Bartlett who is just such a learned musician and indefatigable worker at composition as Professor Paine was in Cambridge, and like *him*, he cannot open his mouth without giving you interesting and valuable information about *music*. I rarely get a chance to meet Bartlett, but always *improve* when I do! He is simple, genial, and unpretentious, and has published over three hundred compositions! *One* short piece he dedicated to *me years ago*, and I am going to practice it and play *it* on my *American* programme. Mr. Bartlett is a good pianist and has an excellent technique and much *dash and fire* in interpreting his piano works. He is also a capital accompanist. He first gave a very interesting little talk, and then sat down and played a very pretty "*Ballade*" of his own. Then Mrs. Lusk sang two of his songs. She was followed by two *males*, one of whom was a *Spaniard* and had the grand name of *Miguel de Castellanos. He was a pianist* and he played a Rhapsody by Bartlett very well. The other *sang*, and was a tall and handsome young man. Mr. Bartlett was happy in the production of his works, and in our warm appreciation of them, and he certainly made himself *most* agreeable and attractive. With the ladies and their male friends sitting in the two drawing-rooms, it was sociable and inspiring, and recalled to my mind how the old composers used to play in the drawing rooms of the Vienna aristocracy in the days when *concerts* were not so lavishly given as now! I am going to try and have *more* such evenings, where *one* artist can exploit himself or *herself.* I think it would be more satisfactory than the usual mixed programme, provided the artist be interesting enough! I wish Ethelbert Nevin were alive still! He gave so much pleasure with his music in drawing rooms always! It was the "*book of the age*" he told me, that started him on a musical career! He read it when he was sixteen, just the impressionable age, and said it was *then* he resolved "to make something out of his own talent." How is the printing of *your book* getting on, and are you doing anything about it? I am *most eager to read it*, and as I am *now* at a good age to die, I wish you would *hurry matters up!* I *may* be in *another world* if you don't publish *soon!* . . .

I invited Laura to spend a week with me at my boarding house, but she persisted in hurrying home, so I suppose she was crazy to get back to *Mr. Fairchild*, to whom she is *absolutely devoted!* I had bought a ticket for Paderewski's concert for her the end of the week, but *nothing could stop her!* It was the most remarkable performance he *ever gave*, and he went *far beyond himself*, even! This was the general verdict of the critics: he even admitted himself that he rarely succeeded in playing *"every piece"* on the programme as he did that day, with *equal perfection*. The proceeds of the concert he presented to the Tuberculosis Clinic. Every inch of standing room was taken and I stood up myself, although I had *three* tickets! I sold *two*, and the *third*, an expensive one, was stolen from my desk drawer mysteriously! I do not know if by one of my Jewish pupils, or the darky who waits on table! I left the house at a quarter before two o'clock in the afternoon, and returned at a quarter past-seven! With the exception of the ride on the cars going and coming from Carnegie Hall I was on my feet all those hours, yet had no sense of *fatigue*, so *life-giving* was Paderewski's playing! I stood under the gallery near the *central* door, and could *hear splendidly there*, being right on a line with the piano. The stage was kept darker than ever, and it was impossible to distinguish his face even with a good opera glass! It was a *"twilight of the gods,"* but as Paderewski *is one*, I suppose it is all right! The red gold has all gone out of his *hair*, unfortunately, and it is now grizzled and the papers no longer call him a *"chrysanthemum."* The audience was the most elegant and distinguished looking I ever have seen in New York. *Exquisitely dressed women*, and the men with talented faces, and an "air!" Nobody was insignificant. Franzen, the painter, was in one of the back seats near me. He now has his studio in the expensive building for artists on 59th Street of Central Park. I can't just think of the name. He gets two and three thousand dollars for portraits now-a-days! He is coming up to my Mondays again.

I have just been down to get my luncheon (Sat.) and found a letter from you on the table, much to my joy! You ask about my Piano Conversation before the *"Iowa New Yorkers' Club,"* which I had forgotten all about! I am happy to say it was a *brilliant* success, and the *entire* audience came up to congratulate me afterwards and to express their pleasure! The president made a speech *full of feeling*, and said it was "the *most beautiful* afternoon the Club *ever* had enjoyed." What pleased *me* was her conclusion, in which she said that she found herself left "in the *loveliest frame of mind*, somehow," and that she did not think she would do anything *bad* for a *long while!* That was an original way of putting it, wasn't it? She is Mrs. James L. Clarkson, of Montclair, New Jersey, a rich woman, they told me. She gave me *beautiful* flowers and entertained me in the dining room of the Astor hotel after the concert with tea and refreshment, and it came *opportunely*, as I had not time to eat my luncheon! Melanie and Elsie Murdoch were present, as was also Edith Hopkins and *Miss Mather* (*of all* people!) but *she* simply *doats* on my Piano Conversation since I sent her tickets to one a long while ago! I was *surprised* she had the energy to come! . . .

Mrs. Carlson has just *come in for my washing* and I read her your letter. She is always so delighted to hear from you! What a glorious trip Addie Wilkes has started on and how I do *wish* I were along with her! Travelling *is* so *interesting*, and I am always hoping by some twist of fortune to see the world ere I leave it *for good!* I *long* to go to *Palestine.* You would hardly recognize New York could you see it now! Twenty-third Street has been abandoned and all the great stores have gone up to 42nd street. Are not the fashions *bewildering* you? Everyday something new and different. The fashions and the Suffragettes are, to me, the most extraordinary things! This war of the two sexes in England is perfectly *amazing!* The cup and saucer I sent you were from that beautiful Japanese store of Fifth Avenue near 28th Street. They are selling out and moving up town. The cup was hand painted the man told me when I admired it, so I bought it. Only a trifle, of course, but pretty, I thought, and not too large! Give my love to all the family and with best love to yourself.

As ever,

Amy

New York June 11, 1914

Dearest Mudkins,

. . . On Tuesday evening we are to have our *third* meeting of the Women's Philharmonic at the house of my friend Miss Elizabeth K. Patterson, in West 104th Street. She lives close by the Subway, so is quite accessible! My pupil, Eugene Toyner, formerly from Burlington, *Vt.* is going to play. He is an exquisite pianist now, and has grown to manhood. He and his mother have taken a flat in Newark, where he plays an organ in the Catholic Church. You may recall that Eugene's mother was formerly *Ella Gillard* of St. Albans! A sister of the *butcher* there! My pupils are attracting a good deal of attention now, and I have a big reputation as a teacher here. A boy pupil of mine name Meyer Larkin played for the famous pianist, Harold Bauer,[1] a week or two ago and when he had finished his piece, a difficult *Menuet,* by St. Saëns, Bauer remarked to him "All Miss Fay's pupils will be *concert pianists!*" This amused *me* very much! This same boy played for Rudolph Ganz last winter, and he was very much struck with the Deppe finger exercises. I am getting talked about in musical circles as a very wonderful teacher *at last!* . . . Poor Lucy Greenberg has had a hard time with her manager, and Mr. Aronson got her only one engagement, which was at Groaverson Hall, the home of the Duke of Westminster. Only the nobility of England were present, and Lucy made a great hit and was the only artist to receive an encore. Aronson then cooly informed Lucy that he had spent fifteen hundred dollars to give her this engagement, and that his money was at an end! She would either have to return to America or go to Berlin and continue her lessons with Scharwenka till next April or May, as the concert season was over in London! Lucy is now in Berlin again, and is bitterly repenting that she ever left *me*, but she is in for another year abroad. I only hope Aronson will keep his word with her and get her engagements in the spring but I very much *doubt it!* Her brothers are now sending her their savings to pay her board and that of her mother and little sister in Berlin! Isn't it a *shame!* She was all ready to *play* when she left me, and she is being managed just as Laura Sanford was, and all my work undone! She sees her mistake in leaving me but has the European bee in her bonnet! Scharwenka has fine pupils and is *well paid* for his lessons! I hope you are well and in good spirits as also all of Kate's family household. Madeline writes that Laura has *set her heart* on seeing *you* and I hope she will achieve that happiness so *longed for*, poor child.

With much love, as ever,

Amy

---

[1] Harold Bauer (1873-1951), distinguished Anglo-American pianist and one-time student of Paderewski.

New York January 4, 1914

Dearest Cater,

How awfully generous you *are* to send me *ten dollars*, and I don't see how you could spare such a lot of money! A thousand thanks for all your goodness, and you always *are* so good to me! I am ashamed that I never can *return it!* I immediately *gallopped* down to Altmann's store and bought material for *two new* shirt waists, one of black cashmere, and one of a giddy coloured stuff, and I sent them to my dressmaker, the good Mrs. Lennon! She is always very quick and prompt, so in about three shakes of a cat's tail I will have *two brand new winter waists* to come out in, with a new black and white skirt I have had hanging in my closet for some time, *"Oh, very 'andsome!"* This skirt was waiting for a partner, and will now be able to appear! The New Year is opening with good anyway and I am looking for prosperity. Yesterday morning at breakfast I exclaimed, "I wish somebody would bring me a bottle of champagne to-day!" Sure enough, in the afternoon, when I was scurrying around for my *Monday* reception who should walk in but my former pupil, Ada Samuels, a Jewish girl whom I taught for nothing for four or five years, now married and prosperous. In her arms she carried a fine bottle of champagne! . . . The bell rang, and in came Edith Blanc, who presented me with a bouquet, much to my surprise! Mrs. Henry T. Finck, a pretty young woman, wife of the musical critic of the *"Evening Post"* and her mother, Mrs. Cushman, were the next comers, and a singer fresh from Paris, Miss Esthar (her real name is Miss Rath, she spells it backwards). I made *her* sing, and Edith play, and with tea and talk we had a very good time!

Why don't *you* start a *day at home* in Cambridge? with your charming daughters *Zina and Rose* you could be quite an eyesome, and it really is a *very pleasant thing*, to serve tea and see your friends *once a week*. I have kept *mine* up ever since I came here to live, way back in the nineties, and I *never* have been without *somebody* except *once*, last year! It was Helen Peirce (Bertie's wife) who started me on the *"day"* business, at Mrs. Merrill's! People like to come, if they know you have prepared to see them, and a cup of *tea* is an excellent medium for conversation! I know *you have it every afternoon*, but I think a *special day* is more effective! . . . I have got that old *"Reflets en l'eau"*[1] into my head at last! I asked Edith to play, and she quite enjoyed doing so. I think she will come up *often*, now! Tell Rose I *was* so sorry to hear she is miserable and wish you could visit Helen Birch in Florida for a change. Best love to Mousie and to Mudkins and to your dear self from

Amy Fay

---

[1] Piano piece by Debussy.

Felsengarten June 13th 1916

Dearest Mudkins,

The American Years

You have been in my mind *much* of late, and I have been planning a letter, but, somehow, could not seem to get *at it!* Nothing of any *note* has occurred, except the notes of Karl Formes' accompaniments, which I am practicing industriously. He is very capricious about singing, however, so I don't get much *reward* for my efforts! He and his young wife and three little boys are boarding at Mrs. Johnson's down the road, and Formes has made himself quite useful to Rose, cleaning up the place, chopping down trees, etc. He is an energetic nature and likes to be busy! This morning I went to Dr. Tewksbury in Littleton to have my teeth gone over. He is simply *swamped* with patients, and you have to engage him *long in advance* in order to get him. He inquired after *you* with much interest, and made his usual assertion that "*Mrs. Peirce* is a *most remarkable woman!*" He sets great store by you! I told him you were in good health and were getting out your great book,[1] at last! I also told *Mrs.* Morrow, Katherine's mother-in-law at whose house I spent last night, and she was much interested to hear about your book, as she is a great *reader*. She wanted to know what it was about and I gave her as good an idea as I *could* of it! How does it impress you now, *in print, at last*? *Favourably I trust*, I am delighted it *is* out! "*Never say die!*"

The Morrows have such a *beautiful* country place in Littleton now, just this side of the town as you *approach* the town. The house is on a heighth or slope *to the right* of the road to Littleton, overlooking the town. . . . You will recall it, a large square white wooden house. They want an *avenue* and to obtain one have bought the adjoining land also. Very much such a house as the Houghtons, but they are adding to it and changing it. Mrs. Morrow has a *large library*, she is a *book lover!* which reminded me of Walter Scott's, in *his* home. It is so *high*, there was a gallery running around it. Mrs. Morrow's is built on similar lines. She keeps *this* room entirely for *herself*, and does not admit the general public in it! Last night she invited *me*, as a *special honour*, to enter it, and she asked me to autograph one of the copies of my book, which she said was "one of the *first* to buy!" (the seventh copy sold). She lived in Chicago when it came out. I expect she will buy *yours* also, when she gets a chance! . . .

We had the most *terrific* thunder storm, which lasted for *hours* yesterday, and *drenched* the land with *rain!* So far, I find it pretty *dull* up here, this year! I have got *used* to the beautifulness of Felsengarten, and it does not cause me any *special delight* (*No*, I will *take that back!*) The place is in *fullflower*, though, and is gay with poppies and fleurs-de-lis also columbines. We don't *drive*, as we used to, such *long* drives, I mean, as Rose is rather tired of the automobile now! She has not used her *new* machine, *yet*, but contents herself with hiring *Ray's* and letting *him* drive it! Perhaps it is on account of the *wrist* she broke, although it is much better than it *was*.

What do you think of *Roosevelt* commanding a battalion in Mexico? How he does *long* to be *spectacular*, and before the public eye! I can't get up the slightest interest in him anymore. This *war is* so *wearing*, one wonders if it *ever* will *end!* ... Do write me a letter and tell all the news, if there is *any!* Rose joins me in love, and I am as always

Your devoted sister,

Amy Fay

---

[1] Zina's Book.

Index

Index

Index

Index

Index

Index

Index

Index

Index

Index

Index

Wagner, Cosima 67
Wagner, Richard 7, 32, 55, 59, 62, 107
  Berlin Festival 59, 66, 67, 69
Walsh, Mr. & Mrs. 34
Watson, Mrs. (acquaintance) 78, 147
Weber, Carl Maria
  Concertstück 91
  "Perpetual Motion" 92
Wetmore, Charlie 134, 135
Weyman, Wesley 20, 106
White, Mrs. Andrew D. 109
Wickes, Madame Dallage 27
Wilkes, Addie 119, 152
Williams, Mrs. Leonardos 93
Wilmerding, Charles 117
Wilmerding, Katherine 147
Wilmerding, Lily Fay 13, 14n, 28, 35,
  74, 99, 102, 120
Winterstein, Hans 68
Winthrop, Mrs. Grenville 34, 126, 132,
  139
Wolfe, Anna 43
Wolfrum, Phillip 103
Women's Home Companion 33

Women's Philharmonic Society of New
  York 18, 19, 21, 24n, 25, 30, 33, 45,
  70, 72, 76, 81, 83n, 87, 91, 97, 106,
  108, 113, 120, 122, 123, 133, 138,
  141, 142, 145, 146n, 147, 149, 152
Women's Political League 74
Woodman, Dr. & Mrs. 114
Worcester Festival 123
World's Fair, Chicago 133
Wren, Jenny 43

York, Mrs. 43
Young, Professor & Mrs. 119
Ysaye, Eugene 105, 137

Zeichner, M. A. 67
Zimbalist, Efrem 105, 110
Zina. *See* Peirce, Melusina Fay
Zola
  "L'Aouin" 7
  "La Faute de l'Abbé Mouret" 7
Zuck, Emma 18, 19

Sister Margaret William McCarthy, C.S.J., *pianist and organist, has earned degrees from Manhattanville College (New York City), Pius XXI Institute (Florence, Italy), and the Doctor of Musical Arts from Boston University. Since 1961 she has been on the faculty of Regis College, Weston, Massachusetts, where she is professor of music and chair of the music department. She is active as a member of the Music Critics Association, College Music Society, and the Sonneck Society. Some of her other writings include articles on "Scriabin the Mystic" in* Clavier *(1965), "The Afro-American Sermon and the Blues" in* The Black Perspective in Music *(1976), "Two-Piano Music around Beethoven's Time: Its Significance for the College Teacher" (1977) and "Handel and Pope" (1985) in* College Music Symposium. *Presently she is researching the history of the musical "peace jubilee" and is working to promote music as a means toward peace in this nuclear age. Since 1954 she has been a member of the Sisters of St. Joseph of Boston.*